Reading Faulkner
SANCTUARY

READING FAULKNER SERIES

Noel Polk, *Series Editor*

Reading Faulkner

SANCTUARY

Glossary and Commentary by
EDWIN T. ARNOLD AND
DAWN TROUARD

University Press of Mississippi / Jackson

Copyright © 1996 by the University Press of Mississippi
All rights reserved
Manufactured in the United States of America

The paper in this book meets the guidelines for
permanence and durability of the Committee on
Production Guidelines for Book Longevity of the Council
on Library Resources.

Library of Congress Cataloging-in-Publication Data

Arnold, Edwin T.
 Reading Faulkner. Sanctuary : Glossary and commentary / by
Edwin T. Arnold and Dawn Trouard.
  p. cm. — (Reading Faulkner series)
 Includes bibliographical references and index.

 ISBN: 978-1-61703-053-6

 1. Faulkner, William, 1897–1962. Sanctuary. 2. Faulkner,
William, 1897–1962—Language—Glossaries, etc. I. Trouard,
Dawn, 1954– . II. Title. III. Series.
PS3511.A86S432 1996
813'.52—dc20   96-3478
            CIP

British Library Cataloging-in-Publication data available

CONTENTS

SERIES PREFACE
vii

ACKNOWLEDGMENTS
ix

HOW TO USE THIS BOOK
xi

INTRODUCTION
xiii

AFTER WORDS
xvii

Sanctuary
Glossary and Commentary
3

APPENDIX
A Chronology for
Sanctuary
249

NOTES
255

CONTENTS

BIBLIOGRAPHY
265

INDEX
275

SERIES PREFACE

This volume is one of a series of glossaries of Faulkner's novels which is the brainchild of the late James Hinkle, who established its principles, selected the authors, worked long hours with each of us in various stages of planning and preparation, and then died before seeing any of the volumes in print. The series derives from Jim's hardcore commitment to the principle that readers must understand each word in Faulkner's difficult novels at its most basic, literal, level before hoping to understand the works' "larger" issues. In pursuit of this principle, Jim, a non-Southerner, spent years of his scholarly life reading about the South and things Southern, in order to learn all he could about sharecropping, about hame strings, about mule fact and lore, about the Civil War, about blockade running, duelling, slavery and Reconstruction, Indian culture and history. When he had learned all he could from published sources, he betook himself to county and city archives to find what he could there. He was intrigued by Faulkner's names, for example, and over the years compiled a fascinating and invaluable commentary on their etymologies, their cultural and historical backgrounds, and, not least, their pronunciations: Jim is the only person I know of who listened to all of the tapes of Faulkner's readings and interviews at the University of Virginia, in order to hear how Faulkner himself pronounced the names and words he wrote. In short, for Jim, there was no detail too fine, no fact or supposition too arcane to be of interest or potential significance for readers of Faulkner: he took great pleasure in opening up the atoms of Faulkner's world, and in exploring the cosmos he found there.

It was my great fortune and pleasure to be Jim's friend and colleague for slightly more than a decade. In the late seventies, I

SERIES PREFACE

managed to tell him something he didn't know; he smiled and we were friends for life. Our friendship involved an ongoing competition to discover and pass on something the other didn't know. I was mostly on the losing end of this competition, though of course ultimately the winner because of what I learned from him. It was extremely agreeable to me to supply him with some arcana or other because of the sheer delight he took in learning something—anything, no matter how large or small.

On numerous occasions before and after the inception of this series, we spent hours with each other and with other Faulkner scholars reading the novels aloud, pausing to parse out a difficult passage, to look up a word we didn't understand, to discuss historical and mythological allusions, to work through the visual details of a scene to make sure we understood exactly what was happening, to complete Faulkner's interruptions, to fill in his gaps, and to be certain that we paid as much attention to the unfamiliar passages as we did to the better-known ones, not to let a single word escape our scrutiny; we also paused quite frequently, to savor what we had just read. These readings were a significant part of my education in Faulkner, and I'm forever grateful to Jim for his friendship and his guidance.

This series, Reading Faulkner, grows out of these experiences in reading Faulkner aloud, the effort to understand every nuance of meaning contained in the words. The volumes in the series will try to provide, for new readers and for old hands, a handy guide not just to the novel's allusions, chronologies, Southernisms, and difficult words, but also to its more difficult passages.

Jim's death in December 1990 was a great loss to Faulkner studies; it was especially grievous to those of us embarked with him on the series. Absent his guidance, the University Press of Mississippi asked me to assume editorship of the series; I am happy to continue the work he started. The volumes in the series will not be what they would have been had Jim lived, but they all will bear his stamp and his spirit, and they all will try to be worthy of his high standards. And they will all be lovingly dedicated to his memory.

Noel Polk

ACKNOWLEDGMENTS

We wish to acknowledge the curiosity and industry of dozens of students in nearly as many classes who were subjected to our long period of captivity with *Sanctuary*. They were sent off to libraries and asked to make strange calls and hunt in corners of their families for bits and pieces of fact and lore—about insulators, mail delivery, and even badgers. We especially want to thank, in no particular order, Denise Kadilak, Melissa Berry, Emily Searcy, Jennifer Lavy, Henry Tanski, Peggy Lantry, Deb Weber, John Bisheimer, Tom Dorman, Linda Brewton, Gail Walters, Carol Dennis, Becca Barnum, Anita Schmidt, and all the others who frankly shared their mystification and their finds. We also wish to thank Noel Polk, Carey Wall, Dan E. Moldea, Ellen Arnold, Bookie Patrick, Seetha Srinivasan, Roger Creel, Randy Moore, Susan Donaldson, Phil Cohen, and Cathy Moore for kindness and keen insights.

HOW TO USE THIS BOOK

The line-by-line entries are keyed to the page and line numbers of the Library of America Edition of *William Faulkner: Novels 1930–1935* (1985), edited by Joseph Blotner and Noel Polk. Running heads in bold type will locate passages in this text and, following the abbreviation VI, in the Vintage International paperback text (New York, 1993). Cross references in the entries themselves will be identified by page and line numbers to both editions separated by a double virgule (e.g., 358:22//58:11). All line counts start with the top line of text on each page. A reliable locating guide can be made as a bookmark by simply preparing a numbered slip of paper that fits your edition.

We believe that the entries will be of greatest service if they are consulted immediately after reading the story itself; we are confident that a subsequent reading after the entries have been reviewed will provide a manifold increase in a reader's understanding and appreciation of the art of William Faulkner.

INTRODUCTION

William Faulkner began writing *Sanctuary* in January, 1929, just as his third novel *Sartoris* was being published. He had only recently completed revising and retyping *The Sound and the Fury* (it would be published on October 7, 1929). Faulkner wrote the first version of *Sanctuary* in five months (January to May) and submitted it to the publishing firm of Jonathan Cape and Harrison Smith, who were publishing *The Sound and the Fury*. When Smith rejected it, writing (according to Faulkner), "Good God, I can't publish this. We'd both be in jail," Faulkner began work on *As I Lay Dying*, which he finished in December of that incredibly productive year. *As I Lay Dying* was published by Cape & Smith on October 6, 1930, almost a year to the day after *The Sound and the Fury*.

During that time, Faulkner's stories were beginning to appear more regularly in national magazines, and although neither *The Sound and the Fury* nor *As I Lay Dying* had generated much sales for the company, Cape & Smith now reconsidered *Sanctuary*'s viability and, in November, sent Faulkner galley proofs of the novel. "I think I had forgotten about *Sanctuary*, just as you might forget about anything made for an immediate purpose, which did not come off," Faulkner would later claim in his 1932 introduction to the Modern Library edition of the book. He continued, in a passage which would come to taint the novel, "Then I saw it was so terrible that there were but two things to do: tear it up or rewrite it. I thought again, 'It might sell; maybe 10,000 of them will buy it.' So I tore the galleys down and rewrote the book. It had been already set up once, so I had to pay for the privilege of rewriting it, trying to make out of it something which would not shame *The Sound and the Fury* and *As I Lay Dying* too much and I made a fair job and I hope you

INTRODUCTION

will buy it and tell your friends and I hope they will buy it too." Faulkner finished the revision in December; the revised *Sanctuary* was published on February 9, 1931; and although it did better than the earlier books, was bought by Hollywood, and continued to be his best selling novel for years to come, its relative success failed to save Cape & Smith, which folded owing Faulkner more than $4,000 in royalties.

Sanctuary defined Faulkner in the public mind as a writer of violent, sensational, semi-pornographic novels. He became known as the "corncob man," the leader of the "cult of cruelty" in American literature. His Modern Library introduction, with its mock implication that the book was a cynical attempt to appeal to his readers' worst impulses, did little to mitigate that impression. Although some critics recognized its artistry and sensed the deeper moral concerns evident in the book, for far too many *Sanctuary* was a novel to be excused or ignored, a hasty and minor work at best. Today, it can be argued that no other Faulkner novel speaks as directly to its readers, continues to challenge our beliefs, to confront our sensibilities, as does this book. Certainly no other Faulkner novel has experienced the kind of critical re-evaluation and re-positioning as has *Sanctuary*.

This "reading," then, in keeping with the principles established by the late Jim Hinkle, the Founding Editor of the Reading Faulkner Series, attempts to approach the work at its most basic level. Although we have read the scholarship, and have benefited from it, our primary concern is to explore the words and phrases and the sentences themselves: to explain and define and connect where we can; to offer possibilities and suggestions and likelihoods where we cannot. Although *Sanctuary* is probably Faulkner's most dreamlike work, a bleak world of nightmare and fantasy and repression, we feel there is a dark logic to it throughout, an explanation for why people act as they do in the book, no matter how irrational these acts sometimes appear. In our reading, we have sometimes referred to the original *Sanctuary*, as edited by Noel Polk, for possible explanations, although we recognize that the two versions are best seen as separate works. More than in the two volumes

INTRODUCTION

which have preceded this one (*Reading Faulkner: Light in August* and *Reading Faulkner: The Unvanquished*), our volume does sometimes take critical positions on characters—we see Temple Drake primarily as a victim, for example, rather than as a victimizer, and are less sympathetic with Horace Benbow than are many readers. Ours, also, is the first novel for which a glossary of words and terms already exists (Melinda McLeod Rousselle's *Annotations to William Faulkner's* Sanctuary [Garland, 1989], and we have attempted not to repeat much of the information found in that work.

This, then, is perhaps a rather idiosyncratic book, with each of the authors bringing her and his critical skills and overall understandings of Faulkner into play—and as Jim Hinkle understood when he brought different Faulkner scholars together to work on these novels, there is a sense of play throughout the series. Neither of us completely agrees with everything in the book, nor do we expect others to accept all of our explanations or suggestions. We do, however, hope that this reading will aid in basic understanding of Faulkner's world, encourage close examination of Faulkner's text, and arouse further discussion of his intentions and meanings.

Edwin T. Arnold

AFTER WORDS

This book has been in the making for nearly a decade. For the first few years, the shape of the project kept metamorphosing as Jim Hinkle, the Reading Faulkner Series Sutpen (he made us all), kept refining his plans for the series. During the gestation, Jim kept flying to strange cities—like Akron—and summoning people to read with him. Chip Arnold and I, who met because Jim married us to *Sanctuary*, read all of it aloud with Bob McCoy and Jim in Akron over five days, rotating paragraphs, struggling over various sections, phrases, inflections. Chip claims he remembers only cup after cup of flavored coffee and dishes of walnuts. I think I remember making the coffee and filling the dish, but every time I teach *Sanctuary*, I am certain I hear their voices, remember how *Sanctuary* sounded—multivocaled, luxurious, disputatious—the best of all possible talk. This experience—four adults righteously attending to a book we all thought we knew pretty well until we were humbled by the discovery of pieces of Faulkner's prose that defied penetration and yielded perhaps the only consensus such an occasion could hope for—the accord that maybe consensus wasn't even desirable any way—was as joyful and professionally invigorating an occasion as could be wished for. If the readers of this work are ever invited to go anywhere and read aloud, they should, without hesitation, say yes yes yes and go.

This reading-in-the-round changed the way I taught everything—especially Faulkner—but more importantly, I learned how to read and how others read. This, of course, was the effect I think Jim intended to have—making good Faulkner readers better, and making self-satisfied Faulkner readers at least less hazardous in the classroom. Finally he just wanted someone to be responsible—not necessarily for the rightness of an explication, but for candid admissions of insufficiency in our readings. Jim explained this himself in one of his advisories to his explicators: "There is no point in pretending (in the name of academic respectability, of not insulting some hypothetical reader's intelligence, of addressing a more select audience).... I want glossaries whose aim is to be *useful* to real potential users, not ones based on false (or at least outdated) pieties about 'the fellowship of educated men.'"

I'm not sure Jim would be entirely pleased with what Chip and I have wrought. In the final five years of this dark pilgrimage, we had taken to slinking around book displays at literature conferences hoping Seetha Srinivasan, the "she who must be obeyed" at University Press of Mississippi, wouldn't see us and force us to lie again about how much longer it was going to take. In the course of finishing it, Jim died; Noel inherited the project in the will; Chip's kids grew up and he went to Japan for a year and came back; I finally saw the queens in the Luxembourg Gardens. We still aren't sure what "dizzent" means.

This summer when I showed some pages of a nearly final draft to a very distinguished French Faulknerian our worst fears were confirmed. The French critic gave me his best Yves-Montand-looking-patient-and-mystified-by-Americans look and said, "It's a sad commentary on the American school system—the need for such a book, isn't it?" Probably so, but I know of no other critical enterprise that could so closely approximate the raking up of leaves for a bonfire. To our readers, we apologize in these efforts for all that will prove to sharper eyes fault and false; but mostly we wish to acknowledge our deep gratitude for the chance Jim, University Press of Mississippi, and Noel gave us to have sat under thunder and rain and read *Sanctuary* with others.

Dawn Trouard

Reading Faulkner
SANCTUARY

Sanctuary

GLOSSARY AND COMMENTARY

Title: **SANCTUARY** A sanctuary is a sacred or consecrated place. In Anglo-Saxon England and other Catholic countries, certain churches and churchyards were recognized as places of refuge. This right of asylum decreed safeguard for criminals or debtors for 40 days; it was sacrilege to remove the person who had gained this protection. In some cases, the accused could during the 40-day period go in sackcloth and ashes before the coroner, confess the felony and take the oath of abjuration of the realm, which meant leaving the kingdom and not returning without the king's permission. Events in the book clearly reflect this concept and practice of sanctuary. As Faulkner said, "In *Sanctuary*, that meant that everyone must have some safe secure place to which he can hurry, run, from trouble."°* Characters in the work are constantly searching for places of escape and safety. The point of Faulkner's title, however, is more ironic than not: in the world of this book, nothing avoids violation and corruption. The title thus sets up false expectations, a pattern followed throughout the story, where hopes for rescue or forgiveness are consistently thwarted or denied. However, in *The Town* (1957) Gavin Stevens defines a sanctuary as "a rationality of perspective, which animals, humans too, not merely reach but earn by passing through unbearable emotional states like furious rage or furious fear. . . ."; this definition may come closer to the meaning Faulkner intended in the title.°

---

*The symbol ° indicates that a source is identified in the notes section following the chronology. Each source is keyed to the page and line number of the note it documents.

CHAPTER I

181:1 **From beyond the screen of bushes . . . emerge from the path and kneel to drink from the spring** Faulkner immediately disconcerts the reader through an unusual time sequencing. In the first sentence Popeye is watching "the man" (Horace Benbow) already drinking from the spring. However, in the third sentence Popeye watches the man "emerge from the path and kneel to drink from the spring." This minor flashback stresses that Popeye has been spying on Horace for some time from behind the "screen of bushes" which conceals him. By underscoring the secret, hidden nature of this locale in these initial scenes, Faulkner establishes the theme of spying, of voyeurism, which runs through the book. This theme is associated primarily with but not limited to Popeye, whose very name implies peeping or observing unawares.

181:2 **Popeye** Popeye is likely based on Memphis gangster Neal Karens (or Kerens) Pumphrey (1904–1931), who was among the most famous Memphis underworld figures of the 1920s. The child of a wealthy cotton man and the daughter of the attorney general of Arkansas, Pumphrey was nicknamed Popeye because his eyes bulged when he became excited. He was first charged with bootlegging in Memphis in 1924 and built up a long list of criminal offenses (including gambling, robbery, and assault) before purportedly committing suicide on October 28, 1931 (eight months after *Sanctuary* was published). Pumphrey seems to have been the gangster described to Faulkner by a young woman in a Memphis nightclub in 1926. As Blotner tells it, the woman was raised in a village called Cobbtown before moving to Memphis and meeting Pumphrey. "Although the gangster was said to be impotent, he still persisted in having relations with women, and he had raped one with a particularly bizarre object and kept her in a brothel."°

M. Thomas Inge makes the most sustained argument that Popeye's name and physical characteristics were also inspired by the cartoon character Popeye the Sailor, who was introduced in Elzie Segar's *Thimble Theatre* comic strip on January 17, 1929. Inge notes that it was "the most widely circulated comic strip in the United States, making some knowledge on Faulkner's part almost unavoidable."° But Faulkner had already used the Popeye character in his unpublished short story "The Big Shot" (1926), where Popeye is described as "a slight man with a dead face and dead black hair and eyes and a delicate hooked little nose and no chin, crouching snarling behind the neat blue automatic. He was a little dead-looking bird in a tight black suit like a vaudeville actor of twenty years ago, with a savage falsetto voice like a choir-boy."° In *Requiem for a Nun* (1951), Faulkner would give Popeye the last name of Vitelli, but he is known only as Popeye in *Sanctuary*. "You dont know his name, noway," Miss Reba later tells Temple (326:31//214:1).

181:2 **A faint path** little used, unaccustomed to traffic. Having grown up in Jefferson, Horace would surely be aware of the Old Frenchman place, so he might at least suspect water is nearby, but it is coincidence or accident that brings him in contact with Popeye. In *Sanctuary: The Original Text*, Faulkner writes that "after not having been passed by a car or passing a house himself in more than an hour, [Horace] left the road to seek water."°

181:3 **Popeye watched the man** The first description of Horace Benbow comes from Popeye's perspective as he watches in secret. Readers, however, see Benbow with but not through Popeye. We never actually enter Popeye's mind here or anywhere else, as we do with both Horace Benbow and Temple Drake.

181:4 **worn gray flannel trousers and carrying a tweed coat over his arm** This outfit marks Horace as a town man, most likely a professional or white collar worker. He is out of place in this rural setting and out of season for the heat of Mississippi May.

181:9 **cane** most likely a kind of bamboo cane, a reed with hard, jointed hollow stems often found in wet or swampy places. Canes can grow more than twenty feet tall and may be so dense as to make passage nearly impossible. Thus, the spot is isolated and enclosed.

181:10 **broken sunlight lay sourceless** The sun itself cannot be seen, hidden as it is by the canopy of vegetation which "breaks" the light into patterns. Like the underground spring and the singing bird, the light has no obvious point of origin.

181:12 **In the spring the drinking man leaned his face to the broken and myriad reflection of his own drinking** a reference to the Narcissus myth, one prevalent in Faulkner's early writings.° The multiple refractions of his image as Horace drinks disturbs the surface of the pool and prepares for the visual distortion when Popeye is described by cubism. See entry 183:22//7:2. Horace's narcissistic self-absorption is reflected in other characters observing themselves in mirrors. Reflection will form a key motif in the book. Also see description of Gowan Stevens (238:9//85:7).

181:14 **them** the concentric circles of water caused by his drinking.

181:14 **the shattered reflection of Popeye's straw hat** Popeye's image, also broken and shattered, replaces Horace's in the water and Faulkner draws the first of many parallels between Horace and Popeye in this scene. As Noel Polk notes, "The second paragraph virtually repeats the description of the spring and the singing bird; the third moves us across the spring, and we look back at Popeye from Horace's point of view, as Horace drinks, then sees in the 'broken and myriad reflection' of the water, not his own face, but Popeye's, in a mirror image of himself. . . . In this way Faulkner places the thematic relationship between Popeye and Horace more directly at the center of the novel's meaning . . . Faulkner directs us at the outset to weigh Popeye and Horace in the same scales."°

181:15 **though he had heard no sound** Though Popeye has come from behind the screen of bushes to stand next to the spring opposite Horace, Horace has not heard him move or detected his presence except by his reflection. Popeye's cat-like, stealthy movements are connected with his spying. His ubiquitousness increasingly becomes one of his most frightening characteristics.

181:17 **a cigarette slanted from his chin** Popeye has a receding chin so extreme that it seems "he had no chin at all. His face just went away, like the face of a wax doll set too near a hot fire and forgotten" (182:26//5:26). The cigarette in his mouth appears to come from the very bottom of his face where his chin would be if he had one.

181:18 **a tight, high-waisted coat** Like Horace, Popeye is wearing conspicuously urban clothes. But while Horace's flannel trousers and tweed coat suggest what Popeye later calls him— a "professor"—Popeye's high-waisted coat and straw hat suggest what he considers himself to be—a Memphis "dude." Both outfits are distinctly out of place in this rural setting.

181:20 **His face had a queer, bloodless color, as though seen by electric light** Although standing in natural (although filtered) sunlight, Popeye still appears unnatural, as though lit by artificial means. An indoor and nocturnal figure, Popeye has a pale complexion suggesting illness or malnourishment. He and three other characters—Temple Drake, the Goodwin baby, and Clarence Snopes—are described as being "putty-faced" (219:13//59:14;221:31–32//62:25–26;360:20//261:11).

181:22 **vicious depthless quality of stamped tin** Stark against the background of sunlight, Popeye in his black suit appears to Horace as if he were a silhouette or shadow. "Stamped tin" reinforces the mechanical nature of his appearance. He seems without thickness but dangerous nonetheless because of his angularity and sharp edges.° Also see a similar image at 198:31//29:21.

181:25 **a sound meaningless and profound out of a suspirant and peaceful following silence which seemed to isolate the**

spot The sound made by the unseen bird gives definition to the setting. It is, in itself, without sense or significance: three simple repetitive notes. However, it takes on a momentary importance because it breaks the "silence" and thus becomes a point of focus between the moments of quiet which precede and follow it. Like Wallace Stevens' jar set on the wooded hill in Tennessee, it becomes "profound" because of its existence, but not because there is any demonstrable purpose or plan behind that existence. Indeed, its lack of apparent meaning adds to its mystery.° See 192; 234; 249 for other uses of this image. "Suspirant" is Faulkner's neologistic variation on *suspiration*: it means "sighing." He suggests that the very absence of sound creates the awareness of sound.

181:29 **The drinking man knelt beside the spring. . . . "I'm asking you," Popeye said. "What's that in your pocket?"** Faulkner's deliberate use of ambiguous pronouns throughout the book blurs identities. The "he" who asks the first question is Horace Benbow, the "drinking man." Popeye appropriates the question and control: "I'm asking you."

181:32 **two knobs of soft black rubber** another indication of Popeye's artificial nature. The description suggests that in addition to the bulging aspect of Popeye's eyes, his pupils are also literally enlarged since there is no mention of the whites of his eyes. Horace is unable to see into his eyes, much less penetrate his intention. See entry 199:4//30:2

182:1 **Dont show me . . . Tell me** Popeye assumes that Horace might be carrying a gun and warns him not to reach into the pocket.

182:9 **like a mask carved into two simultaneous expressions** The image recalls the dramatic mask carved with a smile and a frown. The description also fits the standard illustration of Popeye the Sailor, who usually holds a pipe rather than a cigarette in his mouth.

182:11 **From his hip pocket Popeye took a soiled handkerchief and spread it upon his heels. Then he squatted** The fastidious Popeye wants to protect the seat of his pants from the mud caked on the bottom of his trousers and shoes as he squats. Curiously, Popeye and Horace—both city people—maintain this unnatural position for better than two hours. Faulkner often described country people *hunkering*, which is squatting in a balanced position with feet flat on the ground, but this is not what Popeye and Horace are doing.

182:15 **Now and then the bird sang back in the swamp, as though it were worked by a clock** as if it sounded at regular appointed times, as a mechanical bird marks the hour on a cuckoo clock.

182:20 **I dont suppose you'd know a bird at all, without it was singing in a cage in a hotel lounge, or cost four dollars on a plate** Horace points out how out of place Popeye seems in this setting. Horace's mildly insulting humor seems an attempt to initiate conversation or provoke some response from his strange, silent companion.

182:23 **his right hand coat pocket sagging compactly against his flank** The coat pocket holds his gun.

182:24 **twisting and pinching cigarettes** Although it here appears that Popeye is rolling his own cigarettes, he later takes one from a pack (184). Machine-rolled cigarettes were common in 1929 (the rolling machine was invented by James Bonsack in 1880), but they were not as round and firmly packed as those today; the smoker would automatically twist both ends, as Popeye does, to prevent loose tobacco from falling out or flecking onto the tongue and mouth.

182:25 **doll-like hands** Popeye is a man "of under size" (181:16//4:7), small and delicate though surprisingly strong. The doll imagery is later used to describe Temple Drake. See Ruby's insult to Temple: "you little doll-faced slut" (219:17//59:19).

182:25 **spitting into the spring** Popeye fouls the natural purity of the water from which Horace has just drunk.

182:26 **His nose was faintly aquiline** curved like the beak of an eagle, a physical characteristic Popeye shared with Faulkner himself.°

182:29 **platinum chain like a spider web** a watch chain, although it holds a penknife (209) rather than a watch. Platinum is a less precious metal than silver but often used in jewelry. The comparison to a "spider web" underscores Popeye's sinister nature. In *Sanctuary: The Original Text*, Faulkner was more suggestive in his description of Popeye's accouterments: "with his cigarette and his pistol and his dollar watch loose in his pocket like a coin, with the platinum chain across his vest and a turnip-shaped silver watch which wouldn't run on the end of it, which he had inherited from his grandfather, with a lock of his mother's hair in the back of the case."°

182:30 **Horace Benbow** First introduced in *Flags in the Dust*, Horace is one of Faulkner's narcissistic, overly idealistic, romantic Prufrockians, constantly disillusioned by the harsh realities of the world. In *Flags in the Dust* (1929), he returns from the War in France, where he served in the Red Cross rather than as a combatant. The original version of *Sanctuary*, begun in 1929 shortly after *Flags in the Dust*, concentrates more heavily on Horace than does the revised version published in 1931.° Horace disappears from Faulkner's fiction after *Sanctuary* and his role of "liberal lawyer" is assumed by Gavin Stevens, a lawyer and uncle of Gowan Stevens.

182:30 **Kinston** a fictional town in the Mississippi Delta, fifty or so miles southwest of Jefferson.

182:31 **Jefferson** the county seat of Faulkner's fictional Yoknapatawpha County, central to all of his Mississippi work. Jefferson is based on Oxford and Ripley, Mississippi, the towns in which Faulkner lived most of his life.

182:32 **Anybody in this county can tell you I am harmless** Horace's statement, with its self-deprecating tone, intends to assuage Popeye's curiosity about the stranger. However, Horace, with his idealistic, dreamy manner, will cause considerable harm by failing to appreciate the depth of evil and corruption he faces in a character such as Popeye.

182:32 **If it's whiskey, I dont care how much you all make or sell or buy** "Whiskey" is moonshine, or privately-made corn whiskey. Mississippi was the first state to ratify the Eighteenth

Amendment (1919) which forbade the manufacture, sale, or transportation (though not the actual consumption) of liquor. State law required scientific temperance education "with a special reference to the nature of alcohol and narcotics, and their effect upon the human system." The penalties for breaking prohibition laws were very stiff: "The 1924 session of the Mississippi Legislature enacted a measure making it a felony to own or control or possess a still, or parts thereof, the penalty being a fine of $300 or imprisonment in the penitentiary up to three years, or both fine and imprisonment."°

In his comment, Horace is distinguishing among various moonshining activities. The moonshiner—in this case Lee Goodwin—makes and sells the whiskey; the bootlegger—Popeye—buys in quantity and transports the liquor for subsequent resale at a higher price. It is never completely clear whether Popeye works for someone else or runs his own business, but when Horace asks Tommy who drives the transportation truck, Tommy replies, "Hit's Popeye's truck" (193:33//20:30). In any case, Horace is trying to assure Popeye that he is not a tax agent or revenuer.

183:5 **Popeye put his eyes on Benbow, like rubber** Playing on the previous descriptions of Popeye's eyes as "rubber knobs," Faulkner creates the sense that they "stick" to Horace—Popeye "removes" them at 183:8//6:18. But rubber is by nature more elastic than adhesive. The central idea, in any case, is that Popeye holds Horace still with his eyes.

183:5 **Do you want to run?** Popeye implies that he will shoot Benbow if he tries to escape.

183:12 **a dollar watch** a large, sturdy, nickel-plated Ingersoll pocket watch which sold for a dollar at the turn of the century and which continued to be called a "dollar watch" even after its price increased. Popeye checks the time as dark approaches; he has been on guard near the road, waiting for his moonshine delivery from Memphis.

183:15 **Where the path** the first of many abrupt, often puzzling transitions in *Sanctuary*. After Popeye checks his watch, he and Horace leave the spring, ending the more than two

VI 7:15 / 183:34

hour wait. Why the vigil stops is unclear: perhaps Popeye's shift is over, or he has given up on the truck, or he does not want to be in the woods at night.

183:15 **sandy byroad** This seems to be the driveway which runs from the Old Frenchman place to the gravel highway. The path runs from the highway to the spring and then on to the byroad.

183:15 **a tree had been recently felled, blocking the road** another precaution against a surprise raid. The barrier is Popeye's idea (193:17//20:13), even though it makes it more difficult to load the trucks and interferes with ease of access for customers who would expect to drive up to the house. Gowan Stevens, for instance, will be completely surprised by the tree when he comes to buy liquor in Chap. IV.

183:18 **two shallow parallel depressions, but no mark of hoof** caused not by wagon wheels, which would have been drawn by mule, but by automobile tires (183:20//6:30), those of Popeye's car.

183:22 **modernist lampstand** The modernist art movement emphasized its break with the realist tradition and often employed bizarre exaggeration, repetition, or refraction of images. The cubist effect created by Popeye's reflection in the disturbed water is reinforced here when Horace still sees Popeye as "all angles," more mechanical or artificial than human.°

183:25 **Jack** a tough-guy slang term, possibly contemptuous since Horace has already introduced himself.

183:26 **Why didn't we cut straight across up the hill?** By following the path, they have walked parallel to their destination. By cutting through the denser woods from the spring directly toward the house, they could have gotten there sooner.

183:28 **His hat jerked** Though Popeye is gesturing towards the woods, he is soon described as twitching (183:32//7:13). He is nervous in this situation.

183:30 **Jesus Christ** one of Popeye's most common oaths. Popeye dismisses Horace's question as the sort only a fool would ask.

183:34 **vicious cringing** paradoxical action, a combination of violent aggression and servile fear. Popeye does not simply cower but attempts to maintain some semblance of his earlier fierceness. Compare to the description of the rat Temple inadvertently corners in the barn in Chapter XI. See entry 243:39//93:11.

183:36 **shadow shaped with speed** Because of the darkness, they feel the bird's presence by its rapid movement but can't identify it.

183:36 **stooped** A "stoop" is the rapid descent of a bird. The owl dives down as if to attack its prey.

183:39 **his hand clawing at his coat** ambiguous wording. Popeye is either frantically grabbing at Benbow's coat in childlike search of protection, or, more likely (as seen below), he is grasping in panic for the gun he carries in his right-hand coat pocket.

184:1 **Carolina wren** a large wren with a conspicuous white line over the eye. It sings the loud three-note call Faulkner describes in the opening of this chapter. The swoop of the owl, which so terrifies Popeye, prompts Horace to remember the name of the bird that had sung earlier. In *Sanctuary: The Original Text*, Horace is "trying to remember the name by which country-people knew the joree-bird."°

184:4 **He smells black, Benbow thought; he smells like that black stuff that ran out of Bovary's mouth and down upon her bridal veil when they raised her head** a reference to Gustave Flaubert's *Madame Bovary* (1857): "They bent over to put on her wreath; they had to lift her head a little, and as they did so a stream of dark liquid poured from her mouth, as though she was vomiting."° Emma Bovary has killed herself with arsenic; this "vomiting" is the residue. As André Bleikasten has written, "In both books there is a steady concern with bodily excreta, with oozing or leaking flesh, and with all symptoms of organic corruption."° The readiness of Horace's association has caused some critics to propose that the book Horace has in his pocket is the Flaubert novel.° The story of unhappy marriage and female treachery might very well be the sort of novel Horace would be reading during his own time of trial.

184:12 **Old Frenchman place** a house built before the Civil War by a wealthy Frenchman identified in *Requiem for a Nun* as Louis Grenier (385:1//297:1); one of the two largest and most elaborate plantation houses in Yoknapatawpha County, the other belonging to Thomas Sutpen in *Absalom, Absalom!* (1936). Compare the description in *Sanctuary* to that found in *The Hamlet* (1940): "a tremendous pre-Civil War plantation, the ruins of which—the gutted shell of an enormous house with its fallen stables and slave quarters and overgrown gardens and brick terraces and promenades—were still known as the Old Frenchman's place, although the original boundaries now existed only on old faded records in the Chancery Clerk's office in the county courthouse in Jefferson, and even some of the once-fertile fields had long since reverted to the cane-and-cypress jungle from which their first master had hewn them."° In *The Hamlet* (whose events pre-date those of *Sanctuary*), the Old Frenchman place belongs to Will Varner, the patriarch of Frenchman's Bend. On his map of Jefferson and Yoknapatawpha County, drawn for *Absalom, Absalom!*, Faulkner located the Old Frenchman place about 20 miles southeast of Jefferson near the Yoknapatawpha River. He denied the place was based on any actual site.

184:15 **neighborhood** Frenchman's Bend.

184:16 **digging with secret and sporadic optimism for the gold which the builder was reputed to have buried somewhere about the place** Many Southerners supposedly buried valuables on their property to protect them from pillage by invading Yankee troops. Legends about unrecovered treasures were not uncommon after the Civil War, and Faulkner employed the idea in his story "Lizards in Jamshyd's Courtyard," written in 1930 and published in *The Saturday Evening Post* on 27 February 1932. The story was incorporated into the last chapter of *The Hamlet.*

184:19 **when Grant came through the county on his Vicksburg campaign** Ulysses S. Grant (1822–1885), Union General and later President of the U. S. (1869–1877). Before being named leader of the Union Armies on March 2, 1864, Grant was commander of the Western Federal forces and led the Siege of Vicksburg, Mississippi, from 18 May to 4 July 1863, when the Confederate troops under Gen. John C. Pemberton surrendered. Grant headquartered in Oxford, Mississippi, during much of December, 1862. In Faulkner's version of Southern history, Grant's advance took him through Yoknapatawpha County and he for a time headquartered in Jefferson.

184:21 **Three men** Two of these men would apparently be Lee Goodwin and Tommy. A reasonable guess for the identity of the third would be Pap, but the group is described as "looking at" Popeye and Horace (184:24//8:12). Since Pap is blind, this description would seem to exclude him from this group, but in *Sanctuary: The Original Text*, the third figure is identified as Pap (53).

184:22 **The hall went straight back through the house** The house, also known as a "dog-trot cabin,"° has a "shotgun" hall, so named because you could shoot a shotgun through it without hitting anything. This architectural style was not uncommon. A two-story house with this type of open central hall was called an "I House."

184:25 **Here's the professor** "professor" used here as ironic underworld slang to capture Horace's intelligent, cultured, or scholarly, studious mien: i.e., the stereotyped pianist in a brothel. As Popeye sarcastically explains (185:4//9:8), Horace must be a professor since he has a book with him.

184:26 **crossed the back porch and turned and entered the room where the light was. It was the kitchen** It was common practice to locate the kitchen at the rear of and away from the main house to diminish the risk of fires likely to start in the cooking area.

184:29 **calico** cheap cotton fabric with figured patterns.

184:30 **brogans** a heavy work shoe that reaches above the ankle.

184:35 **pinched and fretted** prepared the cigarette for smoking rather than displayed nervous agitation. See entry 182:24//5:24.

184:36 **bird** slang for a strange, odd person. Here the word choice may be occasioned by the owl which has recently frightened Popeye.

184:39 **Why tell me? . . . I dont serve Lee's customers** Since Ruby is cooking, she is most obviously declaring that she is not required to feed the men who come to buy whiskey from Lee. As a former prostitute, she also seems to be asserting her freedom not to serve men since her comment opens an ensuing round of sexual insults that follow.

185:10 **Was he trying to find this house?** Is he a customer, or perhaps a federal agent? Ruby is concerned with the security of Lee's operation.

185:12 **I'll send him on to Jefferson on the truck** On Faulkner's map, Jefferson is northwest of Frenchman's Bend. The main road to Memphis would pass through Jefferson. Popeye is obviously not worried that Horace is a lawman.

185:15 **You cook. He'll want to eat** There is no reason for Popeye to care if Horace is hungry. His apparent concern is better interpreted as Popeye's attempt to reestablish his authority, lost momentarily in his panic at the owl. Ordering the woman helps him to regain his sense of domination.

185:17 **crimps and spungs and feebs** underworld slang terms: Ruby's paraphrase of "the lame, the halt, and the blind." A *crimp* is a cripple or cheat; *spung* is a variation of sponge and refers to a crook who lives off other crooks; *feeb* is abbreviation for feeble-minded. Pap is the crimp, Tommy the feeb, and Popeye himself (or any of the men who make money off Lee) the spung. Ruby counters Popeye's insults with her own derisive jabs.

185:20 **I'll take you back to Memphis Sunday** located in the southwestern corner of Tennessee, about 75 miles from Oxford. In the 1920s it was infamous for its gangsters, prostitution, and bootlegging and was called the "Murder Capital of the USA," the Southern equivalent of Chicago.° It is significant that Popeye here announces his intentions to return to Memphis on Sunday, the day he does in fact leave the Old Frenchman place with Temple. See entries 246:25//96:26; 247:6//97:15.

185:20 **hustling** soliciting for prostitution. The word connotes the need for hurry in order to make as many contacts as possible.

185:22 **Manuel street** a fictitious street, often identified with Memphis's actual Mulberry Street, located in the red light district restricted for prostitution. Mulberry dead-ends into Beale Street.

185:25 **Ruby Lamar** Ruby shares a last name with noted Mississippi politician Lucius Quintus Cincinnatus Lamar (1825–1893), also mentioned in *Requiem for a Nun.*° See entry 185:26//10:2.

185:26 **Lee Goodwin** Like Ruby Lamar, Lee Goodwin's name recalls the Southern past: Robert E. Lee (1807–1870), Commanding General of the Confederacy, is often seen as the epitome of the Southern gentleman warrior.°

185:33 **He had a sunburned thatch of hair, matted and foul ... a short soft beard like dirty gold in color** Tommy is a blond. See *Sanctuary: The Original Text:* "He had a beautiful face, with pale eyes and a soft young beard like dirty gold. Like Christ he looked: a sort of rapt, furious face."°

185:34 **furious eyes** intense or turbulent rather than angry. Tommy is always watchful, observant.

185:36 **I be dawg if he aint a case, now** "I'll be dog-goned [god-damned] if he isn't funny or strange." Tommy is describing Horace, whom Popeye has already described as an odd character. Although Tommy speaks in pronounced dialect in the book and is clearly slow, he is certainly not stupid.

186:2 **though in plain sight of them, he removed a loose board in the floor and took out a gallon jug** Popeye, ironically, hates drinking and intoxication, in part because he cannot physically tolerate liquor himself but also because of the loss of control it causes. Knowing this, Tommy waits for Popeye to react to the jug provocatively not hidden behind his flank. He wants to see how far Popeye can be pushed: "as though [Tommy] were ready to laugh at a joke, waiting for the time to laugh" (185:39//10:15).

186:7 **baleful** foreboding harm or death. Popeye's exact feelings are hard to read, hidden as they are behind the twisted mask of his face. But he is certainly capable of sudden violence, as Tommy well knows; hence, his "alert diffidence" as he walks by Popeye (186:8//10:24).

186:13 **dummy** a deaf-mute, or simply one who cannot talk: Pap.

CHAPTER II

187:1 **When the woman . . . Popeye and the man who had fetched the jug from the kitchen and the stranger** Only Popeye is identified by name. The others are Ruby, Tommy, and Horace himself. Faulkner emphasizes the anonymous nature of this gathering.

187:4 **trestles** braced frames serving as support; also known as saw horses.

187:10 **an open packing case** where she keeps her extra dishes. We know Lee has been moonshining at the Old Frenchman place for at least four years (193:19//20:9), but this detail—constant readiness to move—underscores the provisional nature of their lives on the margins of society.

187:18 **an old man with a long white beard stained about the mouth** soon identified as Pap, who is probably Lee's father, although it is never authoritatively established in the novel. Lee, however, is the one leading him in to the table. Some readers have linked him to Tommy, who also seems to have no known past, but again there is no evidence, although Tommy also refers to him as "Pap" (209:32//45:22). To compound matters, Pap simply and completely disappears from the book after Lee's arrest for Tommy's murder. In *Sanctuary: The Original Text*, Faulkner emphasized Pap's mysterious nature: "[Horace] never learned who he was nor where he went. He didn't look like any of the others; he was just there, then he was gone, leaving no gap, no hole in the pattern."° See entry 255:23//110:2.

187:24 **cataracted eyes** A cataract is a clouding of the eye lens which blocks the passage of light and ultimately causes blindness. Faulkner turns the noun into a verbal; "cataractal" would be the more common term.

187:33 **and began to suck at it until the woman returned and rapped his knuckles** Ruby attempts to maintain decorum at the table. Pap, like a large baby, must be physically rebuked to wait. The dinner scene is a travesty of a typical family meal.

187:36 **sorghum** a very strong syrup made from the juice of a sargo, a variety of the sorghum plant. Country people commonly used it as a source of sweetening. Since taste is one of Pap's few functioning senses, the sweetness is something of a treat to him.

187:36 **Then Benbow quit looking** Repeatedly in this book, Horace, despite his voyeurism, finds it difficult to witness the unpleasant, horrible, or disgusting. See second entry for 188:21//13:19 and entry 188:24//13:23.

188:5 **she went to the box behind the stove and she stood over it for a time** This is not the packing crate holding the plates (187:10//11:10). By withholding an explanation for Ruby's action here, Faulkner intensifies the mystery of the house and its inhabitants. See 191:31//18:2.

188:7 **lit a cigarette from the lamp** by the flame of the oil lamp. The Old Frenchman place is without electricity, like most rural homes in Mississippi until after World War II.

188:15 **the voice of a man given to much talk and not much else. "Not to drinking, anyway"** Ruby's estimate of Horace. Her quoted words reveal her thoughts about Horace, although she is speaking more to herself than to anyone.

188:17 **He better get on to where he's going, where his women folks can take care of him** Like Miss Jenny and Horace's sister Narcissa in Chapter III, Ruby recognizes Horace's need to be mothered. She also realizes that he doesn't belong at the Old Frenchman place, although he never seems to be in any real danger, protected, almost, by his naiveté.

188:20 **grape arbor** an enclosed bower; grape vines provide leafy walls and sometimes a roof by climbing the latticed structure. Arbors were not uncommon as decorations in Southern yards; they were sometimes equipped with benches and used as secluded meeting places.

188:20 **in the winter I could see the hammock too** because it is no longer hidden by the leafy growth, killed off during the winter months.

188:21 **But in the winter it was just the hammock** Between the cold weather and the loss of seclusion no one—i.e., Little Belle—is in the hammock to see.

188:21 **That's why we know nature is a she; because of that conspiracy between female flesh and female season** Horace sees Spring as the "female season." Reasoning that women's goal is to mate, Horace feels that Spring "conspires" with women to hide their sexual activities, especially young women like Little Belle who are "in season," just beginning to experience their sexuality. In this case, Little Belle can rely on the screen provided by the leafiness of the grape arbor to block Horace's view of her courting activities. We should note, however, Horace's role as a spy in this episode. The arbor growth prevents Horace from indulging in his own voyeuristic impulses, and he feels excluded.

188:23 **So each spring I could watch the reaffirmation of the old ferment hiding the hammock** "Ferment" is a state of unrest, of great activity, and here refers specifically to the renewed growth of vegetation which each spring covers the arbor as part of the annual renewal of nature's sexual cycle in both plants and animals. However, the word also picks up the idea of the grapes themselves, the juices which turn into wine through the act of fermentation. Faulkner suggests Horace's obsession with the sexual activity he suspects is taking place in the hidden hammock.

188:24 **the green-snared promise of unease** Horace is both tormented and stirred by this sexual possibility. The arbor, with all its enticements, is, for Horace, both invitation and trap; sexual excitement is both pleasure and discomfort. He

would seem to prefer a kind of comfortable dormancy. See
T. S. Eliot's *The Waste Land*:

> April is the cruellest month, breeding
> Lilacs out of the dead land, mixing
> Memory and desire, stirring
> Dull roots with spring rain.
> Winter kept us warm, covering
> Earth in forgetful snow, feeding
> A little life with dried tubers.°

188:28 **her—Little Belle's** Horace's stepdaughter, the biological daughter of Harry Mitchell whom Belle divorced in *Flags in the Dust* to marry Horace. Horace not only identifies his stepdaughter, but in his revision of the statement from "her" to a specific name, reminds us that he is conducting this disquisition for an audience.

188:28 **voice would be like the murmur of the wild grape itself** Since the wild grape makes no sound, Horace is employing synesthesia, apparently implying that Little Belle's voice is low, lush and seductive. See entry 294:24//166:29.

188:30 **"It's just Horace." Just, you see** By not introducing her dates, as custom and good manners would dictate, Little Belle fails to show proper respect and courtesy to her stepfather. The modifier "just" shows how insignificant Horace is in her eyes. See entry 189:10//14:19.

188:31 **a little white dress** See Narcissa Benbow Sartoris, Horace's sister, who is also habitually dressed in white, the sign of virginal purity. Both females, with their pretenses of innocence, arouse Horace sexually and increase his guilt and conflict.

188:32 **the two of them all demure and quite alert and a little impatient** To be demure is to feign modesty, pretend shyness. Little Belle and her beau are attempting to disguise their sexual excitement in a false show of modesty, but they are also quite eager for Horace to leave so that they can return to their private amorous activities.

188:33 **And I couldn't have felt any more foreign to her flesh if**

188:35 / VI 14:3

I had begot it myself Although he is related to Little Belle only through his marriage to her mother, Horace shares the feeling any father must experience when he suddenly realizes that he has been replaced in his pubescent daughter's estimation by another male. Little Belle's dismissive "just" (188:30//13:29) leads him to dramatize the appropriate remoteness the culture enforces between father and daughter, through the allusion to incest. However, Horace's use of the word "flesh" also illustrates the fascination and horror he feels in this sexually-charged situation. See entries 293:33//165:29; 293:39//166:4.

188:35 **So this morning ... and this is Tuesday** This is the first indication of the chronology of events in *Sanctuary*. (See Appendix for complete Chronology of the book.) According to the dates given in the novel, the story takes place in 1929, the year Faulkner first began writing the book. In *Sanctuary: The Original Text*, he actually names the year (285). The present day is Tuesday, May 7. The scene Horace recalls took place on the preceding Thursday, May 2. The "four days ago"—the morning Horace leaves Belle—would be Friday, May 3, as further events will prove. That the days between Friday and Tuesday are a blur in Horace's mind illustrates both his drunkenness and his emotional chaos: Horace has been wandering around in a daze.

188:36 **school** the University of Mississippi in Oxford, where Temple Drake also goes to school.

188:37 **if you found him on the train** Little Belle is accompanied by a boy she has just met on the train coming home from school. Horace is shocked at her forwardness and the impropriety of inviting a relative stranger with no social credentials to her home.

188:39 **like the insulators on the poles** round-knobbed glass insulators found on telephone poles. Usually made of green or clear glass, they are now sometimes sold as curiosities or paperweights although, as the inscription on each indicates, they are the property of the telephone company. Horace's feeble effort at humor attempts to reduce the boy to a troublesome but illegal souvenir she has brought home.

189:1 **He's as good as you are. He goes to Tulane** Tulane University in New Orleans. Little Belle further diminishes Horace by making no distinction between Tulane and Horace's alma maters of Heidelberg and Oxford.

189:10 **You're not my father. You're just——just——** Little Belle gropes for an epithet that negates any claim Horace might have to relationship to or authority over her: perhaps "the man who lives with my mother" would complete her thought. Her reiteration of the word "just" again suggests the diminution Horace has long suffered in her estimation.

189:15 **If he'd walked into your room in a hotel, I'd just kill him. But on the train, I'm disgusted** Horace assumes the duty of father-protector to kill any man who compromises his daughter's virtue. However, he implies that on a train Little Belle had the opportunity to avoid the encounter; failing to do so, she has displayed poor judgment and has shamed herself. There is, of course, a good bit of bravado in Horace's pronouncement. In *Sanctuary: The Original Text*, he is less blustering: "If he'd walked into your room in a hotel, I'd just be enraged. But on the train, I'm disgusted."° Compare Horace's sentiment here to Eustace Graham's statements during Lee Goodwin's trial. See entry 376:11//284:2.

189:18 **You're a fine one to talk about finding things on the train! You're a fine one! Shrimp! Shrimp!** Shrimp is slang for a small, weak person, which Horace, physically, at least, is not. Little Belle challenges his vaunted courage, drawing attention instead to his weakness of character and, by implication, his questionable masculinity since he is fetcher for her mother's whims. See entry 191:19//17:19 for further explanation.

189:25 **the slain flowers, the delicate dead flowers** the smell of perfume, made from "slain flowers," in her hair. The image also underscores Horace's connection of female sexuality with nature.

189:26 **and then I saw her face in the mirror . . . watching the**

189:30 **back of my head with pure dissimulation** This complicated description of the act of observing combines voyeurism and narcissism. Little Belle realizes that she has overstepped with Horace. Thus, she reverts to her little girl pose by which she can recover her control and manipulate Horace. She becomes so caught up in watching her own performance in the mirror behind Horace, however, that she fails to notice that Horace, too, can see her "pure dissimulation" in yet another mirror behind her back. Horace witnesses her pretense in the reflection of a reflection: the image which is reversed in the first mirror is corrected by the second—Horace sees the "true" image. See 328:8//216:2 for a similar description of Temple Drake.

189:30 **That's why nature is 'she' and Progress is 'he'; nature made the grape arbor, but Progress invented the mirror** Nature conspires with woman to hide, to deceive, while "male" Progress creates ways for man to discover the truth, as Horace does by looking in the mirror.

189:35 **I thought that maybe I would be all right if I just had a hill to lie on . . . engender money out of it** Horace is repulsed by the rich, fertile and "foul" land of the feminine Delta; he is disgusted by its ripeness and equates the farming of it to a kind of promiscuity. In escaping to higher ground, he metaphorically escapes his wife's lush sexuality. He wants to rise above it, cleanse himself of all its claims.

189:40 **Delta** the Mississippi Delta, the part of the Mississippi River flood plain that extends from Memphis, Tennessee, to Vicksburg, Mississippi.

190:1 **bumps of dirt the Indians made to stand on when the River overflowed** The Delta region is generally flat, but there are ancient Indian burial mounds, built for ceremonial purposes as well as for safety during periods of flooding. See, for example, "Old Man" in *If I Forget Thee, Jerusalem* (1939).

190:4 **set me off** made me leave.

190:5 **He is** either drunk or crazy. See 189:33//15:10.

190:5 **ought not to let——** Lee, as person in charge, shouldn't let Horace drink any more liquor.

190:8 **Belle's room** his wife Belle. Horace's step-daughter is always distinguished as *Little* Belle. He and his wife have separate bedrooms.

190:9 **a handkerchief** the third soiled, dirty rag to be mentioned so far in the book. Horace's repugnance for the unclean is linked to Popeye and Pap.

190:11 **behind the mantel** Horace initially claims that the rag is "stuffed behind the mirror" (190:9//15:28) but later changes it to "behind the mantel." In *Sanctuary: The Original Text*, Horace enters Belle's room and goes to her "night-table": "In a moment he found what he knew he should: a soiled handkerchief with which she had removed surplus rouge from her mouth and stuffed between the mirror and wall."° Belle apparently uses the same rag over and over to wipe off her excess makeup, and is either too lazy or is simply indifferent to Horace's standards of tidiness to be bothered with cleaning up after herself. In either case, this "foulness" is the final straw for Horace. We should note, nevertheless, that Horace is again snooping, prying, searching for evidence of this "dirty" behavior.

190:12 **clothes-bag** a receptacle for dirty clothes. Horace must clean up, put things in order even while deserting his wife.

190:20 **When you marry your own wife, you start off from scratch ... from somebody else's scratch and scratching** To start off "from scratch" means to begin with nothing, without advantage. If you marry a woman with no previous marriage for comparison, you start at zero. But to take on "somebody else's scratch and scratching" means to inherit a past or history other than your own, thus to begin in arrears. Horace, for example, has taken on Belle, her child, and her expectations from a former marriage. Faulkner himself had married Estelle Oldham, a divorced woman with two children, on June 20, 1929, the date on which Lee Goodwin's trial begins. See entry 363:2//264:24.

190:28 **it** the truck which will carry the whiskey Popeye has bought from Goodwin.

190:29   **three of them**   Popeye, Goodwin, and Tommy.

190:31   **the sky, the lesser darkness**   Horace's silhouette is darker than the evening sky which forms a backdrop to it.

191:1   **I lack courage**   Since Horace does show physical courage in the book—during his first meeting with Popeye, for example, and during the attack of the owl which so terrifies Popeye—he seems to be referring to moral courage or courage of character: he recognizes his tendency to run away or avoid unpleasant situations. He shows great self-pity in the following passage which anticipates his complete collapse at the end of the book.

191:2   **The machinery is all here, but it wont run**   Horace unintentionally sets up a comparison between himself, his moral stunting, and Popeye's "machinery," the undeveloped sexual organs, which also won't work. See 392:24//308:23.

191:12   **"Because she ate shrimp," he said . . . small stinking spots on a Mississippi sidewalk**   the source of Little Belle's earlier insult (see entry 189:18//14:26). See *Flags in the Dust* in which Horace thinks of himself as "H. Benbow, M.A., Ll.D., C.S." with the C.S. standing for "Carrier of Shrimp."° See also T. S. Eliot's "The Love Song of J. Alfred Prufrock": "I have measured out my life with coffee spoons." See entry 191:19//17:19.

191:18   **Friday**   Horace gets the shrimp on Tuesdays in *Flags in the Dust*. The change to Friday may reflect the Catholic habit of eating fish on Friday.

191:19   **And I still dont like to smell shrimp**   Faulkner may be alluding here to the misogynist joke comparing the smell of fish and female genitalia. Certainly Horace's disgust with shrimp is a metaphor for his disgust with his wife Belle and female sexuality. See 254:21//108:25.

191:22   **after a while I follow myself to the station . . . and I following him**   An alienated Horace observes himself objectively, distancing himself intellectually from the man engaged in this weekly humiliation. Temple Drake will divorce herself from the events happening to her in the same act of self-protection. See entry 242:25//91:16.

191:29 **he gave back** stepped aside. Horace has been speaking to her in close quarters all this time, even feeling her face like a blind man at one point during the explanation (191:4// 17:4).

191:38 **pinched face** drawn tight in pain or exhaustion.

192:9 **her face not sullen so much, as cold, still** Ruby's expression is no longer resentful but is nevertheless unresponsive, guarded.

192:14 **an orange stick** a pointed stick of orange wood used to manicure the nails. The smallness of the request and her shame about her hands suggest that she is painfully aware of her fall from the luxury of Memphis high life to keep house in this remote Mississippi ruin with Goodwin.

192:16 **abandoned road** the byroad, blocked by the tree, leading to the house. See 193:10//20:6.

192:19 **profound** stark, but also unknowable, mysterious. See entry 181:25//4:16.

192:20 **freshets** an overflowing of a stream caused by heavy rains.

192:27 **I'll be bound** certain, sure.

192:32 **I be dog** I'll be dog-gone, darned. In this scene Tommy pronounces the word as "dog" rather than "dawg," his standard pronunciation. See 185:36//10:13 as example. But also notice Tommy's inadvertent comparison between his fate and that of the dog in the story to follow.

192:33 **skeeriest durn *white* man** an implied racial comparison: Tommy expects blacks to be afraid or superstitious.

192:36 **that ere dog . . . like ere a dog will** *Ere* serves two purposes: 1) that **there** dog; then "ere" adapts to mean 2) **as** any dog will.

192:36 **flinch off** draw away, pull back.

192:37 **whupped out** pulled out hastily. Compare Popeye's reactions to the owl; see entry 183:39//7:20.

192:37 **artermatic pistol** an automatic pistol, one which mechanically ejects the empty cartridge shell and replaces it in the chamber with a new cartridge for firing. By 1911, the U. S. Army issued Colt automatics.

192:38 **dead as a door-nail** absolutely dead. A door-nail is the striking plate of a door knocker. The phrase dates to as early as 1350. In this scene, Tommy speaks in repeated clichés. See 193:2//19:27.

193:6 **shuffling shamble** dragging the feet.

193:13 **Some more of——** The sentence is completed at 193:17//20:13. Faulkner uses this technique throughout *Sanctuary*, interrupting the speaker causing suspense and/or confusion and ambiguity. According to John T. Matthews, the "figure of ellipsis pervades the rhetorical, psychological, narrative, and thematic structures of *Sanctuary*."°

193:21 **Besides gettin that car of hisn outen here again, big as it is** Popeye has set up the barricade after driving his car up to the house. When he leaves with Temple, however, he will have no trouble driving around the downed tree. See 273:15//137:6.

193:24 **"I'd be scared of it too," Benbow said. "If his shadow was mine"** an unintentionally ironic statement, given Popeye's function as Horace's alter ego throughout the novel.

193:26 **guffawed, in undertone** Tommy laughs heartily but attempts to muffle the sound in keeping with the clandestine nature of their enterprise. He laughs to himself. It is worth noting that Tommy catches Horace's joke.

193:27 **impalpable defunctive glare of the sand** The road is becoming harder to see as the light reflecting sand turns into a lusterless powder in the dimming night sky and they go deeper into the woods. See "hushed glare of the road" (194:4//21:11).

193:33 **Sho** sure, of course.

193:37 **piddlin** piddling: trivial, insignificant.

193:39 **makin a run** A *run* can mean one of two things in moonshining: the process of distilling a still's load of mash, and the transportation of the liquor from the moonshiner to the buyers. Tommy obviously has the second meaning in mind. It is more profitable to sell in large quantities to a bootlegger for resale, than in "little quarts and half-a-gallons" to individual customers. Lee does sell to individuals as well, but mostly to promote good will in the neighborhood.

193:39 **gettin shut of it quick** getting rid of the illegal whiskey. This is not only good business but reduces the risk of being caught.

194:3 **a little curious** strange.

194:9 **Two men** Popeye's driver and a henchman.

194:11 **more than midnight** after midnight. It is now Wednesday, May 8.

194:12 **You took your time** The man is annoyed that the planned run is off schedule. It is never made specific when the exchange was scheduled, but it is possible that one of the reasons Popeye was waiting in the woods was that they were expected earlier. Horace's unexpected intrusion may also have caused further delay.

194:15 **Waiting on her back** She is in bed having sex with another man instead of being faithful to the first speaker.

194:17 **Whyn't you fellows hang out a lantern? If me and him had a been the Law, we'd a had you, sho** This statement further illustrates Tommy's sense of humor. He faults these men for not guarding properly and by calling so much attention to themselves by smoking their cigarettes near the main road.

194:20 **mat-faced bastard** At 185:33//10:9, Tommy is described as having "a sunburned thatch of hair, matted and foul." Later, at 205:29//39:1, Temple will see Tommy staring at her, "his mouth open in innocent astonishment within a short soft beard." Still later, after his murder, Tommy will be described as "barefoot, in overalls, the sun-bleached curls on the back of his head matted with dried blood and singed with powder..." (257:26//112:29).

194:28 **lifted his foot for the step** stepped on the running board of the truck.

194:30 **Doc** like "professor," an ironic term of address noting Horace's conspicuity in this group.

194:31 **The second man was laying a shotgun along the back of the seat** He is literally "riding shotgun," protecting the contraband whiskey against lawmen or other bootleggers who might attempt to hijack the truck.

CHAPTER III

195:1 **the next afternoon** Wednesday, May 8.

195:1 **his sister's home . . . ten years old** Horace's sister Narcissa is introduced in *Flags in the Dust*, in which she marries Bayard Sartoris III and moves into his family home "Sartoris." *Sanctuary: The Original Text* specifies the marriage date as August 27, 1919.° In *Flags in the Dust*, Bayard Sartoris is killed while test-flying an experimental airplane on June 5, 1920.° Narcissa gives birth to their child, Benbow Sartoris, on the same day. If the events in *Sanctuary* take place in 1929, as the dates indicate, then the boy should be approaching his ninth birthday. In *Sanctuary: The Original Text*, Bory is nine years old.° In the short story "There Was a Queen," written in 1930 and apparently set in that year, Narcissa says Benbow was born "almost twelve years ago."° Earlier versions of the story, "Through the Window" and "An Empress Passed," were written in 1929.

195:4 **the great aunt of her husband** Jenny Sartoris Du Pre, usually referred to as Miss Jenny, the youngest sister of Col. John Sartoris (1823–1873) and aunt of Bayard Sartoris II (1849–1919), "Old Bayard" in *Flags in the Dust*. Miss Jenny is a main character in that book, in several stories in *The Unvanquished*, and in "There Was a Queen."

195:5 **a woman of ninety** In "There Was a Queen," Miss Jenny dies at the age of ninety in 1930.° In *Sanctuary: The Original Text*, she is 89.°

195:7 **at the window, watching his sister and a young man walking in the garden** In *Flags in the Dust* and in *Sanctuary: The Original Text*, Horace reveals incestuous desires for his sister Narcissa, feelings which are in part transferred to Little Belle

· 33 ·

in *Sanctuary*. The scene of "watching" Narcissa in the garden reminds us of his earlier spying on Little Belle described in Chapter II.

195:8 **widow for ten years** If the events of *Sanctuary* occur in 1929, then Narcissa would have been a widow for almost nine years. It is clear from this and the previous dates that when Faulkner revised *Sanctuary* in 1930 he changed most ages and dates to reflect the passage of another year. He kept his specific chronology keyed to the 1929 calendar, however, the year he first wrote the book.°

195:11 **"I ask you," Miss Jenny said. "A young woman needs a man."** Miss Jenny turns Horace's question back on him as Popeye did earlier. See entry 181:29//4:21. Narcissa is now 36 (261:38//120:2), seven years younger than Horace (253:2//106:3). By Jefferson standards, Narcissa should have remarried by now and this younger man as a suitor is even more questionable. See entry 293:26//165:21.

195:16 **She seems to like children** In his Stevens Genealogy, Cleanth Brooks gives Gowan Stevens's birth date as 1900,° which would make him 29 or 30 at this time, a little old to be just finishing college. In *Sanctuary: The Original Text*, Bory Sartoris says of Gowan, comparing him to his father Bayard, "He went to Virginia, too. . . But he wasn't an aviator like my father was."° In *Sanctuary*, he appears to be a younger man, in his early 20s. Horace's remark is especially ironic considering his own obsession with Little Belle.

195:19 **Gowan Stevens** In *Requiem for a Nun*, Gowan is the nephew of Gavin Stevens, the lawyer who attempts to defend Nancy Mannigoe for the murder of Temple and Gowan's child. In *The Town*, Gowan is Gavin's cousin.

195:22 **At that time** At this point Faulkner shifts, in Horace's memory, to the previous October, when a similar scene involving Narcissa and Gowan took place. Faulkner repeats the phrase "at that time" on four different occasions in the paragraph to emphasize the time shift. This scene continues through 197:10//26:24. See following entries.

195:27 **Stevens wore brown** He wears a blue coat in the Spring

(195:14//24:4). Stevens's clothes serve as another key to the disjointed chronology of these scenes.

195:29 **He's only been coming out since he got home from Virginia last spring** Although Miss Jenny seems to be answering the question Horace asks at 195:17//24:7, set in the present time of the novel, she is in fact answering a similar one Horace asked the previous October. As Faulkner notes, "at that time he [Gowan] was new to Horace" (195:27//24:17). In other words, Horace has, in fact, forgotten who Stevens is, and Miss Jenny is correct in saying that he "ought to remember Gowan" (195:19//24:9). Miss Jenny also indicates that Gowan has been calling on Narcissa since the previous spring, a year before the May, 1929, setting of the present action of the story.

195:30 **The one then was that Jones boy; Herschell** that is, Narcissa's suitor before Gowan. Narcissa evidently has entertained other young men, "college boys," a fact which perhaps connects her to Little Belle in Horace's mind. See second entry 293:26//165:21.

195:32 **F.F.V.** First Families of Virginia, a somewhat satiric description applied to native-born, rather pompous Virginians who considered themselves superior to Southerners from other states because of their leading role in the founding of the United States.

195:34 **the University** the University of Virginia in Charlottesville.

195:37 **Dont let Belle hear you say that** Belle left her older husband for Horace; though Horace is teasing here (October 1928) by suggesting that Belle might also leave him for a younger man if Horace's age were brought to her attention; by May of 1929 it is he who has done the leaving.

196:3 **his sleek head** well groomed, lustrous. Suggestive of the hair tonic Gowan, a dandy, most likely uses. The detail, however, connects him with Popeye, who is careful about his hair and uses Ed Pinaud, a trademarked brand of men's healthcare products. These colognes, scents, moustache waxes, and talcs were popular in barber shops. See 395:32//313:3.

196:10 **Narcissa was a big woman, with dark hair, a broad, stu-**

pid, serene face Faulkner is harder on Narcissa in *Sanctuary* than in *Flags*. There she is described as "tall in her white dress" and as having "that serene repose of lilies."°

196:11 **She was in her customary white dress** Little Belle and her apparent purity are captured by her virginal costume (188:31//13:26).

196:18 **it** it = University of Virginia. Horace counters Gowan's condescending "I've heard of you" (196:15//25:15) with a snobbery based in his own schooling. Miss Jenny manages to neutralize the competition. See entry 196:22//25:22.

196:22 **Oxford** In *Flags in the Dust*, Horace is said to have attended Sewanee and then Oxford University in England as a Rhodes Scholar.° Miss Jenny here speaks of Oxford, Mississippi, where the University of Mississippi is located.

196:26 **jelly** slang 20's term for pretty girl, girl friend, or a steady date of either sex; see "barber-shop jellies" (204:37//37:29). Short for "jellybean" or "jelly roll," which carry a more overtly sexual connotation.

196:27 **A red-headed one** Gowan apparently refers here to Temple Drake, who has red hair (199:3//30:2). Gowan has therefore been dating Temple for at least eight months before the present time of May.

196:29 **She almost said something else** "Have you left her? Why are you here alone?"

196:32 **If you keep on expecting him to run off from Belle . . . He'll do it someday** In *Sanctuary: The Original Text*, it is clear that Horace has abandoned Belle before. Miss Jenny comments, "I've been trying all afternoon to find out myself if he has run away again. . . . You haven't quit Belle in three or four years now, have you?"° Horace's escape attempt in the revised novel carries greater significance since it now becomes the first time he has defied Belle.

196:38 **bucking at the halter** A halter is a device made of rope or leather straps placed over the head of an animal in order to lead or control the animal's movements. A haltered animal will likely "buck"—pull against or arch its back—in an attempt to free itself from this restraint. Miss Jenny suggests that although Horace has been chaffing under the restrictions of his marriage to Belle, he may not be prepared for freedom once he attains it.

197:1 **a small bell rang** announcing that dinner is ready. Sounded by the cook or servant.

197:2 **"Will you forbear, sir?" Benbow said. "Since I seem to be the guest"** "Will you allow me the privilege?" Horace's exaggerated style, almost a parody of the chivalric manner, mocks Gowan's show of politeness at 196:6//25:4. His comments also indicate, however, that he feels Gowan is more a part of his sister's household than he is.

197:4 **Narcissa, will you send up to the chest in the attic and get the duelling pistols? . . . and to have two roses ready** Miss Jenny's joke is ambiguous. She wryly implies that Horace and Gowan are prepared to fight a duel over the honor of escorting her to the table and then extends the play developing a dance protocol: the winner of the duel will then be her partner. In *Sanctuary: The Original Text*, the scene is slightly different. After telling Narcissa to send for the duelling pistols, she holds out her hand for Gowan to kiss. As she does so, she tells Bory (whom she insists on calling "Johnny" in keeping with Sartoris tradition), "Johnny . . . you go on ahead and tell them to strike up the music, and tell Isom to fetch me two roses from the garden."°

197:9 **"There are roses on the table," Narcissa said** The very literal, humorless Narcissa either fails to understand Miss Jenny's joke (as does Bory) or attempts to squelch it.

197:11 **Through the window Benbow and Miss Jenny watched the two people, Narcissa still in white, Stevens in flannels and a blue coat, walking in the garden** The extra spacing before this passage indicates a break in time between the two scenes. Faulkner repeats his earlier description of Gowan (195:27//24:17) to bring his readers back to the present time of the novel. He has suspended present-time action to insert the flashback.

197:13   **The Virginia gentleman one**   Horace continues the line of thought he began at 195:21//24:11. Very little time has passed, although Horace has relived his first meeting with Gowan.

197:16   **scarab**   a scarabaeid beetle, regarded by the ancient Egyptians as sacred and used as a talisman, buried with the dead. Horace speaks of preserving the beetle in alcohol, a kind of pickling or mummification.

197:18   **Gowan Stevens**   Miss Jenny repeats herself (195:19//24:10) in reminding Horace who the young suitor is.

196:18   **They watched the two people disappear . . . it was the boy instead of Stevens**   another repetition of an earlier action (196:1//24:28): Bory takes Gowan's place in the second scene, perhaps reinforcing the idea that Gowan is considerably younger than Narcissa, whose escorts are young enough to be her children.

197:22   **He wouldn't stay**   Gowan's abrupt departure, leaving without dinner and not even saying good-bye to Miss Jenny, suggests that he and Narcissa have argued, perhaps over Temple. If so, the episode provides another underlying motive for Narcissa's later actions toward Temple, Horace, and Gowan himself. See entry 293:26//165:21.

197:23   **Friday night**   May 10, a week after Horace leaves Kinston.

197:23   **He has an engagement with a young lady**   Narcissa's unspecified tone is important in this line. What emphasis does she give "young lady"? Though anger or irritation may inflect the phrase, Narcissa practices studied indifference.

197:26   **I suppose that's why he is going down ahead of time**   Horace implies that Gowan will begin his drinking early to prepare for the dance. However, he also implies that Narcissa may indeed have reason to be jealous of Gowan's activities.

197:29   **Starkville Saturday, to the base ball game**   Starkville, Mississippi, 75 miles southeast of Oxford, the home of Mississippi A & M, the University of Mississippi's "arch-rival" at the time.° Saturday would be May 11.

197:29   **He said he'd take me, but you wont let me go**   There is no reason to think this is a serious offer on Gowan's part, but it is interesting to speculate how Bory's presence would have altered the upcoming sequence of events. Thus, Faulkner underscores the relentless element of chance in the novel.

CHAPTER IV

198:5 **her long legs blonde with running** Temple Drake is characterized by her constant movement especially in the first half of *Sanctuary*. This chapter begins and ends with Temple "running" without achieving distance or goal.

198:6 **Coop** Student nickname for Ricks and Ward Halls, the two women's dormitories at the University of Mississippi at this time. The name involves a sexual joke—that hens are kept in a coop to lay eggs—and anticipates the houses of prostitution in Memphis: the female dorms will be compared to the Memphis bordellos, one of the many ways Faulkner heightens resemblances between proper and improper.°

198:8 **knickers** Temple's underwear, a type of elastic-waist, loose-fitting, long, bloomer-like garments. See first entry to 198:12//29:2.

198:9 **whatnot** whatever. The catchall word here covers all underskirt garments.

198:12 **knickers** Knickerbockers, stylish full britches gathered at the knees which were worn by men in the 1920s and 30s.

198:12 **bright pull-overs** sweaters which are pulled over the head, as opposed to cardigans, which button up the front.

198:14 **pomaded heads** Pomade is a petrolatum-based perfumed ointment used to slick down and style men's hair. See Gowan Stevens, 196:3//25:1 and Popeye 397:35//315:25.

198:15 **with superiority and rage** The Ole Miss male students—the "men"—feel socially and fashionably superior to the town boys, but envy the town boys their cars for dates with college girls on weeknights, since the college boys are forbidden the use of cars on campus.

198:17 **Letter Club** probably the "M" Club, an athletic organization established at Ole Miss and active throughout the 1920s.

198:17 **three formal yearly balls** three formal dances held each year at the University. Faulkner did pen and ink drawings of such affairs, such as the one for the Red and Blue Club, a dancing society, for the yearbook *Ole Miss, 1917–18*.°

198:19 **belligerent casualness** The town boys, shut out of these social events, attempt to project disdain for the whole affair while closely monitoring the course of the evening.

198:20 **black collegiate arms** The college boys are in formal dress.

198:22 **her high delicate head ... predatory and discreet** This passage suggests certain physical similarities between Temple and Popeye—the eyes and chin, for examples. However, Temple is also described as a predatory animal, secretly searching for its victim at the dance. In this social situation she clearly controls her milieu.

198:25 **they would watch her through the windows** The voyeurism motif, introduced in the novel's opening paragraph as Popeye silently observes Horace at the spring, is extended here, to include Temple.

198:26 **as she passed in swift rotation from one pair of black sleeves to the next** The popular Temple dances with many partners, but note that the men are impersonal "black sleeves" rather than identifiable individuals.

198:27 **her waist shaped slender and urgent in the interval, her feet filling the rhythmic gap with music** Between partners, Temple seems without purpose. She impatiently dances alone, keeping her own rhythm, tapping her feet.

198:35 **Home, Sweet Home** song by John Howard Payne, from his opera *Clari, The Maid of Milan* (1823).° Traditionally played as the last number at a dance.

199:4 **Her eyes, all pupil now, rested upon them for a blank moment** Adjusting from the light of the dance to the night outside, Temple's pupils enlarge. However, she is also unseeing, uncomprehending. See Popeye's eyes: "two knobs of soft black rubber" (181:32//4:24).

199:9 **It was a long, low roadster, with a jacklight** A roadster is an open automobile with a single seat in front for two or three people and a rumble seat or luggage compartment in back. A jacklight is a spotlight or lamp mounted on a car.

199:12 **"My father's a judge," the second said in a bitter, lilting falsetto** One of the town boys, later identified as Doc, speaks in an artificially high voice to mock Temple's social snobbery in constantly asserting her father's prominence and prestige. At this point, however, the line makes no sense; it is not until Temple reaches the Old Frenchman place that the meaning becomes evident.

199:19 **He broke the bottle carefully and spread the fragments across the road** to puncture the tires of the college boys' cars, especially Gowan's.

199:26 **three headlights** Gowan's car has the jacklight in addition to the dual headlights.

199:28 **Temple's head was low and close** The meaning of "close" is ambiguous here. Temple is either reclining in the seat, leaning her head on the window nearest them as the car passes, or is snuggled close to Gowan as he drives.

199:31 **"Am I?" the second said. He took something from his pocket and flipped it out, whipping the sheer, faintly scented web across their faces. "Am I?"** Doc produces a pair of panties and implies they belong to Temple and are his souvenir of a sexual encounter with her.

199:34 **That's what you say** The other boys indicate that someone like Doc would not stand a chance with Temple.

199:35 **Doc got that step-in in Memphis . . . . Off a damn whore** Step-ins are panties with wide legs. The reference to a whore foreshadows Temple's abduction.

199:39 **After a while the car door slammed** Gowan and Temple linger in the car necking or plotting Temple's escape from the baseball excursion train. Although the door is slammed, it's not likely they are fighting, because Gowan is in a generous mood as he leaves.

200:5 **You gentlemen going to town?** Gowan's affected politeness is a form of condescension. However, he's also looking for liquor and needs their help.

200:7 **rumble seat** the uncovered passenger seat in a roadster that opens out from the rear of the automobile.

200:15 **I'm a stranger here** Gowan is from Jefferson, but he hopes to be asked where he's from and show off the University of Virginia connection.

200:20 **"Luke might," the third said** Although the question is addressed to Doc, this is not Doc speaking. He is always identified as the second of the three men.

200:24 **Taylor** the first railroad stop, eight miles south of Oxford.

200:27 **Got to get there before the special does** The Special was a train chartered for Ole Miss students and alumni to travel to Starkville for the game, a common practice.° Gowan and Temple apparently have already made their plans for Temple to slip away from the chaperoned group, probably while parked in front of the Coop.

200:30 **stunted blackjacks** a species of the oak tree, which is noted by its blackish bark. Also known as the pin oak (*Quercus shumardii*),° the tree's wood is very hard and it often grows in poor soil so that, like the scrub pine, it is associated with wasted or poverty-stricken environments.

200:37 **"It's as good as that you had tonight," the third said** This is spoken to Doc rather than Gowan. The other two boys are attempting to moderate Doc's antagonism toward Gowan.

201:2 **Virgin——oh, Jefferson** At this point Gowan drops his pose and admits that he is a local boy rather than a Virginian. He is beginning to sense their hostility and drops his pose in favor of ingratiation.

201:14 **"We dont drink rotgut at Virginia," Doc said** Doc now mimics Gowan as he did Temple earlier. Rotgut is cheap whiskey which will "rot" your "gut."

201:17 **He's had a bellyache all night** To bellyache is to complain or grumble. Doc has been in a foul mood because of the dance and his jealousy of Gowan and the more privileged college boys.

201:23 **"The Shack'll be open," the first said. "At the depot"** The Shack was the name of an actual restaurant adjoining the railroad station in Oxford.

201:28 **coca-colas** used as mixers for the moonshine.

201:29 **Cap** short for "Red cap porter," normally African Americans who handled baggage at train stations. However, the title was often abbreviated to "Cap" to refer to any black man in a servile position. It is not clear, however, that the waiter here is black.

201:30 **whiskey sour** a cocktail made of the ingredients Gowan requests. A more sophisticated form of drinking, to his mind.

201:32 **Hasn't got much kick, to me** Gowan suggests he is used to more potent liquor.

201:38 **Up at school they consider it better to go down than to hedge** Gowan, obviously showing off for the local boys, would rather drink "manfully" at the risk of passing out than to drink in moderation and appear hesitant or fearful. A "gentleman" should be able to hold his whiskey.

202:1 **"That's all for him, too," Doc said** Gowan has drunk to his capacity, and he is about to pass out.

202:3 **in my county** Yoknapatawpha County.

202:5 **"That's what they call a drink up at school,"** Doc skillfully pushes Gowan, baiting him to drink himself senseless. Gowan stupidly rises to the challenge.

202:14 **in a cramped dark place smelling of ammonia and creosote, vomiting into a receptacle** After being taken outside for fresh air, Gowan ends up vomiting in the bathroom of the railroad station. Ammonia and creosote are disinfectants used to sanitize the place. This is the first example of vomiting in the book, anticipated by Horace's earlier image of "the black stuff that ran out of Bovary's mouth." See entry 184:4//7:25. Nausea and vomiting play an important role in this novel.° See entry 333:31//223:31.

202:18 **a desire to lie down which was forcibly restrained** Gowan is unable to stretch out in the confined quarters of the bathroom stall.

202:23 **Then he looked at them, wagging his head** The three town boys have followed him into the bathroom and are witnessing his disgusting display. The scene anticipates other similar situations in which people (Pap, Temple) are observed performing bodily functions. See entries 214:6//51:21, 239:22//87:12, 242:23//91:14. Later, when Temple is trapped by Popeye in the barn stall at the Old Frenchman place, he "waggle[s]" his pistol at her. See entry 250:7//102:15 for further discussion of this action.

202:24 **Name girl I know.** It is Temple Drake's name written in the men's bathroom stall, an indication that her virtue is suspect and that her reputation circulates among the males (205:1//38:3). Horace Benbow will also find her name written there (298:23//172:15). The bathroom stall also anticipates the barn stall in which Temple will be raped; the barn itself is used as a bathroom at the Old Frenchman place (242:5//90:26). Though Gowan brags that Temple is a girl who likes to have fun, is a "good sport" who will go with him without a chaperone, Temple is likely a virgin at the time of her assault (279:18//145:11).

202:32 **his eyes were open, waiting for vision to return** Gowan is blind drunk. There are a number of blindness references, which contrast with the images of voyeurism, in the book.

202:39 **quite empty of any sense** Although grammatically the phrase defines the "small clouds rosy with sunlight," it also describes Gowan, who has not yet regained full consciousness, but has, in some fashion, been transported to his car, which is parked in front of the train station. The "low canopy" refers to the retractable roof of his roadster. This reading suggests the unconcern—what Joseph W. Reed, Jr., calls the "indifferent neutrality"—of nature, or, more extreme, its essential meaninglessness. In this way it anticipates both Horace Benbow's and Temple Drake's despair at the end of the book.°

203:3 **fetched him completely to** The blow brings Gowan to full consciousness.

203:8 **his burst collar** Gowan is wearing a stiff celluloid collar which buttons to the neck of his dress shirt. In his drunken state it has broken loose and comically sticks out at an angle.

203:8 **broken hair** The shell of Gowan's hair, which was earlier described as sleek with hair ointment or pomade, is no longer neatly combed and styled. Like the collar, strands of hair stick out from his head. He looks thoroughly disreputable.

203:12 **white folks** a Negro's general term of address to an unknown white man. It indicates a lesser degree of respect.

203:15 **Bout** about.

203:23 **Almost at once he felt better** Gowan is employing the theory that a drink is the best cure for a hangover—the "hair of the dog that bit you." Actually, he is on his way to getting drunk again.

203:24 **six-fifteen** 6:15 a.m., Saturday, May 11.

203:29 **vestibule** an enclosed area at the end of a passenger car on a train.

203:29 **Temple sprang down** By prearrangement, Temple has been watching for Gowan and jumps down as soon as she sees his car.

203:30 **while an official leaned down and shook his fist at her** It is not clear whether this is a university official on the special train or a train conductor. In either case, it means that someone in authority on the train sees Temple get off at Taylor. No one, however, comes forward after Temple's disappearance. Faulkner possibly meant to suggest evidence of a cover-up, especially if it is a university official, since it is later implied that the university cooperates in explaining Temple's disappearance (297:37//171:19), but it is more likely an oversight. See entry 217:17//56:25.

203:37 **overalled men** wearing overalls, loose-fitting denim trousers with a bib front and shoulder straps, often worn by farmers.

204:4 **My canteen** Gowan ironically refers to the empty fruit jar which held the liquor. It anticipates Lee Goodwin's army canteen which Temple uses as symbolic protection at the Old Frenchman place in Chapter VIII.

204:6 **brimless hat** a cloche, a close-fitting brimless hat shaped like a bell.

204:9 **Let's get away from here** Temple's decision to go with Gowan even in his disreputable state seems partly prompted by the "overalled men" staring at her from the otherwise deserted station, which is itself described as "bleak" and "stark and ugly." She feels safer with Gowan, whom she feels she can control, than with these strangers who watch her so intently. Also, at this point, she has no way to return to the train and no reason to feel frightened of Gowan: she still considers herself to be at least marginally in charge. See entry 204:14//37:4.

204:14 **At two oclock that afternoon** Faulkner skips abruptly from 6:30 a.m. to 2 p.m. Temple's demands—"You'd better take me back to Oxford . . . You'd better" (204:10//37:1)—have been ineffectual. She is, in this sense, being taken against her will. The following scene, in fact, parallels that at the beginning of Chapter XVIII in which Popeye literally kidnaps Temple and takes her to Memphis.

204:16 **narrow road between eroded banks** See 192:20//19:5.

204:18 **He wore a cheap blue workshirt beneath his dinner jacket** Gowan has replaced the stained dress shirt with the coarse workshirt bought in Taylor which he now wears beneath the tuxedo jacket.

204:21 **Temple thought His whiskers** Faulkner indicates Temple's unspoken comments by capitalizing the first word, but he does not put them in quotation marks, which would indicate that they are spoken aloud. See Gowan's thoughts at 203:9//34:9. However, Ruby's comments on Horace in Chapter II are apparently spoken, although only to herself.

See 189:20//14:28; 190:25//16:14; 190:33//16:23, for examples.

204:22 **Dumfries** a fictional town Faulkner placed on the route between Taylor and Frenchman's Bend.

204:22 **It was hair-oil he drank** Commercial hair oil contains alcohol and has served as a last resort for desperate drunks. See *Light in August,* in which Joe Christmas tells Lucas Burch, "You ought to be careful of drinking so much of this Jefferson hair tonic" (457).

204:25 **Dont get your back up, now** a cat's arched back as a signal for anger or annoyance. Gowan is anticipating her anger as he prepares to stop at Goodwin's for liquor.

204:26 **It wont take a minute to run up to Goodwin's and get a bottle. It wont take ten minutes** Gowan's jump from one to ten minutes indicates he is trying to pacify Temple but has no intention of heeding her wishes.

204:32 **uttering short, yelping cries . . . plaintive, wary and forlorn** The comparison eerily links the athletic shouts of ballplayers to the frightened cries of birds threatened by an unseen alligator. Are we to assume that this image has been formulated by Temple herself, thinking of the game? Although the language is not hers, the formulation fits the philosophy of the book, in which the most normal of activities—a ball game or a dance or a train ride—can suddenly be interrupted by an unimaginable, unseen horror which has lurked just beyond our knowing.

204:36 **Trying to come over me with your innocent ways** trying to fool me into thinking you are inexperienced, an innocent. Gowan attempts to divert attention from his antics to her reputation.

204:38 **Dont think I fed them my liquor just because I'm bighearted** Gowan implies, falsely, that he tried to get the town boys drunk in order to learn more about Temple's town reputation as a date. In this version of the evening, he was in control rather than hopelessly drunk.

204:40 **badger-trimmed hick** A hick is an ignorant or unsophisticated country bumpkin, a rube. "Badger-trimmed" carries the extra suggestion here of sexual duplicity.°

205:1 **ford** The Ford automobile, invented by Henry Ford (1863–1947), was the most popular and least expensive of American cars and the first to be mass-produced on an assembly line basis. The word in lower case became a generic term for any car, just as "coke" today can mean any soft drink. Gowan is also sarcastically contrasting the common, assembly-line "ford" to his own sporty roadster.

205:7 **By God, I want to see the woman that can—— make a fool of me.**

205:12 **It seemed to her to be the logical and disastrous end to the train of circumstance in which she had become involved** Temple is already denying her own responsibility for this situation, which seems inevitably to grow worse. There is some justification for her belief, as events have conspired to bring her to this end.

205:21 **the one in a suit of tight black and a straw hat, smoking a cigarette, the other bareheaded, in overalls, carrying a shotgun** Although the reader has already been introduced to both Popeye and Tommy, Faulkner here presents them from Temple's point of view as men identifiable only by their clothes. Thus they join the anonymous men from the dance and the train station in her mind.

205:25 **her bones turned to water** Temple is so frightened that her legs will no longer support her although she cannot stop moving.

205:27 **her mouth open upon a soundless wail behind her lost breath** She is trying to cry out but is too short of breath, either through fear or a result of the accident, to make an actual noise.

205:30 **The other man was leaning over the upturned car . . . . Then the engine ceased** Popeye has the presence of mind to cut off the engine and avoid a gas fire or explosion.

CHAPTER V

206:1 **The man in overalls was barefoot also** Temple's point of view, begun in the last chapter, continues in this description of Tommy. Since she—unlike the reader—does not yet know his name, Tommy is simply one of the "overalled men" (203:37//36:18) who have frightened her.

206:3 **splay feet** A splayfoot is abnormally flattened and spread out: a flatfoot. See the earlier description of Tommy at 193:6//20:2.

206:8 **Putty hard walkin** "Putty" here means "pretty": it is pretty hard to walk through the sand, Tommy says. However, see first entry to 219:13//59:14 for a different use of the word.

206:11 **The man watched her, looking at the slippers** The image of the lost or castaway slipper is a recurring one in Faulkner's early work. Pierrot in *The Marionettes* (1920) is pictured with a "woman's slipper at his feet."° David West in *Mosquitoes* (1927) yearns for Pat Robyn while holding her shoe: "It was a slipper, a single slipper, cracked and stained with dried mud and disreputable . . . something of that hard and sexless graveness of hers."° Benjy in *The Sound and the Fury* remembers his sister Caddy: *"I squatted there, holding the slipper. I couldn't see it . . . but my hands could see the slipper. . . ."°* Faulkner might well have had the fairy tale of Cinderella in mind for this image, and, indeed, the story of Temple Drake could be read as a nightmare version of the Cinderella story. See entries 214:19//52:6 and 240:33//89:2.

206:13 **ere two** any two. Temple has small feet; Tommy can insert no more than two of his fingers in her slipper. Tommy's handling of the slipper has sexual implications, a symbolic threat enacting penetration of Temple.

206:15 **Durn my hide** a milder variation of "I'll be damned." The oath indicates amazement or disbelief.

206:21 **He aint laid no crop by yit, has he?** Tommy notes that Temple's figure is too thin and girlish to be pregnant or to have had children.

206:29 **The house came into sight, above the cedar grove beyond whose black interstices an apple orchard flaunted in the sunny afternoon** They are coming out of the dark woods up the hill to the Old Frenchman place. The apple orchard, which lies between the jungle and the house, presents in the sunlight an almost cheerful appearance; however, the closer they come, the more desolate the place appears. See entry 207:23//42:22.

207:1 **I dont want to go there** Temple, sensing danger at the old house, is clearly attempting to keep herself out of harm's way.

207:4 **black man** Popeye, who is dressed in a "suit of tight black" (205:22//38:23). Temple implies no racial identification, but alludes to Popeye's sinister demeanor. Horace himself will later refer to Popeye as "that little black man." See entry 255:13//109:22. In *Mosquitoes*, there is a strange character named "Faulkner" who is also described as a "little kind of black man,"° referring to his deep tan. The niece, Patricia Robyn, also queries the artist Gordon in the book about his dark moods: "Why are you so black?"°

207:7 **Mrs Goodwin's** Women are assumed to be wives. Gowan assumes that Ruby is Lee's legal wife, just as Tommy assumes that Temple is married to Gowan (207:13//42:10). The District Attorney Eustace Graham will manipulate this assumption during the trial (366:26//269:25).

207:13 **fret** worry.

207:13 **Lee'll git you to town** Tommy may be thinking of the courtesy shown Horace four days earlier.

207:15 **They looked at one another soberly, like two children or two dogs** Reinforcing the resemblance between Temple and Tommy, this image underscores their basic naiveté in the face of evil. It also anticipates the description of Miss Reba's two dogs, the objects of her unpredictable wrath later in the book. See entry 286:40//155:19.

207:18 **She entered** Although Temple has been reluctant to approach the strange place, she now boldly and authoritatively enters the house.

207:23 **huge barn, broken-backed, tranquil in sunny desolation** The barn's roof sags in the middle because of a broken beam. This scene of future horror is here described in terms both bucolic and macabre.

207:25 **the corner either of a detached building or of a wing of the house** the kitchen. See entry 184:26//8:18.

207:30 **But the shadow wore no hat** That is, it is not Popeye's shadow. Despite her bold words, Temple is frightened of Popeye.

207:38 **tail of her eye** out of the corner of her eye.

207:38 **thread of smoke** a cigarette trail, an image associated with Popeye. But see entry 208:21//43:29.

208:2 **three square cloths hung damp and limp** diapers.

208:3 **woman's undergarment of faded pink silk** This patched undergarment indicates the extent of Ruby's poverty and fall from "glamorous" Memphis days. See entry 199:35//31:4.

208:10 **two objects like dirty yellowish clay marbles** the cataracted eyes. Compare to Popeye's "two knobs of soft black rubber" (181:32//4:24).

208:14 **He cant hear you** Although Popeye is the first person Temple sees, this is Ruby speaking from inside the kitchen door.

208:17 **fetched up on hands and knees in a litter of ashes and tin cans and bleached bones** Temple literally runs off the porch and falls into the trash heap beside the house. Faulkner employs images of Eliot's waste land in which Temple crawls like an animal, or a baby.

208:19 **slanted cigarette curling across his face** the cigarette smoke.

208:21 **where a woman sat at a table, a burning cigarette in her hand, watching the door** The tell-tale cigarette smoke has led

Temple, and the reader, to believe that Popeye is standing in the kitchen door. Faulkner, however, has fooled us: Popeye has been watching from around the corner of the house, not the kitchen, and the smoke has come from Ruby's cigarette. Ruby, yet unknown and nameless to Temple, is simply "a woman."

CHAPTER VI

209:5 **why cant you take him out back . . . looking like a damn hog with its throat cut** Popeye's concern is not with Gowan's injury but with its offensiveness. He doesn't want to have to look at the blood. His squeamish fastidiousness recalls Horace's inability to watch Pap eat his mixture of food and chewing tobacco. Popeye then begins to clean his shoes, reminding us of Horace's admonition to Little Belle: "You dont soil your slippers, you know" (189:5//14:13).

209:9 **a platinum penknife on the end of his watch chain** Popeye keeps his "dollar watch" in his pocket, a penknife on his watch chain. See entry 182:29//5:29.

209:12 **"You said something about———"** a drink, finding the liquor. Gowan is still pursuing the original purpose of his visit.

209:14 **He began to wink and frown at Gowan, jerking his head at Popeye's back** Tommy tries to warn Gowan against mentioning drinking in Popeye's presence. See first entry to 209:23//45:13.

209:15 **And then you get on back down that road** to stand guard.

209:17 **I thought you was fixin to watch down ther** Tommy's statement confirms that Popeye was standing watch near the spring when Horace first arrived in Chapter I.

209:23 **He jest caint stand fer nobody———** to drink in his presence. Tommy completes the idea at 209:25//45:15.

209:23 **cur'us** curious, here meaning strange, peculiar.

209:24 **better'n a circus to———** Although Tommy's image is appropriate to a country storyteller, the comparison nevertheless indicates that he finds Popeye entertaining—amusing—in his eccentricities. He clearly knows that Popeye is dangerous—

the story of the dog in Chapter II proves that, and also see entry 211:16//47:27—but Tommy also underestimates Popeye's potential for violence. Thus Tommy pushes Popeye, plays games with him, to see how he will react. This idea is made even clearer in *Sanctuary: The Original Text*, in which Popeye, afraid of the dark, "returned to the porch and tried again to persuade the halfwit to get the lantern and take him somewhere and the halfwit refused and the thug stood there and cursed him in a cold, savage voice and the halfwit guffawed and Horace could hear his bare feet scuffing slowly on the boards."°

209:24 **He wont stand fer nobody drinkin hyer cep Lee** cep = except. Thus Goodwin is exempt from Popeye's command, probably because of his primary importance to the operation. Once Lee is no longer necessary, he is as vulnerable as anyone else to Popeye's violence. See entry 267:38//129:5, for example.

209:26 **sup** sip or swallow of liquor.

209:26 **I be dawg ef hit dont look like he'll have a catfit** A catfit is an emotional, angry outburst. In his vernacular, Tommy links himself to a dog and Popeye to a cat, although both are primarily "catlike." But we also know Popeye has killed Tommy's dog and will later kill Tommy himself.

209:34 **His hand came out and fumbled about his knees . . . wrist-deep in shadow** Deprived of the senses of sight and sound, Pap relies on his only remaining senses of touch, smell, and taste to function. Detecting the movement of the sun by the loss of warmth caused by the encroaching shade, he repositions his chair.

209:37 **he bore directly down upon them in a shuffling rush, so that they had to step quickly aside** In one sense this old man, who will later be associated with both Temple's father and with God, represents the force of blind circumstance or fate which simply sweeps aside those unlucky enough to be caught in its path, as are most of the characters in this novel.

210:5 **in a fix** state or condition.

210:7 **galvanised pail** an iron pail coated with zinc to prevent rusting. Such pails were often kept on the porches of rural houses for people to wash up (hence the soap and tin basin) before entering the living and dining area of the house itself.

210:8 **lump of yellow soap** probably made from tallow, rendered from the fat of farm animals such as cattle, horses, or sheep, and often made and used in rural areas.

210:10 **I be dawg ef you didn't drive that ere car straight into that tree** The downed tree, which was meant to block the road, not wreck cars.

210:13 **Mought** there might.

210:14 **po** pour.

210:16 **kitchen garden** a small garden, intended for personal use, as opposed to larger commercial fields.

210:19 **Yon's** yonder is, there is.

210:24 **twell** until.

210:25 **putty rotten** very rotten. See entry 206:8//40:8; however, also see first entry to 219:13//59:14 for another use of the word.

210:27 **Hit's helt all right, so fur** The floor has held together, has not collapsed, so far. Gowan's question indicates that he assumes Tommy comes to the loft for drinks on a regular basis.

210:28 **trap** an opening in the ceiling through which one enters the loft of a barn. There may or may not be a trap door closing the entrance. The word "trap"—and Tommy's statement at 210:30//47:1—anticipate the trap on the hangman's scaffold through which Popeye will drop to his death. Moreover, by descending through this opening in the barn, Popeye will literally "trap" Temple in the stall below. All these meanings recall Horace's earlier discussion of "Female Spring" as a "green-snared promise of unease" (188:24//13:23).

210:37 **Caint call yo name, though** can't remember, recall his name.

210:38 **I've been buying liquor from Lee for three years** According to Tommy, Goodwin has been in business for four years (193:20//20:16).

211:2 **three-fo nights ago** Horace was there four nights ago, on a Tuesday. It is presently late Saturday afternoon.

211:2 **I caint call his name neither** Gowan comes very close to learning that Horace has been at the Old Frenchman place. Such information might have played a significant role in his subsequent actions, or perhaps in the trial itself. In any case, Tommy can't remember, and it goes no further, but it serves as another example of missed connections in *Sanctuary*.

211:6 **After a moment the voice spoke again** Gowan has failed to hear Popeye call after them the first time he speaks. Tommy, however, has heard him.

211:14 **Callin me Jack. My name's Tawmmy** See 183:25//7:5, where Popeye uses the term of address on Horace, and 212:37//49:30, where he uses it on Gowan. Tommy is extremely literal-minded and thinks Popeye has either confused his name or is making some kind of joke. In either case, he finds it highly amusing; he laughs with "silent glee."

211:16 **He jest lief take a shot** He would just as lief—just as soon, just as likely—shoot through the floor as not. Popeye is unconcerned that he might actually hit someone.

211:18 **why didn't you———Here** answer him. Not inclined to be shot playing games with Popeye, Gowan quickly lets him know they are in the loft.

211:33 **grimace of taut, toothed coquetry** Temple automatically reacts by attempting to charm Popeye. Even in the middle of her fear and panic, she instinctively projects the manner which has, in the past, worked best for her.

211:34 **finicking swagger** Finicking is a play on "finicky." The phrase suggests a dainty, almost mincing walk which still imparts the sense of authority or insolence.

212:3 **They've got the cutest little baby in a box behind the stove** We know from an earlier description that the baby is not cute, that it, in fact, has a pinched and sickly appearance (191:38//18:10. See also 262:22//120:25 for a further description). Temple's failure to remark on why the child is kept in a box behind the stove contributes to the incongruities of the situation. The child is not real to her, appears more like a doll which could very reasonably be kept in a box.

212:4 **she said for me not to be here after dark** Ruby's warning is like that conventionally found in Gothic novels and vampire tales. After dark, evil is set loose.° But see entry 239:30// 87:21.

212:8 **That black man** Popeye. See entry 207:4//42:1.

212:15 **because she said if we were married and I had to say we were** Ruby asks whether Gowan and Temple are married. No one has corrected Tommy's earlier assumption that since Temple is traveling with Gowan, she must be his wife. A proper unmarried girl would not accompany a man unescorted. Temple goes along with the ruse for the protection it offers. But Ruby clearly does not believe Temple (see entry 292:2// 163:12). When Ruby first tells Horace about Temple's presence at the Old Frenchman place, she identifies her first as a "woman" and then as a "young girl" (272:31//135:27).

212:16 **"Just to a railroad. Maybe there's one closer than Jefferson," she whispered, staring at him, stroking her hand along the edge of the door** It is ironic that Temple has earlier chosen to go with Gowan rather than stay at the railroad station in Taylor. Temple's stroking the door may be an unconscious or nervous movement; however, there is also a sexual suggestiveness about it that anticipates her later attempt to dissuade Popeye from killing Red. See entry 342:26//236:10.

212:19 **You're all nuts** Gowan directly accuses Temple of being crazy to think he will approach Popeye with such a request, but more generally implies that everyone at the Old Frenchman place is equally mad. See Popeye's equally exasperated statement: "Goofy house. . . . That's what it is" (246:21//96:21).

212:20 **Do you think that ape will?** Do you really think Popeye would agree to drive us into town? "Ape" denotes a large, stupid, threatening character and a "gorilla" is gangster slang. This image doesn't fit Popeye's dainty, deadly image, however.

212:23 **You're crazy as a loon** Loon—a shortened form of lunatic—refers to a simple-minded or insane person. A loon is also a diving bird characterized by its eerie, maniacal cry. In 16th century usage, in reference to a woman, loon meant prostitute or strumpet. See Popeye's subsequent remark: 212:36// 49:29.

212:28 **"Say," she said, "dont you want to drive us to town?"** Temple's question is not so much a request as it is an attempt to manipulate flirtatiously, to get her way. Rather than ask "Will you please?", she tries to impose her wants and needs on Popeye. The boldness of her action also challenges Gowan's lack of courage.

212:33 **Be a sport** A sport is a good-natured person, one who doesn't mind taking a chance or having fun. Gowan has already called Temple this: "Good girl. Good sport" (202:24// 34:24).

212:36 **Make your whore lay off of me, Jack** Although Ruby and Tommy have spoken of Temple as being Gowan's wife, Popeye casts their relationship in terms of pimp and whore, a revelation of his attitude toward them both, his economy of relationship. Though he is directing Gowan to control his property, he is telling her to watch her step, letting her know that she is out of line, and insulting her all at once.

213:4 **Then he quit looking at him** Popeye dismisses Gowan as someone beneath his concern.

213:6 **What river did you fall in with that suit on? Do you have to shave it off at night?** Popeye's jacket has already been described as "tight." Temple suggests that it must have gotten wet and shrunk. Her childish insults, directed at his appearance, are in response to his having called her a whore.

213:8 **her head reverted** as if she were still talking to him, still attempting to insult Popeye as Gowan hustles her away.

213:10 **his head turned over his shoulder in profile** Popeye is watching Temple as Gowan takes her away. She has gotten his attention with her insult.

213:11 **Do you want———** to get us killed? Gowan has already been warned about Popeye's willingness to shoot with little provocation.

213:12 **You mean old thing** Temple is probably directing this childish remark to Popeye, although Gowan is the one dragging her off. Her attempts to persuade either of these men to help her have failed.

213:17 **Shut your mouth** Temple is constantly being silenced by other characters in the novel—by Gowan here, by Ruby in the bedroom (235), by Popeye in the barn (250), in the car (274), and at the Grotto (343). Ironically, the District Attorney, Eustace Graham, encourages her to talk: "Speak out. No one will hurt you. Let these good men, these fathers and husbands, hear what you have to say and right your wrong for you" (377:3//285:1).

213:120 **you're getting all that stuff stirred up in me** The physical effort of restraining Temple is disturbing his stomach, still queasy from too much alcohol.

213:25 **fire-door of the stove** the opening, where wood or coal is fed to the fire inside.

213:29 **She stood on tiptoe, listening** a child-like gesture, as if making herself taller would enable her to hear sounds or voices above her head: the voices of adults, for example. In a moment she will tiptoe to maintain secrecy.

213:32 **her father sitting on the porch at home, his feet on the rail** Temple's image of her father in charge, overlooking the estate, is similar to the earlier description of Pap, the blind and impotent figure to whom she futilely turned for help in Chapter V. See second entry to 250:14//102:22.

213:35 **the shotgun** probably Tommy's shotgun, which he carried while investigating the wreck.

214:6 **a dim, spraddled figure standing at the edge of the porch** Pap is urinating from the porch. Temple will later witness Pap on his way to the barn for a bowel movement (239:21//87:12), and shortly thereafter she will herself be watched in similar circumstances (242:22//91:25). Each event further outrages and violates Temple's security and dignity.

214:8 **Crouching she drew the box out and drew it before her** Temple uses the box and the child within as protection, as a talisman, perhaps, much as she will employ the canteen and the raincoat in Chapter VIII.

214:11 **But she could not think of a single designation for the heavenly father, so she began to say "My father's a judge; my father's a judge" over and over** Temple's panic makes her unable to pray to God the Father, having no appropriate form of address and finding no evidence of His readiness to help her. She replaces this attempt at prayer with a secular mantra which proclaims the social and judicial authority of her earthly father. All conventional tactics are failing; she can rely only on status. See the rape scene in the barn, when Temple is again unable to find rescue from God, her father, or anyone else. See second entry to 250:14//102:22.

214:14 **Goodwin ran lightly into the room** Goodwin's speed is partly explained by the fact that Temple is hovering over his child in the dark. He runs to protect the baby from possible harm.

214:19 **"What are you doing in my house?" he said** a possible allusion to the fairy tale of Goldilocks, who is found hiding in the bed by Papa Bear. This children's story offers a parallel to Temple's own nightmarish situation. See entries 206:11//40:11 and 240:33//89:2.

CHAPTER VII

215:1 **From somewhere beyond the lamplit hall** another abrupt transition. Faulkner does not explain how Temple comes to be with Ruby or what events take place after Lee finds her huddled beside the stove.

215:2 **the harsh, derisive laugh of a man easily brought to mirth by youth or by age** The passage is not entirely clear. The unidentified man (most likely Van, a new character unknown to Temple—see entry 215:13//54:3) laughs easily and scornfully at others. There is a sense that the laughter is rather mindless, the simple giddiness of youth or the merriment of senility.

215:9 **she peered around the door with the wide, abashed curiosity of a child** a continuation of the description of Temple as a child, frightened and yet still compelled to look.

215:13 **Is he your brother?** Temple apparently refers to the laughing man in the khaki trousers, identified as Van in the next chapter. She is trying to impose some form of order on this nightmarish situation, to find some kind of security by establishing relationships among these people. She thinks of her own father and brothers as protectors; she hopes to render Van less dangerous if she can think of him as part of Ruby's family.

215:22 **Judge Drake of Jackson** Jackson, Mississippi, the state capitol, located 150 miles south of Oxford. In so identifying her father, Temple establishes her family's prominence, another form of protection. But now Ruby also knows who Temple is, a potentially important fact at the trial. See entry 366:10//269:9.

215:23 **a linen suit** a light cloth made from the flax plant. The white linen suit is the stereotypical aristocratic attire of the Southern plantation owner. Judge Drake wears a linen suit when he appears in the courtroom during his daughter's testimony in Chapter XXVIII.

215:23 **palm leaf fan** a fan made of a dried and trimmed palm leaf or other plant fiber. Similar fans made of printed cardboard were also customarily sold in local stores or given away by funeral parlors, churches, etc. as a form of advertising.

215:28 **I asked him** him = Popeye. Temple still does not know his name.

215:28 **Gowan wouldn't** ask Popeye for a ride. Temple is calling Gowan's courage and his adequacy as a male companion into question. She is also looking for approval, stressing her own efforts to do what Ruby told her.

215:31 **How could you? . . . Not because I am somewhere I am afraid to stay** Ruby reminds Temple that she *could* have walked away from the house to the road at any time during the day. No one has yet made any move to stop her. Among the reasons for Temple's failure to act are her fear and her dependency on males to do things for her. Ruby also makes it clear that she has chosen to stay with Lee—she also could have walked away at any time. See entry 216:12//55:10.

216:4 **But maybe, with so many of them. . . . . . .** Temple assumes safety in numbers. Since there are many men there, no *one* will prove a threat to her. She might also be thinking of her own home, where she has grown up with five men.

216:7 **He got drunk three times today . . . he got drunk again** See 215:11//54:1. Temple enumerates the times for Ruby in the passage that follows, not including Gowan's present inebriation. Temple talks in run-on sentences, often with little transition between ideas; her confusion and anxiety are escalating.

216:8 **I am on probation and I told him what would happen** "For slipping out at night" (217:26//57:5). Temple has been threatened with suspension from the University if she is caught breaking any other rules.

216:10 **when we stopped at that little country store to buy a shirt he got drunk again** Here Gowan apparently drinks the remaining liquor in the jar. See entry 216:14//55:12.

216:12 **he went into the restaurant but I was too worried to eat**

and I couldn't find him Although Gowan had originally forced Temple to go with him against her will, she here has had an opportunity to get away from him if she wished. See the similar scene with Popeye in Chapter XVIII. See entry 275:14// 139:20.

216:14 **I felt the bottle in his pocket before he knocked my hand away** the bottle of hair-oil he is drinking (204:22// 37:12). See 342:20//236:4, when Temple reaches for Popeye's pistol at the Grotto.

216:15 **He kept on saying I had his lighter** While this episode is further evidence of Gowan's drunkenness, it also fits into the absurd nightmare quality of Temple's experiences and anticipates her confusion about Ruby and the car at the end of this chapter.° See entries 221:9//62:2; 222:7//63:11.

216:26 **she could hear the faint guttering the lamp made . . . the harsh, abrupt, meaningless masculine sounds from the house** Overwhelmed momentarily by the cacophony of sounds in and beyond the kitchen, Temple experiences a kind of aural overload. Faulkner imparts an onomatopoetic quality to the word "guttering," which means, in this case, the low burning of a flame, by conflating it with "guttural," which imparts a sense of thick, heavy sound. Even the noise is gendered.

216:29 **And you have to cook for all of them every night . . . in the dark. . . . . . .** Temple perhaps unconsciously connects the acts of cooking and feeding with the act of sex—Ruby *serves* these men. See entry 184:39//9:4.

216:32 **May I hold the baby?** Temple's fear of sexual violation again causes her to grab the baby as a form of protection. Though she now identifies with the child's helplessness, at the same time she "plays at" womanhood.

216:39 **Will you? Will you ask him?** a noticeable change in stance. This is not at all the abrupt, aggressive manner she previously used with Popeye (212:28//49:21). Perhaps it is because Temple is now dealing with a woman, but it is also clear to her that her earlier strategies have not worked and now she is reduced to pleading.

217:1 **Things like that dont happen. . . . With a little baby** Temple is still unable to believe the gravity of her situation and deals with it through a kind of denial. Though she obviously fears the "otherness" of these people, who are so unlike the people she ordinarily deals with, she still attempts to impose a normal sociological order built on the sanctity and safety of the family.

217:6 **if bad mans hurts Temple, us'll tell the governor's soldiers, wont us?** Temple regresses into baby talk, identifying with the crying child and calling on an almost fairy tale form of protection.

217:13 **precarious dissolute angle** "Dissolute" here means awry, a state of dishabille. Temple's hat (which she has worn all day, despite a leap from a moving train, hours of driving, a car wreck, a fall from the porch, hiding behind a stove, and constant running around) has been pushed back from hugging the baby. She now gives the appearance of dissolution (perhaps even in the moral sense) although she is herself anything but dissolute at the moment.

217:17 **they wouldn't know I wasn't on it, because the ones that saw me get off wouldn't tell** Temple here apparently means her student friends, who were aware of her plans to meet Gowan. But she has been seen by an official (203:30// 36:11). Perhaps she does not know this, but it is also possible that she is playing down the consequences of her actions: "If I can just get back home, everything will be all right, just like before."

217:22 **Daddy would just die** Judge Drake would be mortified if people learned that his daughter was out with a drunk, breaking rules, risking suspension or expulsion from the university. Temple remains concerned with social disgrace despite the imminent real danger in store.

217:30 **because I had a date with a boy she liked and he never asked her for another date. So I had to** lie. This incident says something about Temple's self-centeredness. Apparently Temple, more or less on a whim, so captivates the boy that he loses interest in the first girl. The story establishes her as a disruptive force in relationships, but she tells it mainly to exculpate herself: she is in trouble not for the action itself but because the girl *told* on her.

218:4 **Take all you can get, and give nothing. "I'm a pure girl; I dont do that"** Ruby mocks Temple's teasing pose and implicitly contrasts it with the more honest activities of a prostitute who fulfills her sexual promise for the money or gifts received.

218:12 **her face like a small pale mask** The mask image will be repeatedly used to describe Temple. It apparently derives from her makeup, at least in part, and from her normal indifference to the events around her. Here, however, she is apparently stunned into silence by Ruby's outburst.

218:14 **My brother said** Ruby's brother. Since Faulkner provides no obvious transition and pronouns continue to be ambiguous, and since we know Temple has brothers, this passage may at first seem to be about Temple rather than Ruby. It does draw a parallel between Temple and Ruby, one which Temple will recognize below.

218:15 **he said he would kill the goddam son of a bitch** Ruby harshly contrasts the restrained reaction of Temple's cultured brother and her own brother's more violent response. This is part of her distinction between "boys" and "real men." See entry 344:40//239:16.

218:20 **But I wasn't a coward** Ruby accuses Temple of being a coward. Temple won't leave the Old Frenchman place without a male escort, but Ruby ran away from home to meet her lover. Later, when Temple sneaks out of Reba's house to meet Red, she and Red will act out Ruby's story. See entry 219:27//59:28.

218:22 **When we got back in the buggy I knew it had been the last time** it = lovemaking. Frank and Ruby make love before returning to face Ruby's father.

218:30 **Do you want it too?** to be shot. By her father's measure, Ruby is as deserving of death as her lover Frank. Frank's actions contrast markedly with those of the Virginia Gentleman Gowan Stevens.

218:32 **Get down there and sup your dirt, you whore** "Sup" means to drink, eat or swallow. Ruby's father forces her to acknowledge the results of her actions: this is what you have caused to happen. He is literally telling her to lick Frank's blood, a possible reference to Jezebel, whore wife of King Ahab, whose bodies and blood are eaten by dogs after their deaths: "Thus saith the Lord, In the place where dogs licked the blood of Naboth shall dogs lick thy blood, even thine" I Kings 21:19.

218:33 **"I have been called that," Temple whispered** Popeye has called her whore (212:36//49:29). It is also possible that some of the boys she has dated have done the same in anger or disappointment: her name has been written on the bathroom walls.

218:34 **high thin arms** upper arms, where she is cradling the baby.

218:36 **But you good women** There is no indication that Ruby hears Temple's whisper.

218:36 **Cheap sports** girls out for a good time but unwilling to pay the price, through sex. See entry 212:33//49:26.

218:37 **then when you're caught. . . . . . .** you come running to others for help.

218:40 **kids that give a damn whether you like it or not** Ruby says that the men (as opposed to the children—the "kids"—Temple knows) at the Old Frenchman place don't play by Temple's rules: they expect to be sexually satisfied and would force Temple to comply.

219:4 **Philippines** The Philippine Islands became a protectorate of the United States in 1898, after the Spanish-American war. American troops have been stationed there up to the present time. See first entry 255:5//109:14.

219:5 **nigger women** most likely, a woman native to the islands, not a Negro as such but a non-Caucasian.

219:5 **Leavenworth** Fort Leavenworth, a military prison located in Leavenworth, Kansas.

219:6 **the war** World War I (1914–18). The United States entered the war in 1917.

219:8   **until the lawyer got a congressman to get him out**   Because Goodwin would have been under military arrest, civilian authorities would be of little use.°

219:9   **Then I could quit jazzing again——**   prostituting herself. Ruby has again taken up the trade to pay for Lee's release. Apparently she was practicing before she met Lee, gave it up while they were together, and then started up "again" after his imprisonment, even though Goodwin was betraying her with the native woman. Ruby established a relationship with the lawyer—sex for legal work—similar to the one she assumes Horace will demand. See second entry 219:13//59:14.

219:13   **putty-face**   Here "putty" refers to the color of Temple's face, the makeup she is wearing. Earlier Tommy used the word "putty" to mean "pretty," but Ruby does not speak with Tommy's exaggerated dialect. She is not calling Temple "pretty-face." See entry 221:31//62:25.

219:13   **How do you suppose I paid that lawyer?**   "I lived with the lawyer two months..." (372:14//278:1).

219:17   **doll-faced slut**   A slut is a woman of extremely loose morals. Ruby has already distinguished between herself as prostitute with ethics and Temple as a "cheap sport." "Doll-faced" refers to Temple's makeup, the mask-like quality of her face, but also implies Temple's infantile, childish nature: "an elongated and leggy infant" (219:11//59:12).

219:18   **think you cant come into a room where a man is without him.......**   without his becoming aroused by Temple's presence. Ruby mocks Temple's fears while at the same time validating them and expressing her own fears about Temple's attractiveness. She says that Temple is fooling herself to think these men would find her desirable, but she also warns Temple that they will take her if they decide they do want her.

219:24   **you'd find just what that little putty face is worth, and all the rest of it you think you are jealous of when you're just scared of it**   Ruby accuses Temple of playing at sexual maturity, pretending to want sexual fulfillment while actually being afraid of it. The first "it" seems to refer to this adult sexual pose, the pretense of full womanhood indicated by the makeup and seductive clothes. (Temple "pretends" to be a mother, holding the baby, at the time Ruby attacks her.) The second "it" is the sexual act itself and any concomitant responsibilities or results.

219:26 **And if he is just man enough to call you whore** The irony is that the impotent Popeye has just called Temple "whore," although admittedly in a quite different context, and will later treat her as one. In Ruby's economy, a "real man" is one who has the power to degrade a woman.

219:27 **you'll say Yes Yes and you'll crawl naked in the dirt and the mire for him to call you that. . . . . . .** Such a man could also introduce Temple to yet unimagined sexual passion; he would break down her silly pretenses and release her fundamental emotions. See Temple and Red later in the book (344:16//238:20). Ruby's description, however, also reminds us of her own father after he kills Frank; in one sense she admires her father for his brutal display of authority.

219:29 **her mouth moving as if she were saying Yes Yes Yes** Temple, although her mouth is moving, is not necessarily saying Yes in the way Ruby describes. She is caught up in Ruby's vision, to be sure, and is responding to it. But she is still imitating rather than acting on her own.

219:34 **Temple stood in the floor** as if rooted in the floor. Frozen, transfixed by the image Ruby has conjured.

220:5 **towsack** a bag made of coarsely woven flax or hemp fiber. Sometimes used for clothing or for household needs by the very poor.

220:9 **Will you go out the back and get into it and go away and never come back here?** Here Ruby seems to want Temple to slip away, without anyone's knowledge. She doesn't want Temple to come to the attention of the men any more than is necessary. But see entries 222:5//63:9; 222:7//63:11.

220:14 **Temple could feel all her muscles shrinking like severed vines in the noon sun** Temple realizes the disdain with which Ruby views her; Ruby's stare withers Temple's self-confidence.

The image specifically challenges the strength and fecundity of (feminine) nature introduced in the earlier description of the grape arbor.

220:17 **Playing at it** pretending to be sexually active and available. There will be continued references to Temple's role playing.

220:18 **I didn't. I didn't** In Temple's mind this is absolutely true. She has acted in her usual manner to get what she wants. Her audience has mistaken her manner for a genuine sexual overture.

220:19 **You'll have something to tell them now, when you get back. Wont you?** Ruby believes that even now Temple fails to understand the gravity of her situation, that Temple will turn it into an exciting, possibly comic adventure among the "common people" when she returns to her safe surroundings.

220:20 **Face to face, their voices were like shadows upon two close blank walls** a grammatically confusing sentence. "Face to face" is a dangling modifier. The two women are eyeball to eyeball as they talk, their voices so intense that (employing synesthesia) they practically take shape, throw shadows. As solid entities, the voices could be thought of as replacing the speakers.

220:23 **It's not Lee I'm afraid of. Do you think he plays the dog after every hot little bitch that comes along? It's you** Ruby claims not to be worried about Lee, who has known real women and would not be attracted to a child like Temple. But she is worried about what Temple will do if she remains, what problems and turmoil she will cause as a result of her naiveté and indiscriminate coquetry. Yet, Ruby clearly views Temple as a sexual rival, and seems to be bravely trying to convince herself as well as Temple. Her flagging confidence accounts for some of the contradictions in these passages.

220:26 **All running, but not too fast. Not so fast you cant tell a real man when you see him** Now Ruby accuses Temple of trying to seduce Lee, although she has just said that Lee wouldn't be interested and that Temple doesn't fully understand the consequences of her flirtatious actions. Reemphasizing the fact that Temple could have left already, Ruby suggests that Temple really wants to be pursued and is calling attention to herself.

220:28 **Do you think you've got the only one in the world?** ambiguous use of the pronoun "one." The connection Temple seems to make is to the "real man" Ruby has just mentioned. Temple can respond only with "Gowan," who has continuously failed her. However, the "one" could also refer to Temple's vagina. Thus, Ruby would be saying, "Do you think you're the only woman available? that you're so attractive that men won't notice or consider anyone else?"

220:34 **cooking over a gas-jet** a metal pipe bringing gas into a room. It may be connected to a hot plate by a rubber hose. Ruby has few luxuries.

220:35 **because I promised him** Ruby promised Lee to give up her life as a prostitute.

220:39 **Afraid? You haven't the guts to be really afraid, anymore than you have to be in love** Ruby refers to the commitment necessary for love, the willingness to put the other person first, as she has Lee, despite the costs and even if there is no reciprocity. She is describing love that could be hazardous since it can't be experienced from safety. Temple can't fully appreciate her own risk because she is still unwilling to face the realities of her present situation.

221:1 **I'll pay you** further evidence that Temple still does not hear, or at least does not comprehend, what Ruby is saying. Her response is programmatic: she can buy her way out of trouble.

221:6 **Her mouth laughed, with no sound, no movement of her face** More an exclamation of disdain than an actual laugh—there is no humor in it.

221:9 **I'll get a car. You get away from here and dont you ever come back** Ruby's failure to get a car is one of the most difficult and compelling problems in the book: why does Ruby say this and then not follow up on it—in fact, seem to forget all about it? She is, perhaps, playing with Temple, leading her on in an attempt to punish her. But since Ruby *does* want Temple to leave, perhaps she attempted to get a car, failed, and chose not to explain to Temple. In any case, Ruby's actions do give Temple ample reason to include Ruby among the people who mistreat her. See entry 222:7//63:11.

221:20 **She lit hers at the lamp, someway, Temple thought, holding the cigarette in her hand, staring at the uneven flame** Temple's ignorance is contrasted to Ruby's experience: she does not know how to light the cigarette from the kerosene lamp and cannot tell exactly how Ruby has managed to do it.

221:31 **its putty-colored face and bluish eyelids** a physical connection between the helpless sick baby and Temple herself, who has been called "putty-face" (219:13//59:14; 219:24//59:19). The description will later come to include Popeye.

221:32 **A thin whisper of shadow cupped its head and lay moist upon its brow** refers specifically to the child's hair, which is wet with feverish sweat, but there is also the sense of death hovering over the child. See second entry 221:36//62:30.

221:36 **"He's going to die," Temple whispered** Temple begins to understand, as if Ruby's words are finally sinking in. Since she has already identified with the child, this realization also forces her to face, if only for the moment, her own mortality and danger. It is, moreover, the first trace of pity she shows for another being, although, to be sure, the pity is still largely self-directed.

221:36 **Bending, her shadow loomed high upon the wall, her coat shapeless, her hat tilted monstrously above a monstrous escaping of hair** Once again Temple is described in terms of her shadow, which is horribly distorted against the wall as she leans over the child: she appears to threaten him, as Goodwin seems earlier to have feared when he found her holding the baby's box. Since she will, in effect, be the agent of the family's destruction, the monster image ("monstrously" . . . "monstrous") is not inappropriate. The shadow image also links her with the shadowy Popeye.

222:1 **the voice of the man who had laughed above them, laughing again** Van.

222:5 **"The car," Temple said. "I could go now, while they're eating"** Temple wants to act on Ruby's earlier advice to slip away, without calling attention to herself.

222:7 **"What car?" the woman said. "Go on and eat. Nobody's going to hurt you"** It is as if Ruby had tried to frighten Temple, to string her out as far as she could and then to reverse herself, as if the earlier conversation had never taken place. Only Popeye's car is readily available and he has already refused. What car Ruby intended in her offer is problematic: the Memphis truck, or Vernon Tull's, as she tells Gowan (237:19//84:10) are two possibilities. The curious and unresolved offering certainly adds to the nightmarish quality of Temple's dilemma and the reader's surreal sense of *Sanctuary*.

CHAPTER VIII

223:1 **her face fixed in a cringing, placative expression** Despite critics' charges that Temple constantly draws attention to herself, here she attempts to remain unnoticed as much as possible. Ruby has forced her to enter the room occupied by the men.

223:2 **she was quite blind when she entered** Temple has moved from the darkness of the kitchen to the brighter light of the dining-room and is dazzled and dazed. The blindness also underscores her lack of awareness: she does not yet fully realize the extent of her danger.

223:3 **holding the coat about her** a symbolic gesture of hiding, repeated in various ways during the night.

223:5 **She went straight toward him, as if she had been looking for him all the while** Temple hopes Tommy will protect her since he has already attempted to comfort her (207:13// 42:11). As Faulkner notes, they are "like two children" (207:16//42:13). Ruby, the other woman and thus Temple's most obvious ally, has offered no such reassurance.

223:9 **Here ... you come around here** Rather than protecting, Gowan attempts to assert his ownership of and authority over Temple: she is his girl.

223:11 **Outside, brother** Van usurps Gowan's ownership: "Leave the room; you're out of the game."

223:14 **grinning rigidly at Tommy** in panic and fear. Her gaping facial expression is a mask, a painful rictus, bereft of all meaning.

223:30 **She ran to the road ... just as someone came up the hall** No one tries to stop or even to pursue Temple at this point.

Ruby, in fact, steps aside so that Temple might pass without running into her. The men seem unconcerned, even indifferent; perhaps they are confident that she won't run far.

224:1 **Little bite of victuals** victuals = food; a little something to eat.

224:6 **her face wan as a small ghost in the refracted light from the dining-room** Temple, who has been a vivid, even garish physical presence thus far in the book, begins to take on a disembodied quality which will be emphasized in later chapters. See entry 281:34//148:19.

224:15 **Then he turned his head . . . toward the kitchen** Tommy has come to the front of the house to look for Temple, who is now standing in the path leading from the dirt road. She then runs around the side of the house to the back and then to the kitchen, to the assumed safety offered by Ruby. Tommy can see her as she passes the back door by looking down the hall which runs completely through the house. She is trying to avoid the men altogether.

224:20 **He's trying to get his with a plate full of ham** Van implies that Tommy is using food to entice Temple into having sex with him.

224:30 **'I am,' Goodwin said** Lee is still attempting to keep order in his home. He is also trying to defuse the impending conflict between Van and the drunken, hapless Gowan. It would be bad for business if one of his customers were beaten up. It would also call unwanted attention to his operation, which is apparently left alone by the local law in a kind of gentleman's agreement.

224:33 **little bit** Van's drunken overture to Temple contains a reference to her size, but also suggests his sexual agenda as well: i.e., to "get a little bit."

224:35 **I'm a good guy. Ruby'll tell you** Van wants to diffuse Temple's fear by using Ruby as character witness, although he makes a joke at Ruby's expense, much as Popeye has done earlier. He may, however, also be suggesting that Ruby could vouch for his reputation as a lover.

224:40   **Beyond him Temple stood behind the chair in which the woman sat at the table**   Temple has placed Ruby between herself and Van.

225:10   **With the top of his mind he listened to them**   Tommy is not paying full attention to the talk, although he is aware of what is being said. Tommy, in fact, anticipates the next confrontation between Van and Gowan (225:14//67:24).

225:20   **I never meant———**   Van has made some comment about Temple, surely of a sexual nature given the content of his previous talk. He apologizes to Lee (but not to Gowan) for causing trouble: "I never meant for him [Gowan] to get so worked up, to take it so personally." Or, "I never meant I was actually going to do it."

225:23   **Cant even talk no more**   Gowan is too drunk to speak coherently.

225:25   **Think talk bout my———**   my girl. Again the emphasis is on possession.

225:35   **his whole body writhing in an acute discomfort**   Tommy is certainly concerned for Temple's safety, but he is also sexually disturbed, perhaps embarrassed, by her presence. It is as if he cannot exactly identify the nature of his feelings toward her. His mounting anxiety makes him squirm. See 233:10//78:20; 249:3//101:2.

225:39   **Let every damned one of them. . . . . . .**   "Go to hell?" Tommy's earlier "they" clearly refers to the men who are "pestering" Temple. But Lee's remark seems more directed toward Temple, and toward women in general. He seems misogynistic, blaming women for the trouble they cause among men. His comment also suggests that he, too, is disturbed by Temple.

226:4   **he followed with his eyes the small comet of the match into the weeds**   See "The match flipped outward like a dying star in miniature . . ." (346:6//241:3). The second description appears just before Popeye kills Red. Tommy, his first victim, is also marked by the image of the match (249:38//102:7). See entry 390:7//305:15.

226:5   **Him too, he said. Two of em**   Tommy intuits that even Popeye is interested in Temple, although Popeye gives no outward indication of being so. The "two of em" would seem to be Popeye and Van; Tommy at this time does not suspect Lee. See entry 232:25//77:26. By omitting the quotation marks, Faulkner indicates that Tommy is speaking to himself; the dialect spelling personalizes his voice.

226:10 **Dont nobody never use in there** The room is usually empty, not made use of. Therefore, the light is unusual.

226:12 **he went to the window and looked in** The following scene is from Tommy's viewpoint, although narrated neutrally. It reinvokes the theme of voyeurism: Temple is spied on as she undresses and prepares for bed. Faulkner will later return to this scene, retelling it from other points of view.

226:12 **The sash was down** The sash is the frame in which the window panes are set; the window is closed.

226:16 **her very attitude an outrage to muscle and tissue of more than seventeen and more compatible with eight or ten** Alone in the room, Temple is balled up in the contracted posture of a child, a position which an adult ("more than seventeen") would find very uncomfortable and difficult to maintain. As Elisabeth Muhlenfeld has argued, the emphasis in *Sanctuary* is on Temple's physical, as well as emotional, immaturity.°

226:19 **against which a chair was wedged** The door has no lock (229:6//72:29).

226:23 **lathing and molded shreds of cloth** Lathing refers to the strips of wood which form the foundation for wall plaster. Strips of cloth were sometimes added to the plaster to reinforce its strength and cause it to hold to the lathing; cloth could also be prepared to hold wallpaper. The description underscores the ramshackle state of the house.

226:25 **It turned slowly, as if she were following the passage of someone beyond the wall** Temple can hear through the walls. See 213:37//51:12. Another example of her heightened senses, especially her sense of sound. Stephen M. Ross argues that "Temple's posture as listener invaded by a threatful world embodied as sound, and especially as voice, makes her as much a victim as a genuinely evil character...."°

226:28 **those papier-mâché Easter toys filled with candy** Calvin

Brown describes traditional figurines in the shapes of rabbits, chickens, etc., filled with sweets; children turned and removed the heads to get at the treats inside.° This image suggests that Temple is a kind of toy to be broken in to and enjoyed. It emphasizes the fragility of her body, of her virginity, but also makes her seem mechanical, much like Popeye.

226:29 **Then it turned back . . . and became motionless there for a moment** It is unclear who is walking around outside Temple's door. It could be Popeye, since the other men are on the porch talking and drinking, but Popeye is usually very quiet. Tommy is still looking in the window. Ruby or even Lee are other possibilities.

226:33 **a tiny watch from the top of her stocking** Temple is not carrying a purse; she is wearing a garter which enables her to store her watch in her stocking.

226:34 **With the watch in her hand she lifted her head and looked directly at him, her eyes calm and empty as two holes** She doesn't actually see Tommy, who is outside in the dark. The description again emphasizes Temple's mask-like face.

226:39 **arrowlike** She is as slim and straight as an arrow: "match-thin" (227:8//70:10).

227:5 **She unfastened her dress** Temple removes her dress to prepare for bed rather than for seduction.° She is trying to impose order on chaos. She seems unaware that Tommy is watching her, but in any case, by wrapping herself in the two coats, she is making herself less alluring. She obviously feels that the coats—the second belongs to Van (292:13//163:23)—offer protection.

227:10 **scrabbled** scrabble: to grope about furiously.

227:12 **she whirled and looked straight into Tommy's eyes and whirled and ran and flung herself upon the chair** Again, there is no indication that she actually sees Tommy. Her frantic movements are responses to the sounds of the men's voices. She runs to the chair to make sure it is firmly wedged against the door.

227:26 **faint dry whisper of shucks** Shucks are the husks from an ear of corn. Dry husks were often used as mattress stuffing:

they are quite comfortable, although they make noise with each movement.°

227:36 **She opened the raincoat and produced a compact from somewhere . . . and fastened the raincoat** It is unclear where she has kept the compact: perhaps in a pocket of her own coat. On the one hand, Temple's actions seem inappropriate to her situation. However, there is a ritualistic quality to these actions. Her watch tells her that, in her normal life, it would be time to get ready for a date. Thus, she may be creating her own reality, her own sense of security, by going through this process. She is, moreover, building up her mask; the makeup, like the two coats, adds symbolic layers of protection, of defense, and of authority: she is strengthening her identity. See entry 284:32//152:20 for discussion of Temple's actions at Miss Reba's brothel.

228:4 **a faint, steady chatter of the shucks inside the mattress where Temple lay** The sound is caused by Temple's fearful shivering.

228:5 **her hands crossed on her breast and her legs straight and close and decorous, like an effigy on an ancient tomb** Temple takes on the posture and image of a body prepared for burial. See her comments on this idea at 330:23//219:8. The image also anticipates the "dead queens" at the end of the book. In another sense, Temple's posture is defense against sexual penetration.

228:13 **Tommy heard dry, light sounds like billiard balls** This would have to be a clacking sound. Tommy is focused on the porch, where Van and Gowan are fighting, so the sound could be Gowan's teeth being knocked together by Van's fist. Goodwin then calls Tommy to help restore order.

228:22 **"I got—hah!" he said as Popeye slashed savagely at his face; "you would, would you? Hold up hyer"** a confused series of actions. Tommy appears to misunderstand Lee's directions when he tells Tommy to "Grab him there!" (228:20//72:2). Lee is referring either to Gowan, who has been thrown into the wall and is now falling unconscious off the porch, or to

Van, rather than to Popeye, who is a bystander to the argument. Popeye reacts violently to Tommy's attack out of self-defense, but he is physically no match for Tommy's strength. Tommy's mistake, which humiliates Popeye, is another probable cause for Popeye to shoot him.

228:32 **Hole up hyer. You done whupped him** Tommy, realizing his mistake, wants Van to calm down, acknowledging that Van has already beaten Gowan and there is no need to continue the fight.

228:34 **Now, now; whut you want to kill him fer? You caint eat him, kin you? You want Mr Popeye to start guttin us all with that ere artermatic?** Tommy employs a simple argument here to dissuade Van from further harm of Gowan: you kill only for need, not for pleasure. Tommy also knows how close to violence he has pushed Popeye by his mistake: he is deferential to "Mr Popeye" here as at no other time in the book. "Guttin" would mean shooting in the stomach or gut.

229:4 **"Open the door," he shouted. "We're bringing you a customer"** Van's waggish behavior continues the joke that Temple is a prostitute.

229:11 **His hair was broken about his face, long as a girl's** Van's hair, not his face, is as long as a girl's. See the description of Gowan's "broken hair" (203:8//35:19).

229:37 **He saw Van take hold of the raincoat upon Temple's breast and rip it open** A show of force, certainly; however, this is Van's coat and he needs it to load the truck. Popeye's subsequent actions are more sinister. See second entry to 230:11//74:17.

230:11 **His right hand lay in his coat pocket** The pocket with the gun, an unspoken warning to Lee and the others not to interfere.

230:11 **Beneath the raincoat on Temple's breast Tommy could see the movement of the other hand, communicating a shadow of movement to the coat** Popeye is feeling Temple's breasts under the raincoat in front of the other people. It is possible that he has gotten excited by seeing Van rip open the coat, but there is little evidence that Popeye is aroused at this point. It is more likely a power play than a sexual act. Popeye is stressing his prerogative.

230:14 **"Take your hand away," Goodwin said. "Move it"** As we later learn, Goodwin is afraid of Popeye. His action here shows his courage and his need to keep order in his own house.

230:20 **They lifted Van and carried him out** reversing the action of bringing the unconscious Gowan into the room.

230:27 **While you finish the trick Van started and you wouldn't let him finish?** A trick is a prostitute's customer: "to turn a trick" is to have intercourse or some form of sexual activity for money. Ruby suspects that Lee has stopped Van—and Popeye—so that he can now have Temple for himself. This fear indicates that much of what she earlier said to Temple was bravado rather than complete confidence in Lee.

230:32 **You owe me nothing** Ruby is clearly angry and jealous of Temple and the effect she is having on Lee and the men in the house. Actually Goodwin owes her a great deal, as her earlier story to Temple proved.

230:35 **With the other hand he opened the coat** Faulkner establishes a kind of uneven comparison in this scene between Ruby and Temple. They both are partially undressed under the coats they both wear. Here Goodwin's action in opening Ruby's coat follows Van's tearing open of Temple's coat and Popeye's subsequent running of his hand beneath the coat. Lee's next comment—"Hah . . . Dressed for company" (230:39//75:18)—calls further attention to this possibility. Ruby's nightgown suggests that she is also trying to be seductive. She is competing with Temple, hoping to keep Lee's mind off the younger woman. The wretched state of the garment makes her effort pathetic.

230:37 **the garment on the wire** the panties (208:3//43:10).

231:15 **You little fool!** Lee once again places the blame on Temple, even though she has not consciously caused these problems. It is possible he is doing this in part for Ruby's sake, to show her that he finds Temple to be an irritation, a bother, rather than an attraction. Still, he does blame Temple as the catalyst.

231:28 **her face sharpening out of the approaching lamp in profile** From Temple's perspective, Ruby's face comes into focus in profile as the lamp nears.

231:33 **each respiration choking to a huddle fall** The *OED* lists one archaic meaning of **huddle** as "congested," which fits this passage. Gowan has been drinking heavily and has been hit in the face; his nose is clotted with dried blood. He breathes with great difficulty, and at the end of each breath makes a prolonged pause before he begins again. The phrase also indicates Temple's fear that the one contact to her normal world might die.

231:36 **"They gone down to the truck yet?" Goodwin said.... Tommy watched them enter another door** "They" refers to Van, Popeye and others associated with the truck. Goodwin tells Tommy to check on "it"—the truck. Tommy, however, watches "them"—Ruby and Lee—enter the bedroom and then keeps watch over the men in the kitchen in order to help protect Temple.

232:6 **He was there when Goodwin came out with the raincoat** At this point Faulkner begins to obscure the order of events, to omit obvious transitions, forcing the reader to make the necessary connections. Here, for example, Goodwin has left Ruby in the bedroom and has reentered Temple's room to get the raincoat Temple was wearing over her own coat. Though he has gone in to collect the coat, he—and later Popeye—simulate customers lining up for turns.

232:10 **that stuff** the bootleg whiskey.

232:13 **The woman could see them in the darkness ... where Temple lay** Now it becomes clear that Ruby has not stayed in her room. She is hiding in the dark to see what will happen to Temple, to see if Lee will return to Temple. Thus, she is there when Lee and then Popeye and Tommy come into the room.

232:25 **And Lee too, he said, And Lee too** Tommy is forced to acknowledge that Lee is also a sexual threat to Temple. He is greatly disappointed since he has counted on Lee to protect Temple.

232:26 **Twice he stole along the porch until he could see the shadow of Popeye's hat on the kitchen floor** Tommy is checking on Popeye to make sure he is staying away from Temple.

CHAPTER IX

234:1 **The room was dark** Chapter IX retells the events that occurred in the last part of Chapter VIII, now from Ruby's point of view. She has ignored Lee and has immediately returned to Temple's room. Ruby will repeat the events again for Horace in Chapter XIX.

234:10 **The man came in, without trying to be silent** Unlike Popeye and Tommy, Goodwin is not attempting to conceal his movements. There is nothing in his actions to warrant suspicion. See entry 234:20//80:10.

234:19 **brilliantine** an oily, perfumed hair tonic. This detail anticipates the punch line of Popeye's demise.

234:20 **She did not see Popeye at all . . . until Tommy entered, following Popeye** an unusually punctuated series of phrases. Although Ruby knows from the smell of brilliantine that Popeye is nearby, she is not aware that he has actually entered the room and walked by her to the bed—she is still "waiting for him"—until she finds Tommy next to her. It is Tommy's presence that alerts her to Popeye's movement. Popeye himself remains invisible.

234:25 **They glowed, breast-high** Tommy apparently is creeping behind Popeye, not standing at his full height.

234:31 **The woman stood just inside the door** a close variation of the sentence near the beginning of the paragraph. Her presence literally frames the actions of the paragraph. She is witness (but see entry 234:32//80:22).

234:32 **She could hear no sound from the shucks, so she remained motionless beside the door** This detail sets up a discrepancy in Temple's later version of the scene. Temple remembers vividly the noise of the shucks when she retells the story of this night to Horace. See 330:38//219:24 and 331:22//220:21 for examples. Because Ruby hears no noise, she assumes nothing is happening. She can't actually see, in the dark, what Popeye is doing at "the invisible bed" (234:34//80:24). If Temple were jerking around, as she will remember doing, Ruby and especially Tommy should be able to hear it and would intervene. Tommy, after all, could hear "the mattress crackle" from outside the window (227:29//71:1). Perhaps, then, Temple imagines trying to escape from Popeye's hand while she remains physically still? Since she does struggle as soon as Ruby touches her (235:5//81:4).

234:36 **as though the stealthy evacuation of his position blew soft and cold upon her in the black silence** As Tommy vacates his position next to Ruby, the space previously filled by his warm body is replaced with lighter and cooler air. Ruby is aware of a change in density and pressure. She feels his absence.

235:9 **holding the coat together** Temple thinks Ruby is Popeye or another of the men. She is not passively submitting to rape.

235:19 **Will you get me out of here? Will you? Will you?** Ruby has already promised to help Temple escape and then failed to keep that promise. Temple has every right to suspect her now.

235:36 **she cursed Temple in a whisper** Again the anger and blame are directed toward Temple, as if she had purposefully made all this happen.

236:5 **a dying whisper of fairy feet** There is a kind of Waste Land inverted magic implied here: fairies into rats. See T. S. Eliot's *The Waste Land*: "A rat crept softly through the vegetation/ Dragging its slimy belly on the bank."°

236:5 **Temple whirled, treading on something that rolled under her foot** It could be a rat but more likely a corncob. Both are present in the barn, and both will play significant roles in subsequent events.

CHAPTER X

237:1 **While the woman was cooking breakfast** Sunday morning, May 12.

237:1 **the child still—or already—asleep in the box behind the stove** The baby has either not yet awakened from his night's sleep or has already been awake and has now gone back to sleep. The passage begins to draw a connection between the helpless child and Temple, who has been sleeping in the barn. See next entry.

237:14 **in the crib, asleep** "Crib" has three meanings in this passage. Ruby specifically refers to the crib in the barn, a stall or manger used to house cattle or to store grain. "Crib" also means a child's bed, a meaning which connects Temple with the infant asleep by the stove. A third meaning is that of a prostitute's small, often closet-sized room in a brothel.

237:19 **The nearest one is at Tull's, two miles away** Vernon Tull is a character in *As I Lay Dying* (1930), *The Hamlet*, *The Town*, *The Mansion* (1959) and several short stories. This is possibly the car that Ruby mentioned to Temple the previous night.

238:9 **he knelt there ... trying to examine his reflection in the broken surface** See Horace Benbow (181:12//4:3).

238:16 **I'll get cleaned up some, he said. . . . I passed out twice, he said** Faulkner alternates between two levels of thought here, between Gowan's clearly stated ideas—"I'll get cleaned up some"—and his broader concerns—"thinking of Temple returning among people who knew him." His "gentlemanly" plan to retrieve Temple with a car gives way to greater self-interest when he imagines her "among their common acquaintances," revealing how pathetically he acquitted himself as drinker and protector.

238:27 **whispering eyes** synesthesia. Gowan feels that people will follow him with their eyes and gossip about his shameful behavior.

238:30 **So he engaged the car and directed the man and paid him and went on** Vernon Tull. Though Gowan prefers not to face Temple, he does make an attempt to remove her from the Old Frenchman place. No one comes to get Temple that day, perhaps because it is a Sunday morning. Tull, or whatever driver Gowan enlisted, might have waited until after church to undertake a job for pay; but by that time, Popeye has already killed Tommy and spirited Temple away. See *Sanctuary: The Original Text*: "About noon the car came and he sent word for the sheriff."°

238:31 **a car going in the opposite direction stopped and picked him up** away, that is, from the Old Frenchman place and towards town.

CHAPTER XI

239:5 **rough planks** unfinished, unplaned. See "undressed planks" (239:18//87:10).

239:16 **seventeen** This is the second time Temple's age is given as seventeen. See entry 226:16//69:8; at the trial Temple claims to be eighteen (377:12//285:10).

239:22 **The blind man was coming down the slope . . . clutching a wad of his trousers** Pap is hurrying to the barn to relieve himself. This is the second time Temple has observed Pap under such circumstances. See entry 214:6//51:21.

239:24 **braces** suspenders.

239:25 **gymnasium shoes** tennis shoes.

239:30 **the bright May sunshine, the sabbath peace** Faulkner again contrasts the seemingly benign and even comforting daylight with the horrors of the night before. Ironically, Temple will experience her worst outrage in the daylight, when she—and the reader—least anticipate it. As Robert R. Moore has noted, "She expects evil to operate by a certain logic and erects her defenses according to those expectations, but inevitably her attention is directed the wrong way at the moment evil strikes. Faulkner confounds his readers' assumptions as well in portraying an evil which refuses to play by the rules."°

239:33 **cool, unhurried sound of bells** the sound of church bells which would have been ringing at this time on the campus in Oxford. Temple is also attempting to organize her present experience, find some comfort in it, by linking it to her quotidian markers of daily life at home and school. She will do this again at Miss Reba's. See entry 284:32//152:20, for example.

240:5 **her stockinged feet** She left her shoes in the bedroom.

240:8 **The stove was cold** It is now 9 a.m. (241:5//89:15). Ruby was cooking on this stove when Gowan entered the kitchen; therefore, Gowan must have left very early.

240:14 **dinner** the mid-day meal—lunch—which, in the South, was often the largest meal of the day, especially on Sunday. The smaller evening meal would be known as "supper" (259:37//117:6). Temple has now gone from Friday noon to Sunday morning without food.

240:21 **watching the patch of sun framed in the door** Temple is watching for shadows, especially Popeye's.

240:24 **The bed was empty** Gowan has gone. Temple's failure to ask Ruby about Gowan is curious. Even if the daylight had renewed her confidence, she would surely want to know where he is.

240:32 **iron fire-dog and an overturned stack of bricks** A fire-dog is an andiron, used to stack wood in the fireplace. The "overturned stack of bricks" substitutes for the missing one of the set.°

240:33 **lying on its side, half full of ashes** another allusion to the Cinderella story: the heroine of the fairy tale is forced to sit in the ash heap while waiting for the Prince with the glass slipper to carry her away to the castle. In a perverse reversal of the fairy tale, Temple's shoe is filled with trash and her Prince will be Popeye, who will take her to Memphis. See entry 242:25//91:16.

240:36 **It bore the letters U S and a blurred number in black stencil** presumably Goodwin's army canteen.

241:2 **Now I can stand anything, she thought quietly, with a kind of dull, spent astonishment; I can stand just anything** In *Requiem for a Nun*, Temple states a similar idea: "At first you think you can bear only so much and then you will be free. Then you find out that you can bear anything, you really can and then it wont even matter."° The irony in *Sanctuary*, however, is that at this point Temple thinks she has seen the worst, that she has survived the horror, that she has been tested and survived, when in fact the worst is yet to come.

241:15 **"Hello, baby . . . you wan s'eep all day? Look at Temple"** another example of Temple's solipsism. She disturbs the baby in an effort to make ordinary chat. Temple's vanity is temporarily back at full strength.

241:20 **feeling her insides move in small, trickling clots, like loose shot** birdshot: small metal pellets found in shotgun shells. The lukewarm coffee both makes her queasy and stimulates her bowels.

241:29 **took a mail-order catalogue and tore out a few leaves and handed them to Temple** to use as toilet paper.

241:33 **"They're all gone," the woman said. "They wont be back this morning."** Ruby knows that Gowan left earlier in the morning and she erroneously assumes that the other men, except Pap, are gone. There is no reason to think that Ruby is lying to Temple. She is merely reassuring her that it is safe to go to the bathroom in or near the barn.

241:36 **Unless you're too pure to have to** to have normal bodily functions. Ruby sarcastically counters Temple's primness.

241:40 **She donned the coat and hat and went toward the barn** Temple curiously dresses up to go to the barn. She is again entering the unknown and thus draws her physical defenses about her.

242:5 **She walked right through the barn** She cannot bring herself to use the stalls already used by Pap and the others (corncobs were sometimes used for cleaning up after a bowel movement). She is trying to find the most remote and isolated spot.

242:7 **jimson weed** *Datura stramonium,* a smelly, poisonous plant.

242:8 **Then she began to run** Temple thus has one more opportunity to escape. Certainly the events of the previous night have given her sufficient reason. But in daylight she is now more sure of herself and seems to be looking for an absolutely private place, as far away as she can manage from the house, to relieve herself.

242:15 **Temple stood in the sand, listening to the birds among the sunshot leaves . . . not yet fallen to earth** Temple is in a kind of bower, one that recalls both the spring at which Popeye watches Horace and the arbor in which Horace spies on Little Belle. Temple, of course, will also be observed as she attempts to find some measure of privacy.

242:22 **When she rose** after she completes her defecation. Faulkner elides the scene.

242:23 **the squatting outline of a man** Faulkner intentionally does not directly identify this figure, although later evidence will suggest that it is Lee Goodwin. However, at this point the description of "squatting" (a position paralleling Temple's own) reminds the reader more of Tommy. See entries 246:5//96:5; 246:13//96:13.

242:25 **For an instant she stood and watched herself run out of her body, out of one slipper** Temple is described in another of the stylized tableaus: in her fear she becomes removed from her own physical being, begins to run physically before she mentally can conceive of what she is doing. The lost slipper is another ironic reference to the Cinderella story.

242:30 **When she caught a glimpse of the house she was opposite the front porch** Since Temple left the house from the kitchen at the back of the house, she has circled through the woods to the front. Popeye will follow a similar route when he sneaks to the barn. See entry 247:11//97:21.

242:39 **He was watching me!** Temple does not identify the man for Ruby, nor does she differentiate between the man in the woods and the man at the barn. Faulkner doesn't make it clear if Temple knows who "He" is. The next male named in the text, however, is Goodwin. See entry 243:11//92:12.

243:6 **She looked toward the door . . . and turned and ran toward the door** Temple is now hysterical. Seeing her hand on the cold stove, she assumes that she has burned herself even though she has felt no actual pain, another indication of her withdrawal from her physical sensations, the denial of her body.

243:11 **Goodwin was coming toward the house** coming from the barn. This fact, and Temple's reaction at seeing him, strongly imply that Goodwin was the man watching Temple.

243:20   **Then suddenly she ran upside down in a rushing interval** Temple falls through a weak spot in the loft and plummets downward while still running. Tommy warned Gowan about the hazard (210:30//47:1). The image of static motion is almost cartoonish as well as nightmarish in its exaggeration.

243:32   **it leaped at her head**   See the Goodwin baby: "I have to keep him in the box so the rats cant get to him" (191:34//18:4).

243:33   **treading again on something that rolled under her foot**   Either a corncob or the rat mentioned in next paragraph.

243:39   **the rat's eyes glowing and fading . . . and began to squeak at her in tiny plaintive gasps**   The rat changes from being a demonic creature, its eyes burning in its head, to a pathetic, cornered rodent. In one sense it serves as an analogue to Temple herself: as Albert Guerard suggests, "In the barn loft she is both a girl frightened of rats and herself a cornered rat. But eventually it is the real rat, who has just leaped at her head, that is terrified by the larger animal presence. Its squealing functions, after a first reading, as brilliant anticipation of Popeye's helpless animal sounds."°

CHAPTER XII

245:1 **The woman stood in the kitchen door** Not much time has passed since the end of the last chapter. It would appear that Goodwin has come up from the barn and gone into the house (to take another drink?) while Temple has fled from Goodwin's approach and run back down to the barn.

245:4 **She's not here... You cant find her** Given that Goodwin has just seen Temple in the house (assuming not much time has passed), he clearly doesn't believe Ruby, as he continues to look around the room where he last saw Temple. Ruby is convinced that Goodwin's intentions are sexual.

245:16 **Motionless, facing one another... terrific muscular hiatus** For a moment they are physically frozen, although their postures reveal great physical tension and potential violence. See Temple and Gowan in Chapter VI: "Their feet scraped on the bare floor as though they were performing a clumsy dance, and clinging together they lurched into the wall" (213:18//50:21).

245:21 **her arm flung back for balance... the inert body of the child** Ruby is holding the baby when Goodwin first enters the kitchen (245:1//94:1), and is still holding him when Lee throws her against the table. She grabs for the knife with the hand she has used to catch herself. Lee will next put the baby out of harm's way (245:26//95:19).

245:31 **"That's what I do to them," he said, slapping her** "them" = sluts; though he extends the insult to all women who try to control him. At the same time, Goodwin seems angry with himself, conflicted with his own desires. See entry 247:5//97:14.

246:5 **Tommy was standing in the barn, beside the crib, looking toward the house** Tommy is also in the vicinity and *could* have been the one watching Temple. Certainly Tommy has been doing most of the watching in the book so far, and also is the one who does the "squatting." However, Temple continues to approach Tommy for protection (248:5//99:5), and her fear is now directed towards Goodwin. Ruby apparently comes out the back of the house from the kitchen since she can see Tommy in the barn, but she then circles around the house, passes Pap on the front porch and then walks down the path to the road.

246:13 **Popeye came out of the bushes** A parallel to the first scene with Horace. Popeye's purpose in the woods could be to relieve himself, to spy, to escape the drunken gang, or to stand watch, but he quickly sees from Ruby's appearance that she has had trouble with Lee. In fact, Popeye may have been watching Temple in the gully. Faulkner brings all his principal characters together in this chapter, preparing for the events to come.

246:19 **There ought to be a law** This is likely unintentional humor on Popeye's part since there was such a law (see entry 182:32//6:3), but it also reveals his disgust for the people who buy and use what he transports and sells. A further irony is that Popeye's moral indignation parallels that expressed by the "good people" of Jefferson. See entry 272:9//135:5 and below.

246:21 **Goofy house ... with the telephone directory** This passage further shows Popeye's sardonic, hard-boiled sense of humor. Popeye earlier thought the book in Horace's pocket was a gun (182:1//4:30). To "take for a ride" is a gangster phrase meaning to take a victim to a secluded place and there to murder him. Since this is Sunday, and Popeye met Horace on Tuesday, he is off one day in his computation. Also, the description of Horace as "squatting" vaguely links Horace with the squatting figure watching Temple in the gully and associates him with the group of voyeuristic males.

246:25 **jerking his neck forth as if his collar were too tight** Popeye jerks his head in this fashion when he becomes excited or aroused (289:26//159:10). Thus, he is possibly thinking of Temple back at the house. His next statements to Ruby— "I'm going to town, see? . . . I'm clearing out. I've got enough of this"— (246.30) might therefore be an attempt to set up an alibi, although it has always been his intention to leave on Sunday. It is simply unclear when Popeye decides to rape and kidnap Temple.

246:31 **Somewhere in the swamp a bird sang** recalls the omnipresent bird whose song caught Horace's attention in the first scene.

246:39 **He went on across the orchard, walking gingerly. Goodwin heard him and looked over his shoulder** Popeye is not trying to sneak up on Goodwin: he walks "gingerly" and "with light, finicking sounds" earlier in the woods.

247:5 **Who's down there?** Popeye may or may not know that Temple is in the barn, but Goodwin's behavior apparently tells him all he needs to know. He now also realizes that Goodwin is interested in Temple. The question is why Goodwin has stayed in the orchard. If he wants Temple, why hasn't he simply gone to the barn after her? Ruby has left, and he could have taken care of Tommy, to whom he has already "explained" matters as we learn in the next chapter. Does his hesitation reveal a change of mind, perhaps because of Ruby's reaction? Or is he planning, anticipating the event?

247:6 **I'm clearing out** As with Ruby, it is unclear if Popeye tells Goodwin this to mislead him, perhaps to gain a little time and the element of surprise. But by now he seems to have his plan in mind. See entry 247:11//97:21.

247:11 **Popeye did not enter the house** Popeye's subsequent actions show the deliberateness of his intentions. He has told both Ruby and Goodwin that he is leaving, but he now sneaks around the house, into the woods, through the garden and "weed-choked lot" to reach the back of the barn. He clearly is willing to submit himself to this (for Popeye) discomfort in order to avoid being noticed.

247:16 **Tommy squatted on his heels beside the crib door . . .**

entered a stall quietly Tommy is not aware of Popeye's presence. See 249:28//101:26. This failure to notice Popeye, however, seems unusual since Tommy has proven so alert in the past and so adept at sneaking around on his own. Popeye even smokes a cigarette as he stares at Tommy's back. His invisibility adds to Popeye's overall menace.

247:19 **Above the manger was a wooden rack for hay . . . drew himself silently into the loft** The choice of the word "manger" reiterates Temple's role as martyr by linking her to nativity lore, as perhaps does the word "rack," which is a framework or receptacle for feed but also an instrument of torture. Popeye climbs "into" the rack in order to pull himself through a hole in the floor of the loft. To avoid Tommy's notice he does not use the ladder and trap door.

CHAPTER XIII

248:1 **Tommy was standing in the hallway of the barn** This chapter begins where Chapter XI left off: "Then she got to her feet and sprang at the door, hammering at it, watching the rat over her shoulder, her body arched against the door, rasping at the planks with her bare hands" (244:3//93:15).

248:5 **Then she saw Goodwin** Temple's fear is directed toward Goodwin rather than Tommy, whom she still sees as her protector. This point is worth remembering when we consider Temple's testimony against Goodwin at the trial.

248:7 **her voice making a thin eeeeeeeeeeeee sound like bubbles in a bottle** an hysterical cry. The sound of escaping gas from a carbonated drink, for example. See entry 250:18//102:26.

248:11 **"Lee says hit wont hurt you none. All you got to do is lay down"** Tommy has obviously expressed his concerns about Temple's safety and her fear of men to Goodwin. Tommy appears to be preparing Temple for Goodwin's assault, although his own primitive ideas and urges cause him to put his hand "clumsily on her thigh" (248:15//100:5) as he speaks to her. See entry 248:23//100:13 for further discussion.

248:19 **"Yes," she said, "all right. Dont you let him in here"** Temple interprets Tommy's statement as indicating his own sexual interest in her rather than Goodwin's. Perhaps she seems to accede to him because she feels she can control him better than she could Goodwin. See entry 248:30//100:20.

248:23 **I'll fix hit so caint nobody git to you. I'll be right hyer** Tommy is agreeing to protect Temple from Goodwin and the rest. But his following statement (248:28//100:18), when he repeats Lee's assurances that Temple won't be hurt, again reveals his own interest in Temple. Tommy's behavior confirms that Temple's fear of *all men* at the Old Frenchman place is well-founded.

248:30 **All right. I will** Temple agrees to Tommy's assertion, "All you got to do is lay down." But we have had numerous examples of Temple's responding to statements without apparently comprehending what was being said. It is likely that such is now the case.

248:31 **drive the hasp to** a metal fastener with a slot that fits over a staple. A pin or bolt is then inserted or "driven" through the staple to secure the lock.

248:37 **Tommy's eyes glowed again, the pale irises appearing for an instant to spin on the pupils like tiny wheels** Tommy becomes alert to the possible danger Goodwin represents. He is watching with great care, like a cartoon watchdog, although his eyes also recall those of the rat in the crib with Temple. See the similar description of Dr. Quinn's eyes in Chapter XVIII: see entry 282:35//150:1.

249:2 **his lip lifted a little** Tommy animalistically shows his teeth in response to the perceived danger.

249:8 **and watched Goodwin move swiftly across the corner of the house and into the cedars** This is the same route Popeye used to sneak around Tommy into the barn. See entry 247:11//97:21. Goodwin sees Tommy standing guard. His apparent intention is to circumvent Tommy and make his way to Temple.

249:21 **his hand in his coat pocket** on the pistol.

249:27 **He blinked** He = Tommy.

249:28 **He made to look past Popeye, into the crib** to check on Temple's safety. Nevertheless, it is as if Tommy does not consider Popeye as a possible sexual threat.

249:32 **Didn't I tell you about following me?** a dissonant comment, since Popeye has followed Tommy to the barn. He is, in effect, confusing Tommy, just as he has lied to Ruby and Lee about leaving.

249:33 **I was watching him** him = Goodwin.

249:38 **To Temple ... completely isolating it** The description suggests that Popeye uses a silencer on his gun.° However, Faulkner clearly indicates that this is Temple's perception of the gunshot. Goodwin, outside the barn, hears the shot (270:29// 133:1). He is, at this time, coming around from the woods to the back of the barn. He obviously keeps his distance long enough for Popeye to complete his rape of Temple. Compare to the sound of the bird at the beginning of the book: "a sound meaningless and profound out of a suspirant and peaceful following silence which seemed to isolate the spot..." (181:25// 4:16). Also note the image of the match and compare to Popeye's encounter with Clarence Snopes (324:7//210:15) and his preparation to kill Red (346:6//241:3).

250:1 **and she sat there, her legs straight before her, her hands limp and palm-up on her lap** propped up like a rag-doll or a passive child. Temple is in an attitude of helplessness and expectant sacrifice: her hands are "palm-up" rather than balled into a fist anticipating a fight.

250:5 **the pistol behind him, against his flank, wisping thinly along his leg** the smoke from the gunshot.

250:7 **He waggled the pistol slightly and put it back in his coat** "Waggle" means to wave about, to shake. There are several possible reasons for Popeye's action: clearing the smoke from the barrel before returning the pistol to his pocket; warning Temple to stay quiet and behave; since the pistol, like the corncob, serves as a substitute for Popeye's penis, signaling his sexual intentions.

250:9 **Moving, he made no sound at all ... sound and silence had become inverted** Faulkner again describes the event from Temple's perspective. The absence of expected noise reinforces the scene's nightmare quality. She is pulling back from her physical senses.

250:12 **She could hear silence in a thick rustling as he moved toward her through it, thrusting it aside** It = silence and space, almost the air itself which is all that separates Temple from

Popeye. She can literally hear the ripping apart of the universe as Popeye moves through it. The normal boundaries of her world have now been totally destroyed. See description of Horace Benbow, entry 384:34//296:29.

250:14 **Something is going to happen to me** Temple expresses the sense of fatality, inevitability, and inexplicability of the dark forces of the universe. This refrain occurs in several other Faulkner works, including *Light in August* (1932), *Pylon* (1935), and *If I Forget Thee, Jerusalem* (1939).

250:14 **She was saying it to the old man . . . his hands crossed on the top of the stick** The act moves from the probable to the actual: "going to happen" becomes "is happening." Because sound and silence are inverted, Temple is screaming silently rather than aloud. Her words, which form an accusation, are addressed to Pap, certainly, but are equally addressed to her father, the Judge, who, despite his position and power, has failed to protect his daughter from this kind of outrage. Both men are **blind** to the horror Temple is now facing.

250:18 **voiding the words like hot silent bubbles into the bright silence about them** This continues the motif of the "thin eeeeeeeeeeeee sound like bubbles in a bottle" used earlier (248:7//99:7). The synesthetic "bright silence" intensifies the unreality of this daytime nightmare. As in *As I Lay Dying*, her words simply go off into space, without apparent purpose or result. To "void" means to empty or to evacuate body wastes, a meaning in keeping with the scatological imagery of the novel: Temple's words are no more than gaseous emissions. However, "void" also picks up the concept of the nullity of her existence at this moment: she looks for safety and finds only nothingness. Thus, the blind face she shouts at could also represent the ultimate uncaring God, a blind-deaf father who is ubiquitous but either powerless or unwilling to save her. We do not witness the rape itself, and, as John T. Matthews and others have discussed, information about the rape is carefully withheld from the reader at this point.°

CHAPTER XIV

251:3 **She sat there for about an hour after Popeye left her** Temple enters Ruby's kitchen at 9 a.m., according to her watch (241:5//89:15). Almost immediately she runs back to the barn. Ruby, following her argument with Goodwin, leaves for the spring shortly thereafter. There she sees Popeye, who goes back to the house, talks to Lee, and then sneaks into the barn. Popeye must have killed Tommy and assaulted Temple between 10 and 10:30 a.m. Ruby watches Popeye's car pass soon afterwards, perhaps around 11 since she is already halfway to the house when the car passes her.

251:9 **Popeye did not make any sign . . . Temple looked the woman full in the face, without any sign of recognition whatever** Ruby steps out of the road but does not hide from view. The passage suggests that Popeye sees her there but does not acknowledge her presence. Temple, on the other hand, looks directly at her—the point is repeated—but is too stupefied to process Ruby's brief presence. Still, it is important that Popeye realizes that he has been seen driving off with Temple. Ruby can testify to this fact, although she cannot speak to the actual murder of Tommy.

251:18 **When she entered the hall, she was walking fast** Ruby is aware that something is wrong and might reasonably expect that Popeye has killed Goodwin.

251:20 **He was in the act of putting on a frayed tie; looking at him, she saw that he had just shaved** Goodwin is preparing to contact the sheriff to inform him of Tommy's murder. In order to make the phone call, he will need to go to his neighbor

Tull's house. One possible explanation for his fastidiousness is that, even in this terrible moment, he still abides by the social rules of neighborliness. Another possibility is that he recognizes that, as a formerly convicted murderer, he could very likely be suspected of the crime himself and is attempting to present himself in the best possible light, to costume himself as a responsible citizen. He has recently been drunk and slovenly. He has now changed clothes, shaved, even put on a tie, to take care of this official business with the law. However, given the sense of fatality Goodwin will project after his arrest and throughout the trial, it may also be possible that he is simply preparing to meet his doom in much the same manner Popeye does at the end of the book, wanting to look his best, although in Popeye's case it seems a kind of bravado and in Lee's a sense of propriety.

251:31 **"I'll go," Goodwin said. "You stay here"** Although Faulkner leads us to believe that Goodwin will make the call, it is Ruby who actually contacts the sheriff. This juncture marks Goodwin's ever increasing passivity. Ruby, on the other hand, will take whatever action is necessary to save his life and preserve her world. She also recognizes that Goodwin is in no shape to make the call, despite his best efforts. In *Sanctuary: The Original Text*, Goodwin "sent word for the sheriff."°

251:32 **Tull was the man at whose house Gowan had found a car** "So he engaged the car and directed the man and paid him and went on" (238:30//85:28). Gowan likely had not indicated to Tull that Temple was in danger. He has probably convinced himself otherwise, being more concerned with his own problems than with Temple's. The Tulls are friendly people— they invite Ruby to eat with them when she unexpectedly arrives, and would not likely have taken Gowan's money if they did not intend to fulfill their obligation. See entry 238:30// 85:28.

251:37 **She didn't know the number. "The Sheriff," she said patiently into the mouthpiece** There is no dial on these phones.

Ruby speaks directly to the operator, who will then connect her to her party.

252:2 **This is Mrs Goodwin talking** Ruby is not legally "Mrs Goodwin," but her credibility will be enhanced if she can assume the authority and propriety in being his wife rather than the unmarried mother of his child. Her status will be used against her in Goodwin's trial (366:26//269:28).

CHAPTER XV

253:1 **Benbow reached his sister's home in the middle of the afternoon** This chapter takes us back to earlier the previous Wednesday, May 8. Horace has reached his destination, the Sartoris estate, where his widowed sister Narcissa, her child Bory, and her aunt by marriage, Miss Jenny, live. Faulkner repeats some of the same information in this first paragraph that he earlier gave in the first paragraph of Chapter III.

253:6 **Mitchell** Harry Mitchell, Belle's first husband and a character in *Flags in the Dust*.

253:6 **Benbow would not agree to sell . . . still paying interest** A bungalow is a small, usually one-story house. As a result of the disgrace caused by Horace and Belle's affair and marriage, they have left Jefferson for Kinston where they live in a house obviously inferior to (although perhaps more in fashion than) the Benbow family home in Jefferson. Horace has chosen to go into debt for the Kinston house rather than sell the Jefferson home. Certainly there is an element of sentimentality involved in this decision. Narcissa, on the other hand, is far less nostalgic about the family past, despite her insistence on family honor. See 260:26//118:5 for further explanation.

253:12 **he heard his sister come down the stairs, still unaware of his arrival. He made no sound** Horace intentionally does not reveal himself to his sister. He apparently enjoys the luxury of watching her, and there is the element of voyeurism in his action. Also, perhaps, he wants to delay the inevitable confrontation and conflict over his abandoning Belle.

253:15 **that serene and stupid impregnability of heroic statuary** Although Narcissa sometimes seems unaware or unconcerned, she is not stupid when she feels threatened and is clearly more than a match for her "intellectual" brother. Her static solidity stands in marked contrast to Temple's frenetic movements. She is, in fact, Temple's opposite both physically and emotionally although, like Temple, she is used to getting what she wants.

253:18 **He sat with something of the air of a guilty small boy** Horace has, in this case, been caught in a forbidden act, deserting his wife. His *younger* sister performs the mother's role of chastising him. His first impulse is to ask who told. See next entry.

253:19 **"How did you——" he said. "Did Belle———"** "How did you hear I had left Belle? Did she contact you?" Horace apparently surmises this fact from Narcissa's greeting, "Oh, Horace."

253:21 **She wired me Saturday** Belle sent a telegram to Narcissa on May 4, the day after Horace left Kinston to walk to Jefferson.

253:23 **and had sent for Little Belle** After "going home to Mother," Belle completes the gesture by sending for her child; she is emphasizing that Horace is at fault in his betrayal and compromising behavior.

253:27 **He stayed at his sister's two days** Thus, he would leave on Friday, May 10.

253:28 **living a life of serene vegetation like perpetual corn or wheat in a sheltered garden instead of a field** Faulkner's description of Narcissa emphasizes the protected, controlled, unnatural quality of her existence, secluded as she is at the Sartoris estate. Perhaps one reason Horace is attracted to his sister is her placidity, her "serene vegetation" as opposed to the threatening "trap" of nature he normally associates with the female.

253:32 **After supper** The following scene takes place on the evening of the next day, Thursday, May 9, since Horace will leave the next morning for Jefferson (255:28//110:7).

253:33 **where Narcissa would read the Memphis paper** In *Flags in the Dust*, it is Miss Jenny who reads the Memphis papers. In

Sanctuary: The Original Text, Narcissa reads aloud the "lurid accounts of arson and adultery and homicide, in her grave contralto voice" to Miss Jenny.° Underneath her calm exterior Narcissa apparently secretly enjoys the sins and scandals of the world; it also recalls the titillation she received from Byron Snopes's letters in *Flags.*

253:37 **Not to Kinston** Horace's response to Miss Jenny's recommendation that he "Go back home" indicates that "home"—his family home in Jefferson—has been his destination. His bungalow in Kinston is no longer his home, nor does he intend to stay at Sartoris, his sister's home.

254:5 **"You're right," Benbow said. "Then I'd have to stay at home."** Horace uses Miss Jenny's joke to support his own feeling of confidence. Miss Jenny is "right" in saying that he will come to believe that he doesn't need women to mother or control him. "Home" again refers to the Benbow home; he will start over and live alone in Jefferson.

254:14 **Did you find a man under the bed, Horace?** Miss Jenny wants to know if Belle was cheating on Horace as she and Horace had earlier cheated on Harry.

254:27 **But to walk out just like a nigger** Narcissa is more disturbed that Horace ran away and shamed himself publicly, than by the fact that his marriage has gone bad. She cares nothing for Belle personally. Her racial comparison is meant as a further insult to her brother: he has acted irresponsibly.

254:30 **Unless you're going to walk the streets with that orange-stick in your pocket until she comes to town** Horace has already told them of his adventures at the Old Frenchman place. He has, moreover, kept his promise to Ruby to get her an "orange stick." His scrupulousness is especially annoying to Narcissa: he has kept his word to a prostitute (hence Miss Jenny's emphasis on walking the streets) yet deserted his wife. Miss Jenny's remarks show that she suspects that Horace, carrying the orange-stick in his pocket, is infatuated with the *idea* of Ruby, and she may be right.

254:32 **Yes** Horace is *not* saying that yes, he will walk the street until Ruby shows up. Instead, he, like Temple earlier, seems not to address the actual questions being asked. It is rather a general, vague response, as if his mind were elsewhere: on the story he is about to tell, perhaps.

254:40 **You could feel the pistol on him just like you knew he had a navel** In this strange analogy, Horace proposes that a pistol is as natural to a sinister character like Popeye as a navel is to any living human being.

255:4 **like a sullen and sick child** The image connects Popeye with the sick infant at the Old Frenchman place. But it also links Popeye with both Horace himself, who has acted, and is being treated, like a misbehaving child, and with Temple, who is constantly described in child-like images.

255:5 **a cavalry sergeant in the Philippines** During the Spanish-American War, American forces occupied the Philippines and laid siege to the capital, Manila, which capitulated on Aug. 11, 1898. The United States then purchased the Philippines for $20 million. A second conflict, known as the Philippine-American War, began on Feb. 4, 1899. By early 1900, some 56,000 American troops had landed; civil rule was finally established in 1901, and William Howard Taft became the first Governor-General in 1902. Goodwin would have been stationed there at a later date, closer to the events mentioned below.

255:5 **on the Border** the Mexican Border. General John Joseph Pershing led American forces into Mexico in 1916–17 in a failed attempt to capture the Mexican bandit Pancho Villa.

255:6 **in an infantry regiment in France** The United States entered World War I on April 6, 1917. The first American troops landed in France in June of that year.

255:7 **he never told me why he changed** But Ruby *has* told Temple (219:3//59:4).

255:13 **I know that just like I know that that little black man had that flat little pistol in his coat pocket** For Horace, both facts represent hidden truths, secrets he was alert and savvy enough to discover. In one sense he is telling of his adventure with the same kind of pride—"a sort of naive and impersonal vanity" (328:12//216:6)—he later senses in Temple while she tells her own story. In calling Popeye "that little black man," Horace uses the same description of Popeye Temple has used (207:4//42:1; 212:8//49:1). Again, he is referring to Popeye's dress and general disposition rather than the color of his skin, which is pale and pallid.

255:17 **a harder currency than cash**   her body.

255:23 **I never knew who he was, who he was kin to . . . just left him there when he died or moved away**   It is never clear just who Pap is. See entry 187:18//12:8. Horace's comments, however, do underscore Pap's symbolic role. He is mysterious and ghostly, ironically ubiquitous during Temple's night of horror. He is the dysfunctional patriarch of the house, a bizarre reminder, perhaps (as Horace soon comments), of the Old Frenchman himself. Temple links him to her own father, the Judge. Pap for all purposes does disappear after Lee is arrested. As Horace says, he might as well have been led "completely off the earth." See entry 257:34//113:7.

255:33 **tinned food**   canned food (259:32//116:30).

255:35 **home**   the Sartoris homeplace.

256:2 **I'm the oldest, remember . . . . I have some cover**   Horace asserts his independence but is smarting from Miss Jenny's accusation that he has, in effect, run home to mother. By "cover" he means sheets and blankets (Narcissa sends him more, which he puts in the closet), but he also has "run for cover."

256:14 **he remembered that it was Saturday**   May 11, the same day Gowan takes Temple to the Old Frenchman place. The custom is for country people to come to town on Saturday to buy supplies, see one another, and take a break from their week of labor. The event is both practical and social. Hence, the women stop to prepare themselves before they enter town. See entry 256:24//111:16.

256:21 **locusts covered with ragged snow**   the blossoms on the locust trees. Also, the "foamy screen of locust branches" (257:3//112:5). Faulkner loads the scene with a series of details which emphasize the sense of local color of the town. Horace is easily caught up in hometown nostalgia.

256:24 **the unease of their garments** This refers to their "dress-up" clothes as well, perhaps, as their method of walking "citified." The phrase also recalls Horace's earlier description of Spring's "green-snared promise of unease" (188:25//13:23).

256:27 **tethered wagons, the teams reversed and nuzzling gnawed corn-ears over the tail-boards** When the wagons are tied up, the mules are unhitched and then tied to the back of the wagons ("reversed") so that they can eat over the tail-board from the wagon beds.

256:33 **Slow as sheep they moved . . . without impatience** Faulkner contrasts the country and city sense of time and temperament. The country people, linked to the land, to the natural passage of the seasons, are bemused by the more hectic movements of their city counterparts and calmly reconcile themselves to the rhythms of life. Their faces, however, betray no emotions as they observe: like mindless animals (or "gods," an ironic pairing), they exist "outside" of city time. This scene will be compared to the frantic and hysterical madness which will grip the city people when they come to lynch Lee Goodwin in Chapter XXIX.

257:6 **in unhurried backwaters** Horace has been carried by the "current" of the crowd. He steps aside, out of the movement on the sidewalk and street, to speak to acquaintances.

257:14 **pebble-grain horn-mouths above the rapt faces** the megaphones stationed above the store doors or windows which broadcast the record music. Faulkner's description indicates that they are playing largely country music.

257:16 **lugubrious, harsh, and sad** These adjectives refer to the "disembodied voices" (257:13//112:16) of the records or radio.

257:17 **in May: no time to leave the land** It is still planting season, a very busy time for these country people.

257:26 **He lay on a wooden table** Although public viewings of executed murderers or unusual victims would not have been unheard of at this time, the coroner has Tommy on display in order to identify him, not purely as a grotesque sideshow. The date is Monday, May 13.

257:28 **singed with powder**   indicating how close Popeye was when he shot Tommy.

257:34 **For all general knowledge, he had none**   Based on what people actually know, Tommy might as well have no last name. Like Pap, he is in this way a mystery, especially in a place where family and name are important. The fact underscores how marginal a figure Tommy is in the community and also how invisible Lee's operation is despite his steady clientele.

CHAPTER XVI

258:1 **On the day** Sunday, May 12.

258:9 **natty, shoddy suits** dapper but worn; possibly castoffs or second-hand.

258:13 **him who was already dead** The murderer has been condemned to die. He has, as his refrain will indicate, accepted the finality of his death. In this sense, he is like Lee Goodwin, who will consider himself already dead even before his trial begins.

258:15 **a rich, sourceless voice** During the day the murderer leans out the jail window. At night, since he cannot be seen above the streetlight, he becomes another "sourceless" sound like the hidden bird in Chapter I.

258:16 **heaven-tree** the local name for the royal paulownia (*Paulownia tomentosa*), or "princess tree." Calvin Brown describes its flowers as mauve, trumpet-shaped, and about two inches long. They have "an almost sickeningly sweet odor" and when they fall to the ground, they are "squishy underfoot."°

258:17 **snooded the street lamp at the corner** A snood is a netlike cap worn to keep the hair in place; the tree's flowers form a cap around the head of the street lamp, blocking or dimming its light at night, perhaps forming a halo effect.

258:18 **Fo days mo! Den dey ghy stroy de bes ba'ytone singer in nawth Mississippi** "Four days more. Then they're going to destroy the best baritone singer in north Mississippi." This is the voice of the condemned man himself since the cry comes from the "high darkness" among the trees. If he says this on the day Goodwin arrives, then, according to his calculations, he should be executed on May 15 or 16, a Wednesday or Thursday, depending on where he begins his reckoning. He is, however, executed on a Saturday (269.29), apparently May 25. Therefore, he seems to be singing a ritual song based on sequence ("Ninety-nine bottles of beer on the wall," "We've five more miles to go," etc.). See entry 269:29//131:19.

258:24 **above their steady jaws** chewing tobacco.

258:25 **One day mo** The time sequence here is vague. Apparently Faulkner is telescoping several days in the paragraph, thus giving Goodwin, accused of a capital crime and also facing execution, the time to become irritated with his fellow prisoner's musical complaints when he wants some quiet.

258:25 **Den Ise a gawn po sonnen bitch** "Then I'm a gone poor son-of-a-bitch." Then I'm dead.

258:31 **I didn't do it . . . But if I talk, if I say what I think or believe, I wont be clear** Goodwin refuses to defend himself or to implicate Popeye in the murder. He feels that, since the sheriff has no proof that he committed the crime, in a court of law he can't legally be found guilty (259:7//115:24). However, if he accuses Popeye of the crime, then he is certain that Popeye will, without question, kill him or see to it that he is killed.

259:5 **Did Popeye do it?** Here, Goodwin is obviously playing dumb. But we should also note that Goodwin doesn't know *for a fact* that Popeye killed Tommy. He didn't see him do it: he might "think or believe" it, but he can't be certain.

259:12 **newspaper grift** A "grift" is a job, a business. Goodwin is asking Horace to see to the welfare of his son, a job selling newspapers, if nothing else.

259:22 **Parallel with each seam was that faint, narrow, glazed imprint which another woman would recognize at a hundred yards with one glance** The dress is made over; the seams have been let out in order to fit (260:12//117:21). It is either one of Ruby's old dresses altered, or someone's hand-me-down, selected as part of Ruby's effort to appear proper before the citizens of Jefferson.

259:25 **purple ornament** a cheap, non-descript accessory. However, Temple will also be wearing a "shoulder knot of purple" (376:23//283:14) when she testifies in court. See entry 376:21//284:12.

259:28 **when women ceased to wear veils** Ruby's attempt to appear "proper" in out-of-fashion clothes seems pathetic to Horace.

259:36 **He told his sister and Miss Jenny about the case over the supper table** Horace has already related his adventures at the Old Frenchman place to Narcissa and Miss Jenny. This indiscretion puts Goodwin at risk and is an early clue to Horace's naiveté and ineptitude.

260:1 **have the face** the nerve, the audacity.

260:2 **like a nigger** Narcissa uses this image for the second time in berating her brother (254:27//108:25). Her comments are full of deliberate insults.

260:18 **a moonshiner hasn't got the money to hire the best lawyer in the country?** Miss Jenny, in her own way, is making the point that Horace is *not* the best lawyer for Goodwin under these circumstances.

260:33 **the house where I———** was born. Narcissa completes the thought at 261:3//118:24.

261:1 **It's not that there's litter left; it's that you———that———** In Narcissa's ethical economy, Horace makes social messes through his lack of good judgment and then has to clean up after himself (or have someone clean up for him). But though he will be able to remove the actual debris—Ruby and the child will go away—Narcissa fears that the after trace will linger (like the shrimp droppings) and Narcissa will be compromised by the gossip. In Narcissa's mind, she is the center of the drama and Horace should make her his first consideration.

261:5 **Fiddlesticks** nonsense. Fiddlesticks is a children's game. Miss Jenny is rejecting Narcissa's argument, based on propriety, but also recognizes the weakness of Horace's own argument. See below.

261:6 **collusion? connivance** Miss Jenny brings up a valid objection to Horace's representing Goodwin. Because Horace was at the Old Frenchman place shortly before the murder occurred, and because he has taken Ruby and the child into his own house, he gives the appearance of being more deeply involved in the case than he should. People might think—as they indeed will—that he has something personally to gain by the outcome of the trial. Thus, while Miss Jenny dismisses Narcissa's worry about social appearance, which is a very private and selfish concern, she does recognize that Horace may be endangering his ability to defend Goodwin adequately because of his personal involvement.

261:11 **Mrs Blackstone** Sir William Blackstone (1723–80), English jurist and author of *Commentaries on the Law of England* (1765–1769), which became the standard reference source for lawyers. Horace is admitting the correctness of Miss Jenny's objections while attempting to undermine the seriousness of her charges with humor.

261:25 **It must be because she is one woman you know that dont know anything about that shrimp** Miss Jenny's remark shows that she shares Narcissa's suspicion that Horace is interested in Ruby; just as he obtained the orange stick without knowing whether or not he would see her again, he is now taking Goodwin's case in large part to prove himself to Ruby, who (Miss Jenny assumes) is unaware of Horace's less-than-heroic past. Of course, Horace, by his drunken whining, has already revealed his true nature to Ruby.

261:34 **he had counted on that imperviousness** Horace assumes that Narcissa is so self-absorbed that she will not care too much that he has left Belle.

262:11 **they** the child and the hat.

262:12 **a quality of transience** The unlived-in look of the room (the furniture is covered with sheets to keep off the dust), plus the woman's hat on the bed, give the impression that there is nothing stable or permanent about this situation. Ruby, despite her tangentiality to the scene, has, however, asserted some domestic control even in this barren environment.

262:27 **He was thinking** The following two paragraphs repeat information already given in Chapter II (191–92//118), but from Horace's perspective.

262:29 **of Popeye's black presence lying upon the house like the shadow of something no larger than a match . . . twenty times its size** Popeye's impact, the sense of fear and sickness he inspires, outstrips his actual physical reality: compared to "a match," he is a constant symbol of pending destruction. However, note similar descriptions of Temple's shadow hovering over the Goodwin baby. See second entry 221:36//63:1.

262:36 **outer darkness** somewhere beyond the house and its relative safety, but the phrase also alludes to the biblical state of damnation: "while the sons of the kingdom will be thrown into the outer darkness; there men will weep and gnash their teeth" (Matthew 8:12).

263:7 **I guess I overstepped** presumed beyond her privileges as a guest in Horace's house. Horace has apparently already told her that she and the child must move to the hotel, although he has likely explained it in terms of legal strategy rather than personal pressure.

263:16 **that holding Lee for that killing is just———** ludicrous, a waste of time.

263:25 **"Damn it," he said, "do you think———"** Horace tries to recover through bullying appeal since Ruby has seen through his talk and believes he is moving her to placate others rather than for the legal reasons he has just enumerated.

263:27 **Let me take it** Although Horace knows the child is a boy, he refers to it impersonally as neutered. Ruby pointedly corrects Horace: "I've got him," she answers.

263:32 **Isom** In *Flags in the Dust*, Isom is the son of the Sartorises' black servant Elnora. Thus, ten years later he is still working for Miss Jenny and Narcissa.

263:38 **in which he and Narcissa paddled and splashed** See the Compson children in *The Sound and the Fury*. Noel Polk has drawn further revealing comparisons between Horace Benbow and Quentin Compson.°

263:40 **loblollies** mudholes

264:1 **with the intense oblivion of alchemists** Alchemists were medieval practitioners who attempted, by pseudo-scientific means, to transmute base metals into gold. Their work was often associated with supernatural practices. Horace and Narcissa, as children, attempt to turn mud into something magical. The project is similar to Bayard and Ringo's dirt recreation of the Battle of Vicksburg in *The Unvanquished* (1938).

264:9 **The infrequent lamps mounted to crescendo** The streetlamps become more and more numerous as they move nearer the heart of town.

264:26 **I guess I've got just what was coming to me. There's no use fighting it** Ruby understands that her reputation will hurt Goodwin's chances in court. She can't deny her past, but she does not want to make the kind of grand gesture which Horace, in his naiveté, thinks is appropriate. Horace is showing off, thumbing his nose at the town. Ruby knows how destructive such a display could be to Goodwin's case.

264:28 **But you dont. Or you would have told Isom to drive you to the railroad station** If Ruby truly thought that her presence in town would hurt Lee in court, then she would either never have come or would leave before the trial. Horace overlooks the fact that Ruby always stands by Goodwin and that she might very well feel that Horace would not defend him if she were not there.

264:30 **fretting the blanket** See Popeye, who "frets" his cigarettes (184:36//8:26).

265:1 **drummers** traveling salesmen. See entry 382:32//294:4.

265:4 **Listen, I've got to tell———** At this point Ruby is trying to tell Horace that they can't pay him for his services (265:19//124:24). Although she is concerned about Temple, she is still following Goodwin's lead in keeping quiet about the girl. See entry 272:25//135:21. Knowing nothing of Temple's involvement, Horace is naively confident at this point that he has a simple murder case to handle.

265:20 **That last batch Popeye didn't———** Popeye didn't pay for the last shipment of moonshine to Memphis. This is not surprising given that he had just killed Tommy and kidnapped Temple.

265:29 **passing the narrow street**   the street on which the Benbow house is located. In one sense, Narcissa is attempting to kidnap Horace, to bring him home where she can control him much like Popeye's manipulations with Temple.

265:39 **You might tell her it was not to her I ran**   let her know that he is not retreating from his wife to the haven of his sister. "It wasn't Narcissa I was running to. I haven't quit one woman to run to the skirts of another" (254:1//107:29).

CHAPTER XVII

266:1 **trumpet-shaped bloom** See entry 258:16//115:7 for full description of the heaven-tree.
266:4 **surfeitive** Faulkner's coinage, derived from "surfeit," suggesting the excessive, overpowering smell of the bloom.
266:6 **the general room** a large room in which prisoners could meet together when released from their individual cells.°
266:10 **Nightlily** nightly, another Faulkner coinage, making an adverb out of an adjective.
266:16 **One day mo** See entry 258:18//115:8.
266:21 **On Sunday afternoon** May 19, the Sunday following Lee's arrest. (Brooks incorrectly places this visit on Saturday, May 18.)°
266:26 **galvanic jerks** as if it were being shocked by currents of electricity.
267:6 **adulterer** Goodwin is not actually an adulterer since neither he nor Ruby is married to another partner. The Baptist preacher's objection is that Lee is living in sin with Ruby, by whom he has had a child. The preacher is comingling the sins of fornication and adultery to inflame his congregation.
267:9 **Goodwin and the woman should both be burned** Thus (if Horace's account is accurate), the idea to burn Goodwin originates in a church sermon. Faulkner attacks religious hypocrisy and intolerance as well as social and criminal injustice.
267:15 **They're just Baptists** Miss Jenny dismisses the attitudes of the so-called religious members of the community. The Baptists (the largest Protestant denomination in the South) would tend to represent the more fundamental and conservative church-goers in Jefferson, notorious for a preoccupation with

sins of the flesh. She suggests that they are also the biggest hypocrites. Clarence Snopes will later be identified as coming from a Baptist family (321:24//206:25).

267:19 **Then we'll clear out** Goodwin is apparently putting up a pretense for Ruby. His earlier remarks to Horace indicate that he has little hope of surviving this ordeal.

267:27 **gorilla** a gunman or violent criminal. In thus referring to Popeye, Horace atavistically invests him with threatening, thuggish characteristics which are at odds with his actual physical appearance. See entry 212:20//49:13.

267:33 **rolling his cigarettes with the sack hanging in his teeth** the tobacco sack. Goodwin would have poured loose tobacco in the cigarette wrapping paper and then pulled the draw strings on the sack with his teeth, holding the sack in his mouth while he rolled the cigarette with his hands.

267:38 **I didn't know you were a coward** Goodwin has been making excuses for the wisdom of staying in jail. Horace accuses him of being afraid that Popeye will kill him if he leaves, perhaps in an attempt to bait him into testifying against Popeye by questioning his manhood.

268:3 **there's a corruption about even looking upon evil, even by accident... how it's made her restless and suspicious** Goodwin cannot expect to be found innocent simply because there is no direct evidence to prove him guilty; his presence at the scene of the crime may be enough to convince the people of Jefferson of his guilt. Horace then extrapolates: Narcissa is "suspicious" of Horace, not of Goodwin, whom she has already declared guilty. Because Horace was at the Old Frenchman place, he, too, has been touched by corruption. See entry 268:6//129:13.

268:6 **I thought I had come back here of my own accord, but now I see that———** Horace argues that fate brought him to the Old Frenchman place, made him a part of that situation, so that he could now defend Goodwin in this trial. He has earlier said that one can be corrupted by the proximity to evil, even if "by accident" (268:3//129:11). His suggestion that it was destiny that brought him in contact with Goodwin and Ruby is another example of his romantic attitudinizing and searching for lofty purposes however counterindicated.

268:11   **she's learned that you'll work harder for whatever reason you think you have, than for anything anybody could offer you or give you**   she = Narcissa. Miss Jenny says that while Narcissa might at first have suspected Horace of taking Goodwin's case because of Ruby, she now realizes that Horace is motivated more by altruistic "ideals" than by any desire for personal or sexual gain. See entry 268:14//129:21.

268:14   **she'd let me think they never had any money, when she———**   She = Ruby. It's almost as if Horace understands Miss Jenny to be referring to Ruby rather than Narcissa in her statement above. Horace's unfinished statement might read, "when she actually had plenty of moonshiner's money to hire me." This reading would agree with Miss Jenny's next observation, "Why not? Aint you doing all right without it?" But Horace could also be questioning whether or not Ruby has tried to buy him off with sex, in which case Miss Jenny's retort would still hold true: Horace is presently making do without both money and sex. Miss Jenny implies, however, that Horace is likelier to work hard to be gallant than for either of the other two reasons.

268:27   **You're such a fool**   Narcissa is speaking to Miss Jenny, whose teasing has become exceptionally irritating to her, but her statement could also be directed to Horace.

268:32   **thinking that his mother———**   thinking that Gowan's mother might come to accost Narcissa for robbing the cradle. Miss Jenny is not in the least cowed by Narcissa's anger.

269:8   *I need not say that the hope that you never learn it is the sole reason why I will not see you again*   Gowan will not face Narcissa to spare her the extent of his disgrace. His entire letter is extremely self-serving, places himself at the center of the drama. There is, of course, no mention of Temple. Indeed, his letter denies her existence: "*I have injured no one save myself by my folly*" (269:6//130:23).

269:15 **Someone mistook him for a Mississippi man on the dance floor** Horace sardonically jokes that Gowan must have been mistaken for a graduate of the University of Mississippi rather than the University of Virginia and that the shame was more than he could bear.

269:17 **I think, if I were you———** I would keep my mouth shut. Given Horace's own unseemly public conduct, he is in no position to criticize Gowan.

269:22// **There's only one way** to drop the case and leave Goodwin to his fate.

269:28 **"Go back to Belle," Miss Jenny said. "Go back home"** Miss Jenny's irony is thick. This is what Narcissa wants him to do but he will be a coward if he does it.

269:29 **The negro murderer was to be hung on a Saturday without pomp, buried without circumstance** This chronology disputes that suggested by the man's song. See entry 258:18//115:8. Sir Edward Elgar's (1857–1934) "Pomp and Circumstance" (1901) is the music traditionally played at ceremonial occasions such as graduations.

270:10 **him** Popeye. Goodwin's example continues the "match" imagery associated with Popeye.

270:13 **obstruct———** obstruction of justice. See 271:10//133:24.

270:15 **Let them find the pistol** Popeye has taken the pistol with him. See entry 334:34//225:24.

270:17 **It was me notified the sheriff** Actually, Ruby calls the sheriff. But Lee was *going to* notify the sheriff, and he thinks that this act will enhance his appearance of innocence. See entry 251:31//104:22.

270:17 **Of course my being there alone except for her and Pap looked bad** When the sheriff arrives, only Goodwin, Ruby, and Pap are at the Old Frenchman place. Of the three, Goodwin is the one most likely or able to have killed Tommy.

270:27 **open my head** talk freely, testify.

270:31 **I didn't. I didn't hear anything** Goodwin apparently admitted hearing the shot that killed Tommy before he considered the implications of that statement. Now he denies it in order to avoid involving Popeye. This denial also reminds him not to mention Temple, who raises questions of rape and kidnapping, questions which could further complicate Goodwin's claim of innocence.

271:14 **if Lee didn't tell the truth about an unimportant thing** Curiously, Horace feels that Popeye's being at the Old Frenchman place is unimportant. He either misses the point or he is attempting to appear confident for Ruby.

271:26 **He's only got two days more** The murderer is to be executed on Saturday. This is Thursday, May 23.

272:9 **the last bloom fallen now in viscid smears upon the sidewalk** These smears recall the "fading series of small stinking spots on a Mississippi sidewalk" caused by the shrimp (191:26//17:26). "Messiness" is a theme with Horace, as with Popeye: the smelly shrimp, the shedding trees, Belle's make-up cloth, Popeye's evil odor, Nature's uncontrolled growth. He can't stand life's lack of order. "They ought to clean that damn mess off the sidewalk," he says, echoing Popeye's earlier "There ought to be a law" (246:19//96:19).

272:13 **He was sleeping late the next morning; he had seen daylight** Since Horace has stayed awake all night, he intends to sleep late the next morning but is awakened when the hotel porter knocks on the door at six-thirty, Friday, May 24.

272:25 **The child lay on the bed ... "There was a woman there," she said. "A young girl."** Some of the descriptions of the infant are similar to images earlier used to describe Temple at the Old Frenchman place. Ruby was the last to see Temple with Popeye. She has obviously been struggling with the need to tell about Temple, for both Temple's and Goodwin's sake, and it is the baby's seizure that finally impels her to do it, despite Goodwin's instructions.

CHAPTER XVIII

273:1 **Popeye drove swiftly** This chapter returns to and repeats some of the events of Sunday, May 13, described in Chapter XIV.

273:4 **her hair escaping beneath the crumpled brim in matted clots** as if her hair had been bleeding and is now coagulated.

273:13 **flicking swiftly in and out of Temple's vision without any motion, any sign** As in the barn, Temple does not even turn her head to keep the object in sight. Though she is looking straight ahead, nothing registers. See 249:20//101:18.

273:28 **increasing hiss of gravel** They have turned from the dirt road onto the highway heading north toward Memphis, leaving the Old Frenchman place behind them.

273:30 **feeling her blood seeping slowly inside her loins** Temple's bleeding has proven to many critics that she was a virgin at the time of Popeye's rape, as she likely is. However, the brutality of the rape, as later described, would doubtless have caused bleeding in anyone.

273:35 **as though Sunday were a quality of atmosphere, of light and shade** as if there were a special "feel" for Sunday different from the other days of the week.

274:3 **It was a bright, soft day . . . Temple began to scream** Faulkner contrasts the serenity of the Sunday spring day with Temple's horror. Nature is incredibly rich and sensual: it is a "wanton morning," the clouds are like "gobs of whipped cream," the blossoming of the trees has reached a "crescendo." Faulkner introduces images of childhood fantasy—balloons, basketballs—to capture this riot of nature, which serves as paradoxical backdrop to Temple's abduction. Moreover, this

Nature and the outside world which passes before Temple's eyes are totally unaware of her condition. Temple's reaction is to scream in mindless terror. This scene contrasts with Temple's final scene in Paris's gray Luxembourg Gardens (398:6//316:11).

274:8 **The fruit trees, the white ones, had been in small leaf when the blooms matured . . . in green retrograde before crescendo** "[S]mall leaf" suggests both that the blossoms came out before the leaves had gained full growth, or that the leaves had not had full growth this season and were already in decline ("green retrograde") when the blossoms appeared.

274:26 **Shut it** Shut your mouth. Stop screaming.

274:26 **Look at yourself** Popeye restores order in Temple's world by making her conscious of her self. Her appearance and her concern for it has been a means by which she has reestablished her footing after each outrage. Popeye is canny enough to realize this about Temple. He assumes the role of Daddy to make her behave: "Aint you ashamed of yourself?" (274:35//139:1).

275:4 **pleasure cars Sunday-bent** The traffic is made up mostly of travelers out for a Sunday drive, going nowhere in particular, and so moving in a sharp contrast to Temple's status as rape/kidnap victim caught up in the same traffic.

275:6 **swathed women, and dust-covered hampers** families on a picnic, some of them in open cars. The women are wrapped in long scarves and coats to protect them from the wind and dust.

275:14 **Dumfries** the town where Gowan bought a new shirt and a bottle of hair-oil. See 204:18//37:12. Temple is literally retracing her steps, this time with Popeye rather than Gowan. She was brought to the Old Frenchman place against her will by Gowan; now, she is being taken away against her will, by Popeye. Faulkner draws further parallels between the two trips.

275:18 **I cant———I might———** "I can't get out here. I might be recognized by someone who saw me here yesterday." Temple is more concerned with her embarrassing appearance and condition than she is with being rescued at this particular moment. Though it is a reaction that could be explained by the shock of her past twenty-four hours, it is also in line with her earlier decision to go with the drunken Gowan rather than seek the possible safety of the railroad station. See entry 204:9//36:30.

275:20 **Wait till we get to town** to Memphis, where they won't attract attention. Temple's own needs are discounted by Popeye, just as they had been by Gowan.

275:23 **"I cant get out," she whimpered** There is an element of black humor in this scene. Temple, disheveled and bloody, falls back into her old pattern, and reacts as if she is on a date; she assumes that Popeye, like a good escort, is going to take her into a restaurant for a meal. Popeye, thinking more in terms of a kidnapping, and with a different perspective on "dating," is astonished that she would even consider coming in with him. "Who told you to get out?" he exclaims. "Dont you move" (275:25//140:2). Faulkner contrasts the social expectations of these denizens of two very different social worlds and heightens the tonal discord, the bizarre comedy of manners, played out in this sequence.

275:31 **Candy** Popeye has no interest in brand names and probably doesn't eat candy either. The candy is merely a means to an end, to shut Temple up.

275:32 **a dollar** a silver dollar.

275:35 **Keep it ... You'll get rich faster** See Popeye's reaction to the turnkey in Chapter XXXI: "Keep it . . . . Buy yourself a hoop" (397:30//315:23).

275:37 **changed the sandwich to his left hand** so that he can reach for his pistol with his right hand should Temple's disappearance signal danger for him.

276:3 **"He nearly saw me!" she whispered. "He was almost looking right at me!"** Temple is not hiding from Popeye. She is, in fact, almost conspiring with him to keep from being seen by the boy she thinks she knows. She "whispers" to keep from being heard by others when, if she truly wished to be rescued, she could be screaming for help. Since he has in a sense vanquished all other possible sources of authority, Popeye is naturally the one to whom she must turn. There must, of course, be some question as to whether or not Temple actually sees someone she knows, or whether this is an example of her paranoia.

276:16 **It was as though he were lifting her slowly erect by that one hand** Popeye lifts Temple more by command than by actual strength, although he is quite strong. In other words, mesmerized by fright, she cooperates with him, physically following his lead almost against her will.

276:19 **they appeared as decorous as two acquaintances stopped to pass the time of day before entering church** another example of Faulkner's ironic comparison of these two societies. Rather than enter church, Popeye and Temple will soon enter a whorehouse. See entry 278:19//144:2.

276:30 **I'll get you another coat tomorrow** Popeye understands Temple's complaint to concern her ruined coat rather than her physical loss of blood (which may be the case). He doesn't consider her physical or emotional state in his calculations.

276:33 **"You want some more of it, do you?" he whispered, not touching her. "Do you?"** Popeye reminds her of his power to hurt and humiliate her, but the threat is framed sexually. See Ruby's story of Frank's murder by her father: "I got in front of Frank and father said, 'Do you want it too?'" (218:29//58:19).

276:40 **that round, hopeless expression of a child** Faulkner again suggests a perverse parent-child relationship. Temple eats the sandwich "obediently" (276:37//41:26) at Popeye's command.

277:4 **At the foot of the bluff . . . a young negress in underclothes smoked a cigarette sullenly, her arms on the balustrade** Popeye apparently drives in on Riverside Drive, the road which runs north parallel to the Wolf River at the foot of the bluff. If he takes a right onto Beale Street (or Avenue in 1929), he would then cross Front Street and Main Street before coming to Mulberry Street, which dead ends into Beale from his right and runs to the southwest parallel to South Main one block over. This would be the tenderloin area of Memphis. Beale had once been an exclusive residential area, but after the Civil War and the yellow fever epidemics of 1863, 1873, and 1878, it became the center of Memphis sporting life. One block to the north of Beale, running east parallel to it, is Gayoso, which boasted the more elegant pleasure houses. Mulberry was the site of the less respectable white houses and the Negro houses.° Faulkner's description of the area emphasizes the hellish underworld into which Popeye brings Temple. It starkly contrasts to the earlier description of the lush countryside. In Memphis, Temple sees the "smoke-grimed frame houses . . . set a little back in grassless plots," "gaunt, lopbranched magnolias, a stunted elm or a locust in grayish, cadaverous bloom," "a scrap-heap in a vacant lot." Faulkner compares the vitiated atmosphere of the scene to "a sinister and meaningless photograph poorly made."

277:16 **From the bluff . . . passing high overhead on the river breeze** The central section of downtown Memphis, the business section, started at Main Street. The elevation drops some forty feet from Main down to the Wolf River.

277:25 **the entrance of which was hidden by a dingy lattice cubicle** The lattice probably serves as a decoration but also offers some degree of privacy for customers while they wait for admittance. Fonzo and Virgil Snopes will later mistake the cubicle for the entrance to an outhouse (311:8//191:17). It also calls to mind the hidden grape arbor in which Horace suspects Little Belle's sexual activity is taking place.

277:27 **two of those small, woolly, white, worm-like dogs, one with a pink, the other a blue, ribbon about its neck** miniature male and female French poodles, cartoonish canine symbols of high society. See entry 286:40//155:19.

277:28 **moved about with an air of sluggish and obscene paradox** Small dogs should be jumping around. Their torpidity here, their limpness, is disgusting.

277:29 **In the sunlight their coats looked as though they had**

been cleaned with gasoline Gasoline can be used as a solvent for cleaning blood, for example, from fabrics. The dogs' coats have a smeary sheen.

277:34 **climbing and sprawling onto the bed . . . and tonguing along the metal tankard which she waved** The poodles seem to share Miss Reba's difficulty breathing. Miss Reba's dogs also steal from her beer tankard, as Uncle Bud does in Chapter XXV.

277:39 **Reba Rivers** According to Joseph Blotner, Faulkner met a Memphis madam named Reba when he went to the city with Phil Stone.° Miss Reba also appears in *The Mansion* (1959) and in *The Reivers* (1962), which is set some twenty-five years earlier (1905). In that book the narrator, Lucius Priest, describes her as "a young woman . . . with a kind hard handsome face and hair that was too red, with two of the biggest yellowish-colored diamonds I ever saw in her ears" (98–99). The name Rivers further connects her with nearby Riverside Drive, and perhaps alludes to the whole idea of Memphis, at least this section of it, as a wide-open frontier river town beyond the law.

278:1 **biggest men in Memphis** The political boss of Memphis was Edward Hull Crump (1874–1954). He was elected mayor in 1909, 1911, and 1915, but had to resign in 1916 for failing to enforce Tennessee's prohibition laws. Nevertheless, for the next thirty years Crump's political machine ran the city and to a large extent the state. His organization was strongly linked to the Memphis vice trade.° Faulkner's trips to the city as a young man brought him many stories of corruption and misbehavior.

278:9 **I aint never double-crossed nobody, honey** Since Miss Reba's confidentiality is a key to her success, she will be conflicted over how to deal with Popeye and Temple later in the novel. See entries 331:25//220:22; 365:26//268:16.

278:11 **ringed with yellow diamonds as large as gravel** Like the yellow diamond earrings mentioned in *The Reivers*, these are apparently fake or of low quality. Top quality diamonds are colorless or pale blue; the more ordinary variety are tinged with yellow.

278:19 **She had just returned from church** Faulkner makes a point of who attends church in *Sanctuary*: the righteous, the hypocritical and in this case, ironically, this madam who returns from church to see to her business of prostitution. He had earlier described Popeye and Temple as two churchgoers (276:19//141:6). Miss Reba is apparently a Catholic since she carries a wooden rosary, balanced in the other hand by her tankard of beer.

278:23 **a harsh, expiring, maternal voice** Temple's stay at Miss Reba's becomes a bizarre parody of her former home and college life. Reba acts as a mother to Popeye, encouraging him to find a nice girl and now welcoming the girl he has finally brought home to meet the family. But she also functions as the strong mother missing from Temple's own home, and as the house mother who would oversee the girls in the university dormitory.

278:26 **how many years I been after you to get you a girl, honey** Miss Reba here seems to know nothing of Popeye's impotence and assumes he is highly selective (279:39//146:3). However, see her later remarks (entry 356:26//255:28).

278:37 **The narrow stairwell turned back upon itself in a succession of niggard reaches** The house has three levels (277:24//142:24). Each cramped level requires a tight turn and a climb up a flight of stairs toward the next level.

279:1 **a protracted weariness like a vitiated backwater beyond sunlight and the vivid noises of sunlight and day** There is some resemblance between this image and the earlier description of the spring at the Old Frenchman place (181:7//3:7). The water image is also used to describe Jefferson in Chapter XV (256:39//112:2). In each case the emphasis is on exhaustion and depletion and the utter lack of vitality. It provides counterpoint to the idea of sexual potency that one might expect in a brothel. All energy here (even the poodles) is perverse and paradoxical: nature has become unnatural.

279:3 **There was a defunctive odor of irregular food, vaguely alcoholic . . . beyond each silent door which they passed**

Temple can smell the old odor of food cooked earlier in the house. "Irregular" suggests that meals are not prepared on a regular basis, the workday intervals of breakfast, dinner, supper. The descriptive "vaguely alcoholic" applies to the general "odor" of the house rather than to the "food" itself. Temple, through the funky odor, senses the clandestine business of the house. These activities are carried on in private, hidden from view, but detectable nonetheless. The prostitutes' bodies are "stale" from being "oft-assailed." They are "impregnable" in the sense that they practice sex without emotional investment, not to procreate but to make money. Indeed, the prostitutes would take care not to become pregnant. There is also a fetidness to the sexuality that pervades Reba's establishment, a sense of spiritual and emotional sterility.° Compare Temple's reaction to that of Lucius Priest in *The Reivers*: "It was like any other hall, with a stairway going up, only at once I smelled something; the whole house smelled that way. I had never smelled it before. I didn't dislike it; I was just surprised. I mean, as soon as I smelled it, it was like a smell I had been waiting all my life to smell" (99). In some ways, Temple is as innocent as young Lucius when she encounters this smell, and her reaction is much the same. See entry 313:5//194:5.

279:11 **Later, lying in bed** returns to the scene begun at 277:32//143:3.

279:21 **That blood'll be worth a thousand dollars to you, honey** The blood is symbolic of Temple's entrance into a life of sexual activity. Reba is confident that Popeye will value her lost virginity and that Temple, as Popeye's kept woman, will reap the reward in money and favors. Reba instructs Temple about the sexual economy and valuable markers of the exchange rate.

279:23 **nodding in macabre was hael** *waes hael*, to be healthy. The phrase was often used as a drinking toast; the word *wassail* is a contraction of the words. Miss Reba is, in effect, toasting Temple's loss of virginity, her movement into womanhood, with the greeting "Us poor girls" (279:23//145:16). The dead flowers on her Sunday hat nod in agreement or support, but there is a sense of pity as well as honor in the acknowledgment, a dark congratulation. See Horace's description of Little Belle: "I was smelling the slain flowers, the delicate dead flowers and tears, and then I saw her face in the mirror." See entries 189:25//15:3; 295:7//167:21.

279:32 **district** the red light district of Memphis described above.

280:2 **Minnie'll have them washed and pressed until you wont know it** the knickers Temple was wearing. Minnie will wash out all the blood so there will be no physical evidence of Temple's violation, and they (but not Temple) will be as good as new.

280:6 **though I dont know what she'll do with them except maybe———** It is unlikely that Minnie would wear them. Perhaps they could be used as sanitary napkins, or just as rags for cleaning.

280:13 **you just see if I wasn't———** telling you the truth. Popeye has turned Temple over to Miss Reba for caretaking.

280:27 **You got a boy's name, aint you** Faulkner plays with names throughout this passage. The male and female dogs are named after Miss Reba and her dead lover Mr Binford; Miss Reba apparently considers "Temple" to be a boy's name although a "drake" is a male duck. In any case, Miss Reba's remark recalls Temple's polymorphous sexual nature.

280:33 **the most hardest blood of all to get———** to clean from clothing. Minnie intimates that vaginal blood, especially the blood of a virgin, stains more tenaciously than other kinds of blood stains.

280:38 **I aint going to let no girl of Popeye's———** go without anything.

281:11 **a dull frosting pacing the rise of liquor within the metal** The tankard, probably pewter, beads with condensation as it is refilled.

281:17 **that suh———** son of a bitch.

281:19 **that can put him in jail three times over** Dr. Quinn performs illegal medical practices, including, one would assume, abortions as needed for the prostitutes. There is also a later suggestion that he is a drug addict. See entry 282:35//150:1.

281:23 **terrific slowness** Faulkner intensifies this energized passivity to capture the effort Miss Reba must expend in going up or down stairs. Faulkner used the same image to describe Dilsey's movement in *The Sound and the Fury*.

281:26 **grate filled with fluted green paper** probably a fan-shaped decoration placed in front of the fireplace when it is unused, as it would be during the spring and summer months.

281:27 **It had only one hand . . . as though it had nothing whatever to do with time** Temple has found it very difficult to keep track of time, as when she tries to remember the last day she ate. Although it is the purpose of a clock to tell the time, this one, in effect, denies the passage of time. It has only one hand, which apparently does not move. Thus, although it insists by its position on the "otherwise blank face" of the clock that it has significance, in reality it is without meaning or purpose. It becomes another object of supposed order or authority in collusion with the chaotic world which Temple now inhabits. In addition, the "four china nymphs" holding the ornate rococo clock parody the romantic pretence of the brothel. See entry 283:10//150:15.

281:33 **her ears acute, her eyes a little blind with the strain of listening** Faulkner shows the synthetic toll of Temple's fatigue and stress; her senses no longer work in harmony. The concentration required to listen depletes the energy which would normally be invested in the act of seeing. The aural replaces the visual as her chief method of observation.

281:34 **in a dim mirror . . . a thin ghost, a pale shadow moving in the uttermost profundity of shadow** Because of the weak light in the room (it is twilight), Temple's image is indistinct, almost transparent ("pellucid") rather than sharply reflective. This is another indication of her loss of identity. As noted earlier, Temple judges herself by her physical appearance. Now she is disappearing physically. The mirror gives back a spectral image; she is becoming a shadow figure. Her growing vagueness makes her malleable, receptive to a new identity. See entry 337:22//229:12.

282:1 her face averted not looking at the blood on the towel.

282:3 listening to the secret whisper of her blood Temple is alert to her bleeding; she *feels* the sound of her blood.

282:8 "I cant," Temple said, her voice faint and small. "I'm in bed" a childish lie to avoid an adult directive. See entry 282:21//149:10.

282:21 Count ten, now Temple begs for time with the child-honored practice of counting to ten before beginning a game, like "Hide-and Seek," for example.

282:23 her naked feet in pattering diminuendo The sound of her footfall diminishes as she runs to the bed. This perspective must be from those outside the door, however.

282:27 as though they were of clear glass and worn for decorum's sake another example of false appearance, false "decorum." Dr. Quinn is not a respectable physician, and he too is going to invade Temple's privacy voyeuristically, as have so many other men in this book.

282:29 Make them go out Temple appears to be talking to Dr. Quinn, asking that he make Miss Reba and Minnie leave before he examines her. This seems a strange request, to be left alone with this man, who clearly frightens her. It may be that Temple doesn't want the women there with her during the examination because they are still foreign figures to her, while Dr. Quinn is, despite his oddness, at least a familiar figure of authority.

282:35 Behind the glasses his eyes looked like little bicycle wheels at dizzy speed; a metallic hazel Hazel eyes are bronze with green spokes in them. Dr. Quinn's glasses do not distort the appearance of his eyes; they may be so intense that they seem to Temple, in her fear, to spin. A remote possibility is that Quinn uses drugs, which would be supported by Reba's earlier comment. See entry 281:19//148:4.

282:37 masonic ring indicating membership in the Order of Freemasons, a secret fraternal organization founded in London in 1717. Masons condemned saloons and drinking, swore to live a "blameless" life. Quinn, like the church-going Miss Reba, is (or has been) an accepted member of respectable society. See entries 295:39//168:26; 298:34//172:26.°

283:1 **she began to cry, hopelessly and passively, like a child in a dentist's waiting-room** a bawdy joke in that, like a patient at the dentist, Temple must "open up" (her legs are "close together") if she is to be treated.

283:5 **In the window the cracked shade . . . let twilight into the room in fainting surges** There is a break in the text just before this line. In *Sanctuary: The Original Text*, Faulkner begins a new chapter, XIV, here. The shade is being blown by gentle puffs of breeze, but Faulkner personifies it, allowing it to breathe and yawn, suggesting the almost metaphysical boredom that infects Temple, the sense of being out of time.°

283:10 **The china figures . . . half-past-ten-oclock** The description of the clock connects it with the earlier description of the mirror in which Temple sees herself disappearing (entry 281:34//148:19). The glass face is the one spot in the room where light now collects; it thus becomes a repository for Temple's focus and thoughts, as well as for the events, now lost in time, which have transpired in this room. Thus there is a sense of weariness and waste about the scene, the "voluptuous lassitude" of the cupids, the faux-eroticism of their posture, the "quiet gesture of moribund time" in the face of the broken clock, which is itself compared to a disfigured, physically incomplete casuality of war. See Horace's earlier self-descriptive statement that "I thought anybody with one arm and a pail of water could wash a floor" (255:38//110:18). The clock itself is not running; the hand stays at "half-past-ten-oclock"; the minute hand (we assume) is stationary between ten and eleven on the clock dial (281:27//148:13). Thus, Temple, using the frozen moment as a still point, will soon begin to impose structure on timelessness by reliving her routines in normal life. She will make her present time 10:30 although it is still twilight. See entry 284:32//152:20.

283:19   **Her hair was a black sprawl, combed out now; her face, throat and arms outside the covers were gray**   Temple is red haired, but in the gloom of twilight her hair appears black, just as her skin takes on a grayish tint.

283:21   **she heard the door shut . . . grow twilight colored and die away**   a synesthetic pun: the sounds descend down the stairs, "die away," settle into the dusk as the daylight passes into night. There is a pall of exhaustion and death over everything at Miss Reba's house. See entry 294:21//166:26.

283:26   **lying in a tight knot**   Temple, under the covers, assumes a fetal position, which links her to the Goodwin baby in the box. She is hiding under the covers when Horace comes to talk to her in Chapter XXIII: "She'll smother," he says (326:7//213:6).

283:29   **the serrated palisade of Main Street high against the western sky**   Main Street runs more or less north and south. Mulberry, in the vicinity of Miss Reba's house, runs parallel to it one block to the east. Thus, Main Street's jagged skyline, which is on a bluff or "palisade" (see 277:16//142:16), would be purple against the setting sun to the west.

283:31   **She watched the final light condense into the clock face . . . into darkness lurking with new disasters**   As the light dims, Temple can no longer see the cupid stand which holds the clock; she can see only the glass face which still reflects enough of the weak light to remain visible. The clock face becomes first a "round orifice in the darkness," a word choice which calls to mind the recent abuse of Temple's own orifices—her mouth and her vagina. It next becomes a disc, a globe in space before time or order, the "original chaos." Thus, the clock, an instrument of time, becomes a symbol of *no time*. It then becomes, to Temple, a crystal ball, an instrument of telling the future which is, at this point, totally unfathomable to her. She lacks the ability to read whatever clues or suggestions might be perceived in the "cryptic depths" of the crystal ball. The ball finally becomes symbol of the earth itself—the "intricate and shadowy world around whose scarred flanks the old wounds whirl onward at dizzy speed [recalling the image introduced by Dr. Quinn's eyes] into darkness lurking with new disasters." The world finally exists *in time*, though not necessarily *in meaning*. It is ruled by an "ordered chaos," but it is chaos all the same in which "new disasters" await. The significance of this difficult passage is found in Temple's attitude, so completely changed from the morning when she felt that the worst had happened to her and that she could "stand anything." Now she knows that worse things can and will occur and that there is no preordained or organized form of justice or righteousness or goodness to protect her from it. She sees a "truth" which Horace Benbow will soon have to face himself.

284:3 **powder in the light like chaff in barn-lofts** Temple is already using her experience and knowledge gained in the barn as reference. She is also, apparently unconsciously, comparing the women's dormitory to the scene of her violation and, by extension, to Miss Reba's whorehouse. In other words, Temple is absorbing the events of the past few days, appropriating the experience for analogy, attempting to make sense of them, to find the pattern in them.

284:6 **Some wouldn't . . . They wouldn't say why** The less attractive girls, in general, said they wouldn't walk out naked, but some of the prettier ones also refused. Temple seems to be questioning the pretty girls' decision not to use their sexual advantages.

284:8 **The worst one of all** presumably, the least attractive: "her ugly face" (284:21//152:11).

284:10 **She said the Snake had been seeing Eve for several days and never noticed her until Adam made her put on a fig leaf** The girl argues that clothes excite interest, that Eve naked would be less erotic and suggestive of mystery than Eve hidden by fig leaf. By forcing Eve to dress, Adam, while attempting to possess Eve, actually makes her more appealing to the Snake. This version of the Adam-Eve story has obvious connections to the Popeye-Temple-Red affair later revealed. See Dawson Fairchild in *Mosquitoes*: "When the statue is completely nude, it has only a coldly formal significance, you know. But when some foreign matter like a leaf or a fold of drapery (kept there in defiance of gravity by God only knows what) draws the imagination to where the organs of reproduction are concealed, it lends the statue a warmer, a—a—more . . . speculative significance. . . ."° This idea draws us back to Temple's behavior at the Old Frenchman place where Ruby accuses her of drawing attention to herself by her constant attempts to deflect attention.

284:11 **How do you know** The girl assumes that the question means, "How do you know that is what happened in the Garden of Eden?", but they are really asking whether "boys thought all girls were ugly except when they were dressed."

284:12 **she said because the Snake was there before Adam, because he was the first one thrown out of heaven; he was there all the time** Temple's reconstruction of the girl's explanation of the Genesis story is jumbled and confused. God creates the "living creature after his kind, cattle, and creeping thing, and beast of the earth after his kind" (Genesis 1:24) before He creates man. Milton's *Paradise Lost* portrays Satan's being cast from heaven as a result of his rebellion against God. But Adam and Eve do not cover themselves with leaves until after Eve has been tempted by the serpent and eats from the forbidden tree. Indeed, they cover themselves because of the knowledge gained and the shame that results from that knowledge. The idea seems to be that evil already exists and waits for the innocent to become entrapped in it. This interpretation certainly fits Temple's conception that she has fallen into an almost preordained disaster: "he [the Snake] was there all the time" (284:14//152:3).

284:19 **their eyes like knives** as if her flesh were yielding where the other girls' eyes were piercing it "like knives." The teen girls are anxious to penetrate the secrets of adult sexuality. The scene assumes a quasi-sado-erotic quality as they gang up on "the worst one" for her secret knowledge.

284:22 **until she told them and held up her hand and swore she had** had sexual intercourse or, at the least, been seen naked by a boy. This scene, and the besieged girl's reaction, anticipates Temple's own experience in the courtroom in Chapter XXVIII, in which she is sworn in, surrounded, and forced to tell of her own sexual experiences.

284:25 **they could hear her being sick** Faulkner, emphasizing the link between sex and nausea, prepares for Horace's reaction to Temple's story in Chapter XXIII.

284:29 **the same Sunday** So much has happened to Temple on this day that she is surprised to realize a full day (or perhaps more) has not yet passed.

284:30 **Maybe it was half-past-ten this morning, that half-past-ten-oclock** The clock is *always* at "half-past-ten-oclock." Thus, Temple can relate the time to either occasion: going to church in the morning or getting ready for a dance that night.

284:32 **Then I'm not here, she thought. This is not me** If it *is* ten-thirty on a Sunday (either morning or night), then, according to past experience, Temple would be preparing for either church or a dance. Since it *is* still Sunday, then she cannot be anywhere other than the dorm, where normally she *should* be. Temple attempts to prove that she cannot logically be at Miss Reba's and that the consciousness that *is* at Miss Reba's is not hers. She wants to believe that she is dreaming or imagining her present state. She is wishing and willing that this Memphis experience be nullified since all her previous experience has had her elsewhere at such an hour. Therefore, like Darl Bundren in *As I Lay Dying*, she doesn't know "if I am or not."° However, once again, the clock is broken and in truth it is closer to eight-thirty. See entry 288:22//157:24.

284:35 **She kept the dates written down in her Latin 'pony', so she didn't have to bother about who it was** A "pony" is a simplified supplement to a text, a help-book like *Cliff's Notes* which explain or, in this case, translate. Such a work is often considered an unfair shortcut to actual learning, a form of cheating. Temple is indifferent to the ethics of scholarship as well as to the particulars of her social life. The key is to be popular and scheduled—the date himself is irrelevant.

285:1 **a warped turmoil of faint light . . . she could not see**

herself The diminished twilight—or, by now—a streetlight strikes the clock face so that the clock cannot be read. Temple's own reflection is also displaced by the refracted light.

285:3 **It's this nightie, she thought** Temple blames her disappearance (she has no reflection) and the fact that she is still in Memphis and not Oxford, on the sleep garment. If she were properly dressed for a date, then the date would appear and she would be home again.

285:6 **She drew the bolt quietly** Albert J. Guerard argues that in unlocking the door Temple comes to accept and "anticipate" Popeye's next assault.° However, locked doors have not protected her in the past. Moreover, in one sense Temple is no longer there and has nothing to fear. In another sense, she is back at Ole Miss, waiting on her date to arrive. It is only in the nightmare world of Memphis that this date proves to be Popeye.

285:7 **cradled in her arms** more word-play emphasizing Temple's infant-like nature.

285:34 **"You want me to———"** change Temple's binding. Again, Temple is like a baby with soiled diapers.

285:40 **Mr Binford** Faulkner very likely had in mind Lloyd T. Binford, the notorious Memphis chairman of the Shelby County Board of Censors from 1928 to 1955.°

286:9 **But Mr Binford ketch it sho nough . . . empty Mr Binford's clothes closet** Minnie is referring first to the dog and then to the dead man.

286:28 **machine lace** inexpensive, mass-produced by machine rather than made by hand.

286:35 **a washstand . . . fluted rose-colored paper** a table used for washing, shaving, or other bathroom needs. The flowered decorations and the "fluted rose-colored paper" are used to help disguise the uses of these objects, similar to the respectable appearance of Miss Reba's house (which nevertheless seems to be entered through an outhouse, according to Virgil and Fonzo). The description makes another connection between sex and excretion. See entry 386:6//299:5.

286:39 **the dry complaint of mattress and springs died into the**

terrific silence in which they crouched Although this mattress sits on springs, the image recalls the "faint, dry whisper of shucks" (227:26//70:28) at the Old Frenchman place.

286:40 **She thought of them . . . symbolised by ordinary the licensed tranquility of their lives** The description of the dogs reflects Temple's own situation.° It also (assuming these are Temple's conscious thoughts) reveals a growing awareness on her part. She sees the meaningless self-importance of her former life ("flatulent monotony") as well as her dependence on authority and power to mediate the carelessness of her life. This role, formally symbolized by her father the judge, has now been taken over by Popeye, who both protects and threatens. Temple and Tommy have earlier been compared to dogs (207:16//42:13), and Ruby has said to Temple, "Do you think he [Lee] plays the dog after every hot little bitch that comes along?" (220:23//61:5).

287:17 **some sense—elimination, perhaps—identified as a sweet** Elimination is hardly a sense but a process requiring a combination of senses, in this case sight and smell. By the process of elimination, Temple identifies the indeterminate item on her plate as a probable dessert. She is so confused that she cannot explain to herself how she knows what she knows.

287:21 **and Miss Reba saying that they would go shopping tomorrow. And I've just got two dollars, she thought** The act of shopping is, for Temple, a quasi-familiar prospect, something that makes sense to her. Thus she regrets that she has so little money to spend.

288:1 **a widow's bonnet with a veil** Miss Reba is still in mourning for Mr. Binford after two years. She is apparently still wearing the bonnet after visiting the cemetery, although she has partially undressed and is now getting drunk.

288:22 **Again time had overtaken the dead gesture . . . half-past-ten** There is a break in the text just before this sentence. In *Sanctuary: The Original Text*, Faulkner starts a new chapter, XV, at this point. The hand on the broken clock has not moved but "real" time, as told by Temple's watch, which does work, has now caught up. For the moment both time-pieces agree. Now it *is* ten-thirty at night.

289:16 **as though she were bound to a church steeple** This image contains the idea of crucifixion, the innocent suffering in isolation but displayed for all to see. The church steeple would also be the community symbol of morality and virtue, much as the courthouse tower would remind one of judicial order. Faulkner presents Temple as being sacrificed on the communal alter. See entry 333:26//223:15.

289:16 **She grinned at him, her mouth warped over the rigid, placative porcelain of her grimace** porcelain = enamel of her teeth. Temple again hopelessly resorts to her only defense, the hope that she can cajole or manipulate Popeye with her charm. She smiles this toothy grin out of terror.

289:19 **"No, no," she whispered, "he said I cant now he said . . . ."** he = the Doctor. She cannot have sexual activity since she is still bleeding from the earlier violation.

289:22 **her palms lifted** image of supplication which also suggests crucifixion: the palms are parallel to the floor and open for penetration.

289:22 **her flesh beneath the envelope of her loins cringing rearward in furious disintegration like frightened people in a crowd** This curious image suggests that Temple is arching away from Popeye's hand, that her flesh draws back from the intrusion, in essence flees in panic. Temple later describes her violation in the bedroom of the Old Frenchman place to Horace: "my skin started jumping away from it like those little flying fish in front of a boat. It was like my skin knew which way it was going to go before it started moving, and my skin would keep on jerking just ahead of it like there wouldn't be anything there when his hand got there" (330:12//218:27). Both images are the reverse of her fantasy of growing a penis: "Then I thought about being a man, and as soon as I thought it, it happened. It made a kind of plopping sound, like blowing a little rubber tube wrong-side outward" (331:11//220:8).

289:28 **He gripped the top of the gown . . . making a high whin-**

nying sound like a horse   Again Faulkner does not describe exactly what Popeye actually does to Temple, but we later learn that he has used his hand to molest her at the Old Frenchman place (330:10//218:25) and likely does so here. This is the third time Popeye has attacked her in twenty-four hours.

CHAPTER XIX

290:1 **"But that girl," Horace said** This chapter returns to the discussion between Ruby and Horace begun at the end of Chapter XVII (272:31//135:27). This is Friday, May 24, nearly two weeks after Temple's kidnapping.

290:3 **He was just giving her a lift to town** Horace is, of course, horrified to discover that Temple was at the Old Frenchman place, because of the complication it adds to his defense of Lee Goodwin. He also doesn't want to face the possibility that Popeye might have done something to Temple. He uses the fact that Popeye had earlier given him (Horace) a ride to town as support for his contention that he was possibly doing the same for Temple, as she had earlier, in fact, requested.

290:7 **as though it had died in the presence of an unbearable agony which had not had time to touch it** Agony functions as an entity, whose very threat kills. It is as if the child had dropped dead at the *prospect* of pain rather than because of the pain itself. Temple, however, the other "infant" in this book, has so far managed to survive, to live through the agonies she has experienced.

290:18 **with men pitching dollars back and forth between holes in the bare earth** Pitching coins was a common pick up game at the time. In this version, men attempt to toss their silver dollar into a small hole. In another version, they would see who could come the nearest to a line drawn in dirt or on the sidewalk without going over.

290:27 **Little shirt-tail boys** careless youngsters playing hard without regard for responsible actions. Ruby is specifically referring to Gowan, who has played at being grown-up, but surely includes Temple in her general condemnation.

290:27   **that think because Lee breaks the law, they can come out there and treat our house like a. . . . . . .**   Because Goodwin breaks the law by making liquor, people like Gowan act as if they have no need to observe common rules of courtesy. They treat the house as if it were a public establishment.

290:34   **I'd hang every man that makes it or buys it or drinks it, every one of them**   This is Ruby's version of the "There ought to be a law" pronouncement also made by Popeye and Horace. In her anger and exasperation she makes a sweeping call for mass execution of any and all who traffic in alcohol. Though this would include Lee, she likely blames his actions on the fact that he had been drinking.

291:11   **that he was getting nowhere, and he would have these spells like last night**   The first "he" is Lee Goodwin, who is not making much of a living at moonshining; the second "he" is the child, who has been having fits.

291:15   **she had that spent immobility of a chimney rising above the ruin of a house in the aftermath of a cyclone**   After a fire or a terrific storm, a chimney is sometimes the only part of a house or shack left standing, the sole remaining mark of the structure's previous existence. Through this image Faulkner marks Ruby's fundamental strength: despite the absolute and total devastation that surrounds her, she is intact, although momentarily exhausted by her outburst of anger.

291:17   **"Standing there in the corner . . . 'It's me—the woman'"**   Ruby recounts the events previously described by the omniscient narrator in Chapter VIII. She even uses one of the narrator's images: "with her eyes like the holes in one of these masks" (291:21//162:20).

292:2   **What fault is it of mine if you're not married?**   Ruby's point is ambiguous. She either means that if Temple were married to Gowan, she would not be considered fair game to the men at the house, or that she would be safe at home with her husband rather than out with college boys. See entry 212:15// 49:8.

292:3   **I said 'I've lived my life without any help from people of** your sort; what right have you got to look to me for help?' Ruby rephrases what she said to Temple in Chapter VII (218:1//57:20).

292:18   **that stuff on his hair**   the pomade.

292:24   **I could just hear little faint sounds, from the shucks, so I knew it was all right yet**   the sounds caused by Gowan's labored breathing. Ruby assumes nothing happened since there was little activity and Popeye was by the bed for such a short time. In her later account, Temple claims that Popeye has been molesting her with his hand. See entry 330:18//219:4.

292:33   **It's me—the woman**   In this house of threatening men, Ruby does not identify herself by name, but by sex, since Temple would not really know her by name anyway.

292:40   **people on the slow and unhurried pavement below the window**   The passers-by move leisurely on the sidewalk outside. "Slow" and "unhurried" logically though not syntactically modify "people" rather than "pavement."

293:2   **quiet tables**   the people eat quietly, without turmoil or disagreement. Like Temple at Miss Reba's in the preceding chapter, Horace here contemplates simultaneous time: during Temple's night of terror, ordinary people (himself included) lived unmolested lives.

293:6   **Narcissa will———**   be surprised? pleased? to see you.

293:12   **By God, when I think that I had the opportunity———**   to put Gowan in his place. Horace again strikes a blustery pose as avenger of females. His reaction here is similar to his earlier threat against Little Belle's beau: "If he'd walked into your room in a hotel, I'd just kill him" (189:15//14:23).

293:15   **If it hadn't been for that woman———**   Horace still assumes that nothing abusive has actually happened to Temple, that Ruby was successful in protecting her against the men and that Popeye took her to safety.

293:18   **a balloon-tailed suit**   formal dress, like a tux with the extended tail.

293:19   **On any train or in any hotel, on the street; anywhere, mind you———**   These phrases continue Horace's earlier train of thought: "people like that walking the earth with impunity" (293:16//165:11). He is lamenting the ubiquity of Gowan's irresponsible kind and their disregard for decency. However, these phrases also make clear that Horace has Little Belle in mind as much as Temple, in that the reference to the train and the hotel comes from Little Belle's, and not Temple's, experiences (189:2//14:10). Miss Jenny recognizes the shift in focus with her reply, "I didn't understand at first who you meant" (293:21//165:16).

293:22 **that last time he was here, just after you came?** Wednesday, May 8.

293:26 **He asked Narcissa to marry him** If this happened (and there is no substantiation for it), Gowan and Narcissa were likely having the conversation while Horace and Miss Jenny watched from the window. Narcissa is given the upper hand in the break-up, at least as she has apparently related it to Miss Jenny. While Gowan's failure to say his good-byes suggests an abrupt and perhaps a disgruntled departure, he had already scheduled his date with Temple for the Friday dance. Any such "proposal" on his part could be Narcissa's explanation for Gowan's failure to return, so that she doesn't appear to have been thrown over.

293:26 **She told him that one child was enough** her child, Benbow Sartoris. The insult underscores Gowan's adolescent nature; however it also acknowledges the difference in ages between Narcissa and Gowan. In *Sanctuary: The Original Text*, Horace says of his sister, "She seems to keep them not only in hand, but she contrives by some means to make them friends with one another. It's like a club. I wonder if there's a grip, password. . . . . No: she's like a very mature little girl playing dolls."°

293:30 **So he got mad and said he would go to Oxford, where there was a woman he was reasonably confident he would not appear ridiculous to** Gowan has already arranged to date Temple, but by this account Narcissa's rebuff contributes to Gowan's irresponsible actions toward Temple. He is, in part, reacting against the humiliation he has received from Narcissa and attempting to recoup his manliness by his bragging, drinking and general recklessness. He does, of course, once again make a fool of himself.

293:33 **I'll declare, a male parent is a funny thing, but just let a man have a hand in the affairs of a female that's no kin to him.......** Miss Jenny resolves the two threads of conversation: Horace's on Temple and Little Belle, hers on Narcissa and Gowan. She frames it as if "male parent" were her target, but in fact the set includes all men. Horace is a "male parent" but is not Little Belle's actual father, nor is he in any sense Temple's father. But he does "have a hand in the affairs" of both women. Temple's experiences represent a worst-case scenario of what could very easily happen to Little Belle, who is very much like Temple.

293:39 **and thank God she isn't my flesh and blood** The "she" is still primarily Little Belle, although Temple remains a secondary reference. This statement recalls Horace's earlier comment, "And I couldn't have felt any more foreign to her flesh if I had begot it myself" (188:33//14:1).

294:1 **I can reconcile myself . . . involved with a fool** A scoundrel is at least intelligent and plays by some form of rules, no matter how deceitful those rules might be. A fool is utterly unpredictable and invites chaos, as indeed Gowan has. Horace assumes that girls have defenses against scoundrels, but not against fools.

294:4 **Start some kind of roach campaign?** an ordered attempt to exterminate roaches or other vermin, usually on a large scale. This campaign would be against young male fools.

294:6 **I'm going to do what she said; I'm going to have a law passed . . . that makes, buys, sells or thinks whiskey.......** The "she" is Ruby Lamar (290:33//161:24). To some extent Horace has been quoting Ruby throughout his entire tirade. However, he is also, unknowingly, echoing Popeye, who has already said, "There ought to be a law" (246:19//96:19).

294:11 **He returned to town** apparently without seeing Narcissa. Whether his original intentions were to discuss his concerns about Narcissa's involvement with the likes of Gowan or his own problems, Horace does not warn her about Gowan.

294:12 **new-fledged cicadas** *Fledged* means newly-covered with feathers, as a young bird. Faulkner here means newly-hatched, as these insects would have been.

294:15 **a photograph of his step-daughter, Little Belle** The picture Horace takes from Kinston is one of the young girl he is fascinated with rather than the wife he has just left.

294:16 **highlight** a reflection of light on the surface that obscures the photograph.

294:19 **looked in turn at something just beyond his shoulder** just as Little Belle was observing herself in the mirror over Horace's shoulder in the earlier scene (189:26//15:4).

294:21 **voices darkening into silence** synesthetic description of the couple's voices softening, lowering secretively as he, the stranger, approaches.

294:22 **who meant them, her, no harm** Horace remembers coming into the grape arbor. In his present state of mind, Horace *might* mean harm to Little Belle's companion, but he still tells himself that the girl has nothing to fear from him.

294:23 **who meant her less than harm, good God** Horace reaffirms his benign intentions towards Little Belle, but he can't stop thinking about his potential for such behavior. He stands self-accused by his insistent denial.

294:24 **darkening into the pale whisper of her white dress** The "murmur of voices" fade away into the night—"darken"—as they hear him near and only the rustle of her dress makes a noise.

294:24 **of the delicate and urgent mammalian whisper of that curious small flesh . . . seething sympathy with the blossoming grape** Horace's thoughts become overtly sexual as he imagines Little Belle in the arbor. Her blood, or at least some female effluence (the "sympathy"), courses in harmony with nature. The "murmur of the wild grape" (188:29//13:27) and the "urgent mammalian whisper of that curious small flesh" combine. Faulkner's syntax illustrates Horace's movement from conscious recounting of past events to unintentional awareness of his physical desire for Little Belle. Thus his revulsion in the following scene.

294:29 **He moved, suddenly . . . beyond his shoulder** These lines detail Horace's abrupt shifting of perspective, similar to his sudden realization of Little Belle's deception when he caught her watching herself in the mirror in Chapter II. From one angle, Little Belle appears innocent and sweet; from another, secret and sinful. The phrase "like something familiar seen beneath disturbed though clear water" recalls Horace's seeing Popeye's reflection in place of his own at the spring in Chapter I. Horace is horrified by both her (he assumes) experience and his relative ignorance. But he also recognizes that he is projecting these thoughts and interpretations onto the picture.

295:3 **The railroad station was three quarters of a mile away** The railroad station in Oxford is three quarters of a mile from downtown. This would be on Saturday morning, May 25.

295:7 **a new hat trimmed with rigid and moribund flowers** See Miss Reba: "the flowers on her hat rigidly moribund, nodding in macabre was hael." See entry 279:23//145:16.

295:15 **day coach** a passenger car with upright seats as opposed to a Pullman which has overnight berths for sleeping purposes.

295:22 **among unshaven puffy faces washed lightly over as though with the paling ultimate stain of a holocaust** The faces of the newly awakened appear pale in the weak daylight of the "primrose dawn." However, this paleness is connected to death. Earlier they slept with their throats open to the knife (295:18//168:4). Now they are presented as victims of some massive slaughter. Horace is aware of their vulnerability.

295:24 **blinking at one another with dead eyes into which personality returned in secret opaque waves** The passengers come back from the death of sleep, regaining their individual personalities as they awake. With consciousness comes guarded expressions to protect and mark their more vulnerable selves.

295:30 **Horace rose quickly and went forward into the smoking car** The old man's expectoration is like Pap's removal of his quid in order to eat. In both cases, Horace is too delicate to abide the situation.

295:32 **jim crow car** the car reserved for blacks on the segregated railway line. "Jim Crow" was a racist term for a black person, the crow being a black bird. "Jim Crow" laws were originally enacted in Tennessee in 1881 and were implemented throughout the South until 1917 when they were ruled unconstitutional. Nevertheless, they continued to be enforced by custom.°

295:36 **the blue acrid air in which white men sat** blue with cigar and cigarette smoke.

295:39 **small cryptic badges** fraternity pins or emblems. The well-to-do fraternity boys are part of a higher organized and privileged community just as Dr. Quinn, who works for Miss Reba, is a Mason.

296:2 **surrounded each by bright and restless bees** The bees would be the college boys themselves. Women, like flowers, in this metaphor, give off a scent that attracts males. The old trap of Nature is being stressed, but it would appear that this image arises from Horace's own consciousness, since it agrees so neatly with his own attitude toward the Female and Nature.

296:5 **their cold faces still toothed with it** Their mouths are opened in laughter. All of these college students are completely self-absorbed.

296:16 **plaintive, fretful cries, like a bird** See the earlier description of college students' "short, yelping cries like marshfowl disturbed by an alligator . . . short meaningless cries, plaintive, wary and forlorn" (204:32//37:23).

296:31 **Gordon hall** The men's dining hall at the University of Mississippi in the 1920s.

296:34 **Then he just squalled . . . cryptic, headless and tailless evocations on the mind** The noise and rudeness confuses Horace. He is overcome by the seemingly senseless patter and racket. Horace's sensibility is completely out of step with this generation; he cannot possibly hope to understand them, despite the fact that his own step-daughter could easily be among them—in fact, has been. He finds them all crass and vulgar.

297:3 **to punch mine** to have sex.

297:5 **"Do you like liver?" "I can't reach that far"** a crude phallic joke: My penis (or finger) won't reach as far as her liver.

297:24 **cold, blank eyes** Faulkner's point seems to be that Temple, who is also characterized by her cold stare, is merely typical of her generation. Temple is not that much more thoughtless or careless than are her fellow students.

297:26 **At the top of the hill three paths diverged . . . . The broader path led to the postoffice** This description is an accurate representation of the University of Mississippi at the time of the book. Faulkner himself worked at the university post office in 1921–22.°

297:35 **I probably just missed her, didn't I?** Horace is attempting to cultivate a casual conversation without making people suspicious, but there is also his hope beyond hope that she is really there, that something terrible hasn't actually happened to her.

297:37 **She quit school about two weeks ago** Horace is at Oxford on Saturday, May 25. Temple disappeared from the train on Saturday, May 11, two weeks earlier. She could have been withdrawn at any time during those two weeks. In any case, she has been accounted for in bureaucratic terms.

298:3 **Are you another detective?** Temple's family has apparently hired a detective to find her.

298:4 **"Yes," Horace said, "yes. No matter. It doesn't matter** Horace appears to claim that he *is* a detective, which, in a sense, he is. It is also possible that he is beginning to realize how late he is, that events have assumed their own momentum. He may, then, be answering as Temple earlier answered Ruby, simply agreeing without fully comprehending the questions.

298:10 **savage identical paint upon their mouths** the bright lipstick used to form a cupid's bow on their mouths works as tribal coloration in the sexual hunt.

298:10 **like music moving . . . . It's finished** This lengthy description is taken from Horace's perspective, filled as it is with his jejeune, despondent romanticism. The emphasis is on loss—of youth, of love, of innocence. What Horace sees is "slow ruin" all around him. He realizes that his defense of Lee Goodwin is now much more complicated than he had ever realized. He, in fact, gives up at this point, at least for the moment, since it seems hopeless in all respects.

298:21 **a filled but unlighted cob pipe in his hand . . . slowly fingering the unlighted pipe** Horace had earlier forgotten his pipe (295:10//167:25). He must have bought this cheap pipe at the station. Ironically, it is a corn cob pipe, a bit of foreshadowing since, at this point, the reader does not know that Popeye used a corn cob to rape Temple, although cobs and shucks have played an important role in her ordeal. Though it is filled with tobacco, it is unlit, non-functioning, and Horace is "fingering" it as he reads Temple's name on the bathroom wall. All of these images continue to link Horace to Popeye, specifically in impotency.

298:27 **their blonde legs monotonous . . . of the young** A replication of the first descriptions of Temple (198:4//28:4). Temple's kineticism and provocative nature are shared by most of the young college girls, at least as Horace perceives them.

298:31 **pullman** a passenger car with berths for sleeping.

298:34 **an unlighted cigar in his ringed hand** The unlighted cigar recalls Horace's unlighted pipe, while the ring connects Snopes to the corrupt Dr. Quinn, who wears a "masonic ring." See entry 282:37//150:4.

298:36 **passing the sleek crowns in increasing reverse** the stationary heads of the students on the platform which are left behind as the train picks up speed.

299:1 **Like with a guillotine** in a stark straight line, as if his hair had been cut with the blade of a guillotine. Yet another image of death by blade in this scene (295:19//168:4).

299:8 **The train checked speed; a jerk came back, and four**

whistle-blasts The train is signaling that it is coming to a stop, alerting the next station. The passengers experience the braking.

299:14 **Aint this Judge Benbow?** Clarence Snopes addresses Horace as "judge," although Horace is a lawyer. Horace's "I'm afraid you anticipate a little. Hope, rather" (299:24//173:26) indicates that Horace has aspirations to become a judge. There is a "Judge Benbow" mentioned in *Absalom, Absalom!*, *The Unvanquished*, and *The Hamlet*. In *Absalom, Absalom!*, Judge Benbow's son's name is given as Percy. See entry 364:3//266:9.

299:22 **I'm Senator Snopes, Cla'ence Snopes** In *Flags in the Dust*, Clarence is identified as the son of I. O. Snopes, who runs the Snopes restaurant. Clarence is described as having a "hulking but catlike presence,"° which sounds more like Tommy than the state senator of this book. Clarence Eggleston Snopes also appears in *The Mansion* (1959), where he is eliminated from a congressional race by the machinations of V. K. Ratliff. Faulkner also gives more background on him in *The Mansion*. In a 1959 letter to Albert Erskine (who was attempting to coordinate the chronologies of *The Hamlet*, *The Town*, and *The Mansion* for their joint publication), Faulkner described Clarence as being "20 to 25, maybe a year or two more, in Sanctuary, in the whore house business, roughly about 1925 or so."° See entry 300:25//175:8.

299:26 **the third finger discolored faintly at the base of a huge ring** indicating that the ring is a cheap imitation. See Miss Reba's diamonds; see entry 278:11//143:22.

299:36 **an express truck** a hand-propelled truck used to load and unload express trains.

299:39 **Course you aint in my county no longer** Horace lives in Kinston rather than Jefferson and Yoknapatawpha County and thus is no longer a constituent: Snopes has nothing to gain politically by helping Horace.

300:3 **the big town** Jackson, the state capital

300:14 **Any time you're in the city. . . . . . look me up.**

300:18 **"Why not ride back here?" Horace said** Horace apparently asks Snopes to ride with him not because he wants his company but in order to question him and garner Jackson intelligence. He sees by Clarence's questions that the Senator stays up to date on gossip and information. He is also taking some perverse pleasure in making Snopes uncomfortable.

300:23 **Holly Springs** a town approximately 30 miles north of Oxford. They must change trains in Holly Springs to continue to Jefferson.

300:25 **Horace remembered him ten years ago . . . elected him to the legislature without recourse to a public polling** See *The Mansion*: "So Uncle Billy Varner had to do something with Clarence so he got a-holt of Manfred de Spain at the bank and all three of them got a-holt of enough folks to get Clarence into the legislature in Jackson, where he wouldn't ever know nothing to do until somebody Uncle Billy and Manfred could trust would tell him when to mark his name and hold up his hand."°

301:6 **You got a pretty tough case up home there** Clarence is referring to Lee Goodwin's trial for murder, not Temple's abduction. "Up home" means in the upper part of the state, where Jefferson is located.

301:10 **One of her best friends is no longer in school there** There is no evidence that Temple is in fact a good friend of Little Belle, but given the small student body at this time, it is not an impossibility. Horace's strategy, however, is to disguise his interest in Temple since she is, at this time, not publicly associated with Lee Goodwin's case.

301:16 **Ran back home, did she?** from Oxford to Jackson. Horace is fishing for information.

301:18 **When it come out in the paper** See entry 301:27// 176:22.

301:19 **companionate marriages** a trial marriage program devised in 1927 by Judge Benjamin Lindsey. Serialized in *Red Book* magazine, the program advocated "legal marriage with legalized birth control, usually without payment of alimony."°

Also known as "marriage of cohabitation," it promoted the idea of marriage as an art, and supported sex education and instruction on the "art of love," in the schools to better prepare young people for the "serious duties of marriage and parenthood."°

301:27 **Her paw sent her up north somewhere, with an aunt. Michigan. It was in the papers couple days later** approximately May 13 or 14. Part of the family's cover-up to give the private detective time to find Temple. At this point they probably do assume she has run off with someone. Gowan may even be a suspect since his letter to Narcissa indicates that he has dropped out of sight. Horace now learns that Temple is not accounted for, and so not safe.

301:33 **You was at Oxford trying to locate her?** Clarence rephrases Horace's earlier statement in an attempt to trick him. In trying to garner information from Clarence, Horace has inadvertently given away more than he wished.

302:3 **stool in hand** for the descending passengers to step on.

302:5 **George** similar to Popeye's "Jack."

302:15 **Thank' suh** Horace tips the porter with money, in contrast to Snopes's tip of his used cigar, and commiserates with him over the state senator's bad manners.

302:21 **two youths in new straw hats** identified in Chapter XXI as Virgil Snopes and Fonzo Winbush.

302:28 **seat at the rear, facing backward** so that he cannot be seen by anyone from the front of the car.

CHAPTER XX

303:3 **I'll give you a ride, this time** The driver will not charge Horace, who cannot drive a car (263:32//122:16), because Horace is a good customer. See entry 381:11//292:1.

303:6 **only twenty minutes past eight** This is still May 25, a Saturday.

303:27 **Of course, with me———** As a self-proclaimed enlightened and tolerant man, the driver doesn't normally worry about the character of the people staying in the hotel. He does, however, acknowledge the force of the church women.

303:28 **if there was a man———** who would stand up to the church ladies. Horace implies that he is the one to do it. However, see next entry.

303:36 **And I know some more folks around here that better do the same thing** The proprietor means Horace, who originally let Ruby stay in his house but then gave in to his sister's demands and moved Ruby and the child to the hotel. He draws a parallel between himself and Horace, indicates Horace's own complicity in the matter, while attempting to justify himself on grounds of righteousness.

304:8 **a pigeon-hole** one of a network of cubicles on the wall behind the reception desk. The proprietor would keep messages, mail, or keys for the guests. He has taken the bill from the cubicle corresponding to Ruby's room.

304:13 **She said you'd pay it** Ruby is not taking advantage of Horace here. It is likely that she does not have the money. As we later learn, she has every intention in paying Horace with sexual currency.

304:20 **How did———Did———** How did you know who I was? What I wanted?

304:23   **I knew that someone—— I didn't believe that——** that someone would be good enough to take her in. I didn't believe that the people of the town were totally without goodness or pity.

304:26   **I dont keer whut Ed says**   Ed must be her husband, the jailer; Mrs. Walker will do as she pleases.

304:32   **On the next afternoon**   Sunday, May 26th.

304:33   **I'll have to take her home now**   As Narcissa's following comment indicates, Horace is referring to the family home in Jefferson, the Benbow house; and not her home, the Old Frenchman place.

305:6   **She ought to be used to that**   since she has been a streetwalker.

305:13   **I know that nobody in Jefferson knew it except——** Narcissa and Miss Jenny, both of whom Horace has already told.

305:15   **"You were the first I heard tell it," Miss Jenny said. "But, Narcissa, why——"**   Miss Jenny points out that Horace was the first to give away the information and that, if it were so important, he should have been more discreet. Her comment to Narcissa is not so clear. She is obviously implying that Narcissa told others, but she may also be asking Narcissa *why* she told others, which is how Narcissa's response indicates she interprets it.

305:19   **dry, light voice**   Horace is shocked at Narcissa's treachery and his own foolishness. He is angry but controlled.

305:21   **I told her I'd come for her at the jail and. . . . . . .**   take her somewhere else, the Benbow home.

305:22   **Well, I dont suppose it matters. I hope it doesn't**   Horace's decision is a failure of moral courage, as he himself recognizes. He does not want to face Ruby at this time.

305:25   **"I could even tell her I had a puncture," Horace said. "Time's not such a bad thing . . . of each hand**   Temple has already manipulated time to help her deal with her own experiences. If, by using the flat tire as an excuse, Horace can buy himself a little time, maybe things will resolve themselves. Instead of tragedy being stretched, extended and connected, enough time will pop the band and reduce it to two wads of rubbish.

305:32 **He was in bed... felt rather than seen or heard** Time has elapsed. Horace has taken to bed, hiding from his moral responsibilities. Dramatically, the scene reverses Temple's night at the Old Frenchman place, with Horace in Temple's position and with Narcissa replacing Popeye.

305:36 **How much longer are you going to keep this up?... You know what I mean** Horace deliberately misunderstands his sister. She means, "How much longer are you going to stay away from Belle and play at being a lawyer?" He pretends to understand, "How much longer are you going to hide out in my house?"

306:4 **You can send Isom in to hide in the canna bed** to spy on me. There is an irony in the statement, given Horace's own voyeurism.

306:7 **The question is, where I live** Narcissa suggests that Horace, as a man, escapes some of the social consequences of consorting with criminals and defying community mores that, as a woman, she cannot evade. Furthermore, despite what she says, Narcissa is determined to return Horace to Belle and propriety.

306:18 **I ask you to have consideration for our father and mother** both of whom are dead. She wants to protect the Benbow name and reputation. As Narcissa says, she is truly *not* concerned with what devilment Horace actually does. It is that he is doing it *publicly* that humiliates her.

306:19 **They say you refused to let the man have bond to get out of jail** Though the charge is untrue, Narcissa points out the growing scandal resulting from Horace's actions. The townspeople are gossiping that Horace has compromised himself as a lawyer, keeping Goodwin in jail so he can consort with Ruby.

306:21 **You can think of a lie to tell him about that, too** Narcissa refers to the lie Horace thought of telling Ruby about his absence from town when she needs him. Or she means that Horace must have already lied to Goodwin about the possibility of bond, so now he can lie to him about Ruby.

306:29 **And over her, of course** Horace means Ruby, since the townspeople at this time do not know that Temple was at the Old Frenchman place. They could speculate that Goodwin killed Tommy in a contest for Ruby: the motive is sex.

306:30 **Do they say yet that it was I killed him?** The next step in the gossip, Horace sarcastically suggests, will be that Horace killed Tommy out of jealousy over Ruby.

306:32 **I dont see that it makes any difference who did it** Narcissa's own moral indifference is made clear by this statement. Justice is much less important than propriety, or the *appearance* of propriety.

307:3 **She wont know it** that Narcissa will pay, but also that Horace abandoned the case under Narcissa's pressure. The offer is significant. Narcissa really doesn't care whether Goodwin is found innocent or guilty at this point. She will even help set him free if Horace will withdraw. It is only when Horace refuses that Narcissa feels forced to destroy his case. As she asks Eustace Graham, "So the quicker he loses, the better it would be, wouldn't it. . . . If they hung the man and got it over with" (362:25//264:6).

307:8 **You wont leave before breakfast** almost a command. Narcissa is making up her mind what to do. Since she now knows that Horace is not going to give up the case, she will have to act and is measuring her time. See entry 360:33// 261:24.

307:10 **The next morning at breakfast** Monday, May 27th.

307:15 **the district attorney, who had also been raised in Jefferson** Eustace Graham. In *Flags in the Dust*, there is a Eustace (no last name) who is a lawyer and a cripple, as is Eustace Graham in *Sanctuary*. Bayard Sartoris III, who will marry Narcissa, insults this Eustace with his comment, "Taught us in groundschool never seduce a fool nor hit a cripple."°

307:17 **I believe he was at the bottom of that business night before last** Horace says this despite all evidence that Narcissa had a major hand in it, as Miss Jenny has already pointed out to him (305:15//182:24).

307:33 **an effluvium of pomade** an aura, a reeking of hair oil, which connects him with Popeye.

307:34 **an imitation ruby stud** See 347:37//243:27 for a description of Gene, the proprietor of the club where Red's wake is held. These physical characteristics continue to link Clarence Snopes to the corrupt underworld of the novel.

307:38 **the idea that he had been dry-cleaned rather than washed** Despite the outward appearance of neatness, Snopes is actually quite filthy. See 300:12//174:24

308:5 **the church aint got no place in politics, and women aint got no place in neither one, let alone the law** Snopes suggests that women have no place in politics or in church, and neither the church nor women have any place in politics, which is a dirty business and best left to those who know how to work it. Women also have no place in law which, like politics, has its own secret rules, its own ways of doing things, which are best not looked into by outsiders. Wherever women are, they complicate men's lives. Snopes is commiserating with Horace over Narcissa's interference in her brother's affairs.

308:9 **and what he does aint nobody's business but his. What you done with her?** What Horace does with Ruby is nobody's business, but Clarence, presenting himself as a like-minded confidant, assumes Horace will share his exploits with him.

308:17 **Like that girl gittin her paw all stirred up, running off like she done. I reckon he done the right thing sending her clean outen the state** Snopes is following up on Horace's earlier mention of Temple. See entry 301:10//176:5. He has clearly made the connection between the Goodwin case and Temple's disappearance, thanks, in part, to Horace, who is the only reason at this time to connect them.

308:29 **Memphis. Anything I can do for you?** As we will later learn, this is Clarence's third trip (at least) to Memphis looking for Temple. See entry 323:10//209:8. At this point he has not yet found her and is still fishing for information.

308:30 **he could not see at all** Horace is in a blind rage, at Clarence, but also in general frustration at the growing complexity and ugliness of the situation. Note again the image of blindness, failure to *see*.

CHAPTER XXI

309:1 **As the train neared Memphis** Chapter XXI continues with the characters introduced at a distance in Chapter XIX. This is apparently late Saturday afternoon, May 25.

309:1 **Virgil Snopes** In *The Town*, Virgil is identified as the son of the local schoolmaster and the brother of Byron Snopes, who appeared in *Flags in the Dust*. In *The Mansion*, Virgil's father is given the name Wesley, and the story of the boy's exploits in Memphis are recounted and expanded. Faulkner's ironic use of classical names for some of the Snopes—in this case, Dante's Virgil, or in the case of Byron, The Romantic Poet—has been noted.

309:3 **paraffin-paper package** waxed-paper.

309:8 **shaven necks** Their freshly cut hair suggests that they are rubes in the big city. They have come to attend barber's college, but the description also connects them with Clarence Snopes (298:40//173:3).

309:9 **Fonzo** Alphonzo Winbush Snopes, a character in *The Mansion*.

309:20 **I bet you aint never bu———** bu = been here at all. Virgil has been lying about his knowledge of the big city. Fonzo is challenging Virgil's purported knowledge. See 309:18//189:8.

309:26 **It wont be open till eight oclock in the morning** the barber's college.

309:35 **The Gayoso hotel** Located at 139 South Main Street in Memphis, the hotel was named for Don Manuel Gayoso de Lemos, Spanish explorer and the last governor of the Spanish territory in Louisiana. The hotel opened in 1844 and closed in

1960. During the Civil War the Gayoso served as headquarters for both the Confederate and the Union armies.°

310:1 **"Look out," he said, drawing it back** Fonzo is fearful that the redcap, the porter, is a thief. Faulkner is employing all the old jokes about the rube in the big city.

310:3 **Which way is it, now?** the Gayoso Hotel.

310:4 **saw Virgil in the act of turning away from a cabman** Virgil is asking directions to the Gayoso.

310:27 **They left Main Street. At the next corner Virgil turned again** They are walking south on Main. They apparently travel down Linden or Pontotoc for one block and turn into Mulberry.

310:30 **monkey niggers** the bellhops, dressed in porter uniforms, who attempted to take their bags at the Gayoso. Similar costumes were sometimes worn by organ grinder monkeys.

310:37 **At five-thirty they entered a narrow dingy street of frame houses and junk yards** Mulberry street.

311:1 **mother hubbard** a full, loose gown.

311:7 **This hyer's the back. Dont you see that privy?** Virgil mistakes the false entrance for the disguised front to an outhouse.

311:27 **quivering high in the serried windows against the tall serene western sky** "Serried" means pressed or crowded together in rows. The building is between them and the river.

311:32 **"Durned if they didn't," he whispered** Fonzo assumes the man and woman are entering a bathroom together.

312:25 **"I can let you have a room, but I'll have to charge you extra whenever you do business in it** Miss Reba must see the steady rate she can extract from them for the room occupied for a full month as sufficient compensation for the lost prostitution work. In fact, Miss Reba does make the girls behave around the boys. She later complains to Misses Lorraine and Myrtle. See entry 354:4//252:11.

312:31 **"The barber's college"** Miss Reba again suspects she is being made the butt of a joke, hence her response: "you little whipper-snapper": a rude or audacious youth. Barbers are a traditional subject of bawdy humor, often associated with prostitution and sexual matters. Note that a fellow barber-student first takes Fonzo and Virgil to a brothel (314:31//196:16).

312:39 **kimono** a loose fitting gown, suggesting the exotic and sensual. Estelle [Franklin] Faulkner wore kimonos following her return from Shanghai, China after divorce from first husband, Cornell Franklin.°

313:1 **a trail of scent which she left** See entry 279:3//144:26 for the importance of smell at Miss Reba's. This erotic scent refers to the girl's perfume but also keeps the comedy of Virgil and Fonzo's failures as sexual hunters present.

313:4 **hen-house** Compare to the "Coop," the girls' dormitory in which Temple has been living. Fonzo's comment, a play on "fox in the henhouse," once again connects Miss Reba's brothel with the dorm. See entry 198:6//28:6.

313:5 **They didn't go to sleep for some time that first night ... "Hear them?" he whispered** Faulkner compares the first night at Miss Reba's with Temple's in Chapter XVIII. Like Temple, Fonzo is bewildered and yet strangely intrigued by what he senses in the house. Also, we should remember that Fonzo and Virgil are in the house at the same time as Temple. They may, in fact, be on the same floor. Their story can be seen as a comic counterpoint to Temple's. See entry 313:9//194:9.

313:9 **colored coiling shapes of splendor ... and strange nostalgic promises** The "shapes of splendor" refer to the bright city lights reflected in the streets and through the windows. Virgil and Fonzo see in the lights the projections of their wildest hopes. The women, the prostitutes, are just beginning business for the evening and offer their customers—and, by extension, Fonzo and Virgil—both traditional pleasures and the possibilities of undiscovered sexual experiences. Compare the boys' erotic reveries with Temple's nightmares, both drawn from the same sources of sound, sight, and smell (287:6//155:26).

313:14 **the apotheosis of his youth assumed a thousand avatars** Fonzo's supreme, idealized youthfulness is manifested in a thousand forms, each performing some magnificent imagined sexual act.

313:15   **Maybe it'll begin tomorrow, he thought; maybe by tomorrow night. . . . .**   Fonzo's imagination will become reality; like Temple on her first night, Fonzo is also manipulating time.

313:27   **On the third day**   Tuesday, May 28 or Wednesday, May 29.

313:39   **"They're all married. Aint you heard them?"**   Virgil and Fonzo can hear the girls having sex. Virgil assumes that they are therefore all married. Compare to Tommy at the Old Frenchman place, who assumes Temple and Gowan are married since they are traveling together.

314:3   **She's a dress-maker   she** = Miss Reba. They think a woman has been having a fitting in their room and has forgotten her underwear.

314:17   **he would rise and unlock the door and leave it ajar, but nothing happened**   Faulkner contrasts Fonzo with Temple, who locks her door when she first arrives but later unlocks it. Fonzo makes his room accessible in case one of the women should wander in. See entry 285:6//153:5.

314:19   **On the twelfth day**   probably Wednesday, June 5, since Fonzo uses "prayer-meeting" as their excuse (see below): Baptist prayer meetings traditionally meet on a Wednesday night.

315:12   **We been to prayer-meeting**   The act of fellatio is sometimes described as "prayer-meeting" since the performer may be on his or her knees. Faulkner may have inserted a bit of wishful bawdy into Fonzo's alibi.

315:19   **the women on their twinkling blonde legs**   The women are prostitutes. The description of their legs recalls the earlier description of the college girls Horace sees and, beyond that, of Temple herself (see 198:4//28:4; 298:27//172:19, for examples).

315:21   **How about that three dollars now?**   As they watch the women, Fonzo asks Virgil if it would not be worth another three dollars to have sex again.

315:26   **They waited two nights. "Now it'll be six dollars," Virgil said**   Virgil's calculations are not completely clear. He is possibly saying that after tonight they will have spent a total of six dollars, or that since they have missed two nights, they will have to do it twice that night to catch up. Thus, two acts at three dollars each = six dollars apiece.

315:32 **She caint eat us** Faulkner joke plays out two ways: 1) a sexual joke concerning oral sex and; 2) the hazards of vagina dentata and women's genitalia biting off penises; although "eating" is also used as a traditional metaphor for conflict: "I'll eat you up and spit you out," for example.

315:39 **"I caint eat that six dollars, noways," Virgil said. "Wisht I could"** Because the sexual pleasure seems ephemeral, Virgil feels he has nothing to show for the six dollars. Another version of his earlier statement, "Aint nothing worth three dollars you caint tote off with you" (314:37//196:22).

316:8 **There's Cla'ence** According to the information given in this chapter, the date is probably Friday, June 7. There is, however, a problem with this chronology. Clarence calls Horace with news on Sunday, June 2, saying he discovered Temple a "[c]ouple days ago" (see entry 320:16//205:7). At this time Popeye catches him looking through the keyhole and burns him with a match (324:10//210:18), and Clarence runs away. When Horace comes to interview Temple on Monday, June 3, Clarence waits outside to speak to him but is obviously afraid to enter the establishment (entry 322:4//207:5). Popeye keeps Temple at Miss Reba's until June 17, when Red is murdered; in fact, according to Miss Reba's account in Chapter XXV, Popeye brings Red to Temple from June 6–9 (see entry 358:23//258:19). Therefore, Clarence should be worried about Popeye's presence at this time and would not likely be carousing so openly. See Chronology.

316:20 **They crossed a street of negro stores and theatres and turned into a narrow, dark street** They are walking into the Beale Street district of town, segregated for the black houses of prostitution.

316:31 **This stuff is color-blind** The money doesn't distinguish between blacks and whites; it can be spent on either.

Faulkner used a variation of the joke in *The Reivers* when the man who pulls Boon, Lucius, and Ned out of the mud charges them two dollars apiece. Boon protests that Ned is a Negro and thus shouldn't cost as much. "Son," the man replies, "both these mules is color-blind."°

CHAPTER XXII

317:1 **On the third day of his search** Wednesday, May 29.

317:3 **unbroken jungle** Compare the description and operation of this house to the Old Frenchman place. Like Lee, the old woman sells special goods to a specific clientele. She is suspected of being a moonshiner, but is instead a maker of potions.

317:20 **the woman** Ruby Lamar.

317:28 **Do you think that would——that I'd care a damn what——** that would stop me, that I'd care what others thought.

317:30 **You have to live here** In her attempt to absolve Horace of guilt, Ruby employs a variation of Narcissa's argument as to why Horace should distance himself from Goodwin's case and from her.

317:32 **and if these uxorious. . . . . . .** the men in town who allow themselves to be ruled by their wives.

317:35 **which seems at first to be mere affinity for evil but which is in reality practical wisdom** This is Horace's view on it rather than the narrator's. Women are naturally suspicious of other people's motives not necessarily because they are evil themselves but because they are wise enough, have the practical wisdom, to know that most people act out of selfishness.

318:3 **dont you let them. . . .** beat you down. Horace is reacting to Ruby's stoic futility: "There's not anything else I could do" (318:1//201:29). But the vehemence of his reaction—"Bitches"—reveals his anger toward Narcissa and women in general.

318:5 **The next day he had the telephone installed** Thursday, May 30. See entry 318:5//202:3.

318:5   **He did not see his sister for a week ... a week before the opening of Court**   Court opens on June 20 (365:1//267:1). A week earlier would be Thursday, June 13. However, as Cleanth Brooks and others have pointed out, Horace needs more than a week between Snopes's call and the beginning of the trial to do the various things he does.° Other evidence indicates that this call takes place on Sunday, June 2, four days after the phone is installed in Horace's house on May 30. See Chronology.

318:9   **he thought it was Narcissa**   Even though he has not informed his sister of the telephone, Horace assumes she has kept him under watch closely enough to know about it.

318:16   **leaning above the instrument ... whispering into it behind a soft, huge, ringed hand, the telephone toylike in the other**   The "instrument" must refer to the speaker part of the telephone; the toylike "telephone" is the receiver placed to his ear. This would be a wall telephone with the speaker attached to the main body and the detachable hand-held receiver connected by a cord.

318:23   **That would interest a couple of parties**   Judge Drake, for example, and perhaps Eustace Graham. However, see entry 363:25//265:19.

318:32   **"All right. I'll be down town in the morning. You can find me somewhere." Then he said immediately: "Hello!"**   Horace attempts a bluff of indifference but loses his nerve and fails to bring it off.

318:37   **dicker**   to negotiate, as in a trade.

319:4   **He walked down to the gate**   Horace does not want Snopes in his house. In his disdain for Snopes, he is also enacting his earlier admonition to Little Belle: "But you dont bring them home, you know. You just step over them and go on. You dont soil your slippers" (189:4//14:12). However, Narcissa's objections to having Ruby in the Benbow house are based in the same feelings.

319:9   **plaintful**   a Faulkner coinage; variation of plaintive. A "plaint" is a complaint or lamentation.

319:15   **until I tried to call you out to Mrs Sartorises**   Narcissa is called by her married name from her marriage to Bayard Sartoris. Thus, Clarence has already spoken to Narcissa (likely on June 2, the same night he calls Horace; see 362:29//264:10), who will use the knowledge that Snopes wanted to talk to Horace. Also, he likely got Horace's number from Narcissa, and this supports Horace's earlier suspicion that Narcissa has been keeping tabs on him (318:5//202:3).

319:19   **toward the house**   Snopes masks his eagerness to be invited into the house by intimating the need for privacy. Horace is unusually rude to Clarence throughout this meeting but also recognizes that he doesn't need to be seen with Snopes.

319:35   **Keeping batch, are you?**   living as a bachelor.

320:3   **"She's not here," Horace said, "if that's what you're hinting at"**   Ruby is not in the house. Snopes has implied that Horace has moved to the empty house so that, away from Belle and Narcissa, he can enjoy Ruby in private.

320:16   **Couple days ago I come onto a piece of information**   If we take Snopes's remark literally, the date he acquired the information would be May 31 or June 1.

320:28   **he'd try to sell to the State**   to the district attorney, who represents the state in court proceedings. Horace's failure to imagine a third possible buyer beyond himself and the prosecution will leave him utterly vulnerable to surprise at the trial.

320:36   **He raised his hand and drew it across the back of his neck**   Clarence is apparently feeling the place on his neck where Popeye burned him (321:15//206:16; 324:10//210:18). See entry 324:7//210:15.

321:4   **Horace shut his hands and put them in his pockets, shut against his flanks**   to prevent Snopes from shaking hands again and to deny, symbolically at least, that he is entering into a deal with such a contemptible character.

321:16   **If she aint—hasn't been there, you can git your money back**   Snopes's qualification makes it clear that he suspects that Popeye will not keep Temple at Miss Reba's for long, especially now that others—Snopes included—know of her presence. She will, however, remain there until June 17, another two weeks.

321:22 **Where is——** Where is she? The question is completed on 321:26//206:27.

321:22 **Wait. Are you a Baptist, by any chance?** Horace thinks back to his conversation with Miss Jenny (267:5//128:2). His experience with Baptists is that they are more devious and treacherous than even thugs and politicians.

321:24 **I aint hidebound in no sense** Hidebound = extremely strict, conservative: "hardshell." I was raised as a Baptist but one who can break the rules (see 363:29//265:13).

321:27 **I'll trust you** to pay me after I tell you. However, Snopes apparently does not tell Horace in which brothel Temple can be found until Horace has paid.

CHAPTER XXIII

322:1 **As Horace entered Miss Reba's gate** Monday, June 3.

322:4 **Around an adjacent corner Snopes' head peered, turkey-like** Snopes has good reason to be careful. Popeye has already caught him looking through the keyhole to Temple's room, and has burned his neck as a warning. See entries 316:8//198:25; 323:10//209:8.

322:9 **Boys will be boys, wont they?** Although Snopes knows perfectly well why Horace is going in Miss Reba's establishment, he pretends that it is as a customer. He is perhaps suggesting to Horace that this is something which Snopes could use on him at some later date if Horace should prove an enemy. See entry 322:22//208:14 for further support for this reading.

322:22 **married and all and not being sho where his wife is at** Snopes angles for any psychological advantage. He pretends that he has caught Horace cheating on his wife, but he also acknowledges that Belle is not in Kinston (he has obviously checked) and could herself be cheating on Horace.

322:26 **Only I hate to see a good———** I hate to see a good man spend more than he needs to when there are cheaper whorehouses available.

322:31 **Higher'n Monte Carlo** Monte Carlo, in Monaco, the premiere gambling center in Europe at the time.

322:31 **I'll show you a place where———** no doubt the Negro whorehouse where Snopes will take Virgil and Fonzo on June 7. See 324:25//211:3.

323:1 **pie-face-ted man** pie-faced Clarence Snopes. See 320:13//205:4.

323:10 **He turned up here about two weeks ago** Miss Reba's approximation causes a problem in the chronology. Two weeks ago would be Monday, May 20, but Virgil and Fonzo arrive at Miss Reba's on May 25, only nine days earlier. Since the boys come to stay at Miss Reba's by accident, there would be no reason for Snopes to come looking for them before that time. See *The Mansion*: "And since the Memphis red-light district is not all that big, it was only the course of time until they and Clarence turned up at the same time in the same place...."° But according to Miss Reba's account, Snopes visits her house four times. The first time is "about two weeks ago" (May 20). Then a "couple of nights later" (323:16//209:14)—approximately May 22—he returns, and Reba tells him he needs to spend money if he's going to hang around the house. These two dates would be before Clarence meets Horace on the train, before he has any reason to be searching for Temple. The "next time" (323:19//209:17) Clarence comes is not specified by Miss Reba, but Clarence tells Horace that he is going to Memphis on business on Monday, May 27 (308:29//187:22), and this time he specifically asks questions about Temple (323:36//210:4). The last visit is the afternoon when Popeye catches him, May 31 or June 1 (320:16//205:7). Clarence will return on June 7 and this time find Virgil and Fonzo, approximately two weeks after they have arrived (316:8//198:25). This is obviously a confused and implausible scenario, and it seems likely that Miss Reba (or Faulkner) simply miscounted. See Chronology.

323:18 **has got to get on the train now and then** To "pull a train" means to take on a series of sexual partners. Reba is saying that people need to hire a girl and spend money if they come to her place.

323:31 **I done seed too many now** penises.

324:7 **So Popeye goes on upstairs on them cat feet of his** Popeye's surprise attack on Snopes acts as a comic parallel to his earlier murder of Tommy, with the match substituting for the pistol, which "was no louder than the striking of a match" (249:39//102:8). Clarence is also yet another voyeur spying on Temple.

324:19 **going wump-wump-wump inside like one of these here big dray-horses, and he pawed at the door for about a minute, moaning to himself like the wind in a chimney** A dray is a heavy cart or sled without sides which would be dragged, usually by a horse. The sound the terrified Clarence makes suggests he has recently eaten and his insides are bouncing around. In his haste to escape Popeye, Clarence unknowingly reenacts Temple's panic in the barn, "pawing at the door" and moaning.

324:34 **But all in the way of my business, not theirs** Miss Reba's dealings with lawyers has not involved hiring them to do legal work for her; instead they come to her establishment to employ *her* services.

324:38 **You may be guilty right now of harboring a fugitive from justice** not Temple but Popeye. See Miss Reba's reply: "Then let them come take him. . . . What Popeye done outside is his business" (324:40//211:18). Horace has attempted and failed to pressure Miss Reba in cooperating. She knows too much to be intimidated in this manner: "I had too many police in this house to be scared of them" (325:1//211:19).

325:13 **"It better not been born at all," she said. "None of them had."** Horace has attempted another ploy, to gain Reba's sympathy for Ruby as a widow with a child. Again he fails. Reba has seen too much of the world to be moved by this image. It was common practice for prostitutes to send their unwanted or unexpected children to families or homes that specialized in illegitimate births so that the child wouldn't be aware of its mother's profession and so the mother could continue to work. See first entry to 331:36//221:4.

325:17 **You aint lying to me, are you?** about Ruby and the child. Reba *expects* a lawyer to lie; truthfulness surprises her.

325:25 **The mantel supported a wax lily . . . a meek-looking man** with an enormous moustache This is a memorial to Mr. Binford. The wax lily is either preserved from his funeral or simply artificial do-it-yourself shrine decor.

325:38 **This aint hers** Temple does not want to have anyone invade her room, or to be seen in her room. We later learn that Popeye keeps his clothes there, and probably other evidence as well. See entry 334:25//225:15. Another possibility, however, could be that she doesn't want Popeye to know that she has had visitors. By exercising this prerogative, she exerts some control, determining when and where she will agree to be seen.

326:9 **I couldn't a stayed in my business without learning to be deaf and dumb a long time before this** Compare to Clarence Snopes: "Now, now, Judge. I aint going to tell this at home. . . . If us boys started telling what we know, caint none of us git off a train at Jefferson again, hey?" (322:16//208:7).

326:17 **I'll promise before you tell me a thing that you wont have to testify in Court unless they are going to hang him without it** without her testimony that Popeye, not Goodwin, killed Tommy. Since it is highly unlikely that he can save Goodwin without Temple's testimony, Horace is being naive. He takes the same position Lee takes: the prosecution has got to prove Lee did it. See *Sanctuary: The Original Text*: "He need only arrange to procure her if things went wrong. Whatever he did, the evidence against Goodwin was not strong enough to convict him as it was now. . . . "°

326:24 **And you with diamonds, and her with that poor little kid** Reba employs Horace's earlier line in an attempt to convince Temple. She seems to have been moved by the image more than she admitted. But Miss Reba speaks to Temple in her identity as a mobster's woman—"They aint going to catch Popeye, honey" (326:30//213:30)—while Horace addresses her as a disgraced Jackson girl—"You can use a different name, wear clothes nobody will recognize you in, glasses" (326:28// 213:27). See entry 326:36//214:7.

326:36 **Her head was tousled . . . a savage cupid's bow**

Temple's appearance when she suddenly reveals herself is shocking. She is cheaply and grotesquely made up, almost a caricature of her former co-ed self. Brazenly appropriating the costume and make-up of a whore, she will use much the same strategy when she appears at Goodwin's trial. See second entry 376:30//284:21.

327:19 **your——he——** Horace doesn't know how to refer to Popeye. Your male companion? Man? Boyfriend? Horace doesn't know, and doesn't want to know, what relationship actually exists between Temple and Popeye.

327:20 **"Dont think I'm afraid to tell," Temple said. "I'll tell it anywhere"** Temple, probably drunk, asserts her independence, her willingness to tell the truth. Her bravado is ironic, in that at the trial she will barely speak, and when she does, she will lie.

327:29 **Now and then Horace would attempt to get her on ahead to the crime itself, but she would elude him** Since Horace does not yet know what has happened to Temple, he misunderstands her reluctance to deal with the morning of the crime. To discuss Tommy's death, she will have to deal with her own attack.

327:35 **"Yes, that," she would say. "It just happened"** "That" is the murder of Tommy, the "crime" Horace wants to talk about.

327:38 **There were two of them there** two rats.

328:6 **You can feel them like you can in a car when they begin to look for a good place to stop—you know: park for a while** You can sense their sexual excitement without actually seeing or touching them. Her analogy brings the world of conventional dating into the underworld, but also draws a comparison between the sexual politics of dating and the act of rape.

328:14 **like a dog driving two cattle along a lane** Temple is directing, manipulating, controlling Horace and Miss Reba with her story. But she is also in a sense explaining herself, validating herself. She sees no personal shame: she was the *victim* in the event, and now she is center stage as narrator.

328:16 **those shucks** the corn shucks in the mattress.

328:21 **That's because breathing goes down** down into the body and thus into the bed on which she is sitting.

328:26 **Like the mashed-in place on the pillow after you got up** Temple connects aural clues so she can make sense of what is happening. She can imagine what the men are doing on the other side of the wall by the sounds they are making (226:25//69:16). In a similar way, the indentation in the pillow identifies the recent presence of someone's sleeping head.

328:30 **I'd try to make like I was a boy** "Make like" = pretend. If she were a boy, she would not be so vulnerable to sexual attack, she thinks.

328:33 **you look at him** the teacher or professor. Temple largely thinks of authority as male. She wants to please the man in control: "Call on me. Call on me."

328:36 **kissing your elbow** the folklore belief that if you kiss your elbow, then you will change your sex.

328:37 **and I'd wonder if I could tell when it happened** whether she could feel the moment of transformation, when she had changed sex, developed a penis.

328:39 **I'd strike a match and say Look** so that they could see her changed sex in the dark. There is no electricity at the Old Frenchman place, so she would have to "strike a match" to bring light. But the idea of the match is also closely associated with Popeye. She would in effect be turning his own weapons back on him. See entry 329:27//218:2.

329:4 **Now I am. I am now.** a boy.

329:7 **Because I thought how much I'd done for them, and now they'd gotten me into this** Temple anthropomorphizes (and morselizes) her legs, addressing them as her most attractive physical features, and the main object of the men's attention and desire.° But she is also objectifying herself, assigning guilt to her legs while denying any responsibility she might have. See entry 341:31//235:5.

329:10 **Then I'd think maybe I couldn't tell it and I'd get ready to look. . . . Then I'd think if I didn't look at the right time, it** would be too late   Temple uses counting games to gain control. Since her transformation from a boy to a girl is not taking place, she assumes she has gotten part of the spell wrong.

329:19   **a kind of iron belt**   a chastity belt or girdle; a padded, metal device intended to insure female fidelity, used during medieval times.

329:22   **put it in the———**   in the bed or raincoat with her, quite likely between her legs as a kind of substitute chastity belt.

329:27   **long sharp spikes on it and he wouldn't know it until too late and I'd jab it into him**   Since Temple cannot actually become a male with a penis, she wants to have the ability to do the penetrating, the destroying. Her defense would be a kind of reverse rape. Although the "him" is specifically Popeye, the reference could also be extended to men in general: she will "teach" them all a lesson.

329:31   **I didn't know it was going to be just the other way**   that she would be the one to be "jabbed."

329:36   **Oh, yes; this was something else funny I did**   In retrospect, in the telling, Temple recognizes the apparent absurdity of her actions. She means "funny" in the same sense as "crazy" earlier (329:7//217:12). Also see 330:23//219:9; 330:25//219:11.

329:36   **She told**   At this point Faulkner quits Temple's first person narrative and, for a time, uses third person, yet the narration continues to be extremely subjective with Temple's point of view governing the account.

329:38   **listening to the shucks . . . and she could feel her nostrils going alternately cool and warm**   cool as she breathes in, warm as she exhales. Temple is hypersensitive to everything, all her sense experiences are intensified.

330:2   **Then he was standing over**   over the bed, over Temple.

330:3   **and she was saying Come on. Touch me.**   Temple is apparently saying this to herself, not aloud. Certainly neither Ruby nor Tommy hears her say this to Popeye; but it is unclear whether Temple is aware whether she speaks aloud or not.

330:10   **Then it touched me, that nasty little cold hand, fiddling**

around inside the coat where I was naked Temple has removed her dress and is wearing only "scant undergarments" (227:8//70:10) under the raincoat. Popeye's hand is turned into an object, "it" rather than "he." See 330:11//218:27.

330:11 **It was like alive ice** Popeye's hand, which is without human warmth.

330:17 **Then it got down to where my insides begin** to the vaginal opening.

330:18 **my insides started bubbling and going on and the shucks began to make so much noise it was like laughing** The language suggests that Popeye is masturbating Temple, or at least that Temple is responding physically to Popeye's disturbing touch. But also note that Ruby and Tommy, who are in the room when this happens, do not hear the shucks rattling: "She could hear no sound from the shucks, so she remained motionless beside the door, with Tommy squatting beside her . . ." (234:32//80:22). Ruby implies that if she had detected Popeye's actions, she and Tommy would have attempted to stop him.

330:25 **I could see myself in the coffin** This image ties Temple to Horace's earlier image of Emma Bovary vomiting the bile of her rigor mortis onto her white gown.°

330:31 **and I could see all the people sitting around the coffin, saying Dont she look sweet. Dont she look sweet** Temple sees death as another way to avoid her fate, but even in death she seeks approval from those around her. The emphasis on "sweetness" suggests that Temple would like to think of herself as lovable, innocent: like a sweet child. But the image is also ironic. Compare to Miss Myrtle's comment on Red's corpse in his coffin: "Didn't he look sweet?" she wailed. "Didn't he look sweet?" (352:29//250:14). Red's death and funeral will not take place for another two weeks (June 17 and 18).

330:35 **I got mad, because he was so long doing it** If Temple is reporting her feelings accurately, she seems to have instinctively recognized Popeye's impotence. Her imagination foreshadows the victim-victimizer relationship she will have with Popeye. See entry 330:40//219:26.

330:40 **I'd talk to him like the teacher does in school . . . and it was a little black thing like a nigger boy** Temple imagines that she is a school teacher scolding her student. She sees herself as a middle-aged woman ("forty-five years old"), authoritative, punishing, and invulnerable. Popeye, the student, becomes an "it"—small, inadequate, and black (Temple thinks of Popeye as "that black man")—but the ambiguous pronoun might also refer to the penis—"and it kind of drawing up and drawing up like it could already see the switch" (331.6)—reacting to threat of castration. See entries 331:2//219:28, 331:6//220:2, and 331:8//220:4.

331:2 **Because I'd say How old am I? . . . and I never could wear gray** In her effort to unsex herself, Temple imagines herself to be middle-aged, menopausal, matronly. She is also now a figure of authority, in control of the errant schoolboy.

331:6 **And I was telling it what I'd do, and it kind of drawing up and drawing up like it could already see the switch** Popeye is now identified almost entirely as the flaccid penis itself, which, anticipating the punishment it is about to receive, is shrinking even more.

331:8 **I ought to be a man. So I was an old man, with a long white beard** Temple moves from girl to boy to matron to old man in her imagination.

331:14 **It felt cold, like the inside of your mouth when you hold it open** Temple imagines the penis as the vagina turned inside out, made of the same kind of soft, membranous tissue found inside the mouth (or the vagina).

331:16 **how surprised he was going to be** when he touches a penis instead of the female genitalia he expects.

331:19 **Then all of a sudden I went to sleep** In her panic, Temple apparently becomes catatonic until Ruby comes to take her away.

331:25 **I wish you'd get her down there and not let her come back. I'd find her folks myself, if I knowed how to go about it. But you know how. . . . . . . back home in Mississippi, where she belongs.** Why Horace doesn't at this point take Temple away from Miss Reba's, where she is still at the mercy of Popeye, is a crucial question. Miss Reba apparently does not know who Temple is; it is highly unlikely she would allow her to stay if she knew of Temple's prominent connections and the risk Reba was running in keeping her. Her concern here is humanitarian, and she is in fact issuing a challenge to Horace to rescue Temple. But Horace does not follow up on it. If he were to take Temple to Mississippi, he would have to turn her over to her father, Judge Drake, and thus run the risk that Judge Drake would not allow her to testify in court if Goodwin needed her. (Clarence Snopes will go to Jackson on June 4, the day following this interview, to sell his information to Judge Drake; but Drake apparently makes no attempt to remove his daughter during the next two weeks she remains at Reba's. See entry 363:25//265:18.) However, Horace has already said that he doesn't intend to use Temple unless he simply has to, and his later actions show that Temple's testimony is not part of his intended defense. See entry 326:17//213:16. Indeed, Temple's rape at the Old Frenchman place greatly complicates Horace's case, which is still a relatively simple murder trial. Even as a defense witness, Temple would have to explain her presence at the murder scene, even if her identity and the rape itself could be concealed. It's maybe as simple as Horace's disgust with and horror of Temple (and all women), his desire that she be kept hidden from sight. He later says, "Better for her if she were dead tonight" (331:35//221:3). Thus, his choice is to leave her despite Miss Reba's warning, "She'll be dead, or in the asylum in a year, way him and her go on up there in that room." See first entry to 331:36//221:4.

331:29 **way him and her go on up there in that room** Reba apparently means sexual activities, although she might also be thinking of arguments Popeye and Temple might be having.

331:31 **She wasn't born for this kind of life** Miss Reba says that this kind of behavior is unnatural for Temple and she acknowledges that Temple has been forced into an unusual role.

331:36 **For me, too** It would be better for Horace if Temple were dead. Not only does she complicate his case, she is also forcing him to face a truth about life, and about himself, which he cannot, or does not wish, to comprehend. Horace is repeating Miss Reba's earlier comment on helpless, unwanted or abandoned children (325:13//212:2).

331:36 **He thought of her, Popeye, the woman, the child, Goodwin, all put into a single chamber ... indignation and the surprise** It would be better if everyone involved in this sorry episode could be quickly and simply removed from the world, exterminated in a gas chamber. Horace thinks in terms of mass execution, as he did on the train to Oxford (295:16//168:1).

331:39 **And I too** This time Horace is including himself in the group which should be exterminated, since he has also been corrupted by the event.

331:40 **Removed, cauterised out of the old and tragic flank of the world** Horace imagines a surgical excision of this group, as if they were a cancer on the world. Not only should they be removed, the space they occupied should be cleaned and scarred closed by burning. See "the ordered chaos of the intricate and shadowy world upon whose scarred flanks the old wounds ..." (283:36//151:15).

332:11 **thinking of the expression he had once seen in the eyes of a dead child ... profoundly in miniature** This image recalls Temple's view of the broken clock in her room at Miss Reba's, the face of which changes "from a round orifice in the darkness to a disc suspended in nothingness, the original chaos" (283:34//151:12). Here, the "globes" are the sightless eyes of the dead child, in which are still trapped the last images at the moment of death. The passage also invokes the description of the Goodwin baby in its throes of unbearable agony. The child recognizes the inevitability of disaster, the design of evil, which is at the heart of the world: so thinks Horace.

332:21 **He thought of the other morning when he had crossed it** May 25, when he went to Oxford looking for Temple.

332:32 **The house ... writhed like cold smoke** This long passage repeats many of the same images already associated with Temple at Miss Reba's (283:5//150:11). Horace wonders how, or whether, he should go on living in a world which has no meaning, or at least no justice. He feels that time is coming to a halt, that the universe (which he supposed was ruled by some omniscient power) has been abandoned. Goodness has fled. The "chemical agony of a world left stark and dying above the tide-edge of the fluid in which it lived and breathed" elaborately suggests the image of a fish left stranded on a beach, or, perhaps, an aborted fetus. Its bleakness recalls the earlier image: "Removed, cauterised out of the old and tragic flank of the world" (331:40//221:8).

333:9 **sweet chiaroscuro** Little Belle's picture is in black and white. Photographs could be painted or touched with color, but color film was not widely used in the 1920s and 30s.

333:10 **cardboard** the backing on which the photograph is printed.

333:10 **by some quality of the light . . . shallow bath of highlight** Horace's movement causes the light on Little Belle's photograph to blur the picture, to make it seem alive in his hands.

333:13 **beneath the slow, smoke-like tongues of invisible honeysuckle** The highlight on the picture, coupled with the movement of Horace's hands, makes the picture come alive to Horace. Immediately he remembers the grape-arbor, the smell of the garden, and all the sexual connections he has invested in that place.

333:15 **the small face seemed to swoon in a voluptuous languor** Horace imagines that he is holding Little Belle's face in his hands and that she is becoming aroused, as he obviously is.

333:16 **blurring still more . . . like a scent itself** Little Belle's image is lost in the highlight, but the memory stays imprinted on Horace's eyes (like the final image of death imprinted on the unseeing eyes of the infant corpse mentioned earlier. Sex and death are strongly connected in Horace's mind). Horace momentarily gives himself over to his desire for Little Belle. In his imagination, he makes love to her. This act, however, immediately links him with Popeye, who has actually raped Temple; Horace will be sickened by the recognition that he shares this base and corrupt desire to violate Little Belle (Temple's counterpart in the book).

333:20 **that sensation in his stomach** The "hot ball on his stomach" (332:18//221:27) finally causes him to vomit.

333:24 **and leaned upon his braced arms while the shucks set up a terrific uproar beneath her thighs** Horace is reliving the event Temple has described to him. At this point, he is braced over the girl (Temple/Little Belle) as she writhes beneath him.

333:26 **Lying with her head lifted slightly . . . roaring out of her pale body** Horace now identifies with the girl(s), the victim(s) of the act. He is the one being raped, violated, and as he vomits, the expelled matter is connected with the blood flowing from the assaulted female(s). The image also recalls Horace's initial assessment of Popeye: "He smells black . . . he smells like that black stuff that ran out of Bovary's mouth and down upon her bridal veil when they raised her head" (184:4//7:25). The crucifix image recalls the earlier description of Temple "bound to a church steeple" (289:16//158:30). See entry 333:28//223:18.

333:28 **She was bound naked on her back on a flat car moving at speed through a black tunnel** Though Horace's nightmare (and all of *Sanctuary*) is shot full of Freudian symbolism, whether Faulkner actually read Sigmund Freud is another question. Certainly he was aware of Freud's general ideas and uses typically Freudian images as the corncob, the pistol, the train racing through the tunnel, for his own artistic purposes. Here Horace comes to identify completely with the "she" and merges with Temple's enforced passivity.°

333:31 **The car shot bodily from the tunnel . . . filled with pale, myriad points of light** Horace's act of vomiting is orgasmic. He seems literally to reach climax as he vomits, both sickened and thrilled by his imaginative reconstruction of Popeye's act.

CHAPTER XXIV

334:13 **The table beside it was littered with cigarette stubs . . . the single ruby eye where Popeye's mouth would be** Although Temple smokes, Popeye also spends much of his time simply sitting and smoking beside her bed, watching her. His actions indicate a kind of obsession with Temple, a deep involvement which parallels Horace's obsession with Little Belle. We later learn that Temple has been left alone for the past week, that neither Red nor Popeye has been to her room, and she is now, in Miss Reba's words, "wild as a young mare" (358:25//258:21).

334:19 **It was midmorning** Monday, June 17.

334:22 **with that quality as of spent breathing which it had in midmorning** the main activity takes place through the night; the mornings at the brothel are time for rest and rejuvenation from the previous night's work.

334:25 **she saw one of Popeye's innumerable black suits lying across a chair** The clothing suggests that Popeye is living with Temple in the room; Temple's earlier reluctance to meet Horace there becomes clearer. See entry 325:38//212:27.

334:29 **closet improvised by a print curtain** Either a closet opening is covered with a curtain which can be pushed aside to reveal clothes or a section of the room, a corner perhaps, has been made—"improvised"—into a closet by hanging a curtain.

334:34 **automatic pistol** Popeye obviously has more than one pistol. He would not leave the room without one on him. See entry 340:27//233:20.

335:6 **smug orange gleam of banknotes** The banknotes are gold certificates issued between 1882 and 1922. They were bright yellow or orange on the back and were thus often known as yellowbacks.° Popeye has apparently given the money to Temple since she had only two dollars with her (287:22//156:12).

336:5 **John Gilbert** Gilbert (1897–1936) was a famous silent screen actor, noted especially for his romantic roles opposite Greta Garbo. Minnie finds Popeye to be "right pretty," an estimate not supported by Faulkner's descriptions.

336:26 **The street was empty . . . in a door beyond it** The man in the cap is apparently Popeye's man, stationed to keep an eye on Temple while Popeye is absent. The cab driver might be as well; when he looks at her "interrogatively" (336:30//228:8), he could either be offering her a ride or following her. Or he could be asking if she is for sale, since she is in the brothel district and looks like a prostitute. In any case, Temple is again being "eyed" by a number of men.

336:30 **She turned into the drug store . . . to the house** Although Faulkner does not tell us whom Temple calls, we later surmise that it is Red (344:36//239:11). However, she could call anyone—her father, her brothers, the police—but does not do so. She appears to have decided to run away with Red.

336:35 **When that cab over there started up, I got ready to pack up too** As Minnie suggests, it would also have been quite simple for Temple to hop in the cab (she has plenty of money) and go wherever she wished. This assumes that the cab driver was not in Popeye's employ and that Temple did not fear this was the case.

337:22 **spying herself in the mirror. She turned before it, studying herself, puffing at the cigarette** Compare to the earlier description of her reflection in Chapter XVIII (281:34//148:19). Temple has now regained a sense of identity, although it is now the identity of a Memphis prostitute. She occupies herself by "studying" her new self-image in the mirror.

338:29 **"I wont!" Temple said. "I wont!"** get in the car or go back in the house.

338:32 **You're scared to!** to face Red.

338:36   **"I'm giving him his chance," he said, in his cold soft voice. "Come on. Make up your mind"**   By this Popeye seems to mean that he is allowing Temple to decide Red's fate. That is, if she goes back in the house and forgets about running off with Red, he lives. If she gets in the car and goes to the Grotto, where she has arranged to meet Red, he dies. Appropriately, the name of this establishment, Grotto, derives from the Latin for *crypta* meaning vault or crypt. Therefore, Temple's choice is a momentous one. See entries 340:10//233:3; 340:32//233:25.

338:39   **daddy**   "Daddy" is slang for an older male lover, a "sugar daddy," usually one who is wealthy or powerful and keeps his younger consort in high style in return for sex or public companionship. Temple's habitual dependence on a male authority figure makes it easy for this substitution to take place. Popeye becomes her "daddy," and she is attempting to sneak away with a "boyfriend" in much the same way she likely did it at home and certainly at school. The identification does, of course, have incestuous sexual overtones. See entry 219:27//59:28.

339:3   **You wont do it. You're afraid to. He's a better man than you are**   Temple justifies her decision. She baits Popeye, provocatively insisting that Red is bigger, stronger (she has just felt Popeye's "frail" arm), "a better man" than Popeye, who will not actually face Red man-to-man.

339:5   **"Where?" he said. "Grotto?"**   Where are you supposed to meet Red? The Grotto is a nightclub-roadhouse.

339:12   **You couldn't fool me but once, could you? No wonder I bled and bluh———**   At the time of Temple's rape, she didn't realize that Popeye was not using his penis. Popeye has subsequently assaulted Temple at Miss Reba's (289:19//159:3) before bringing in Red as surrogate.

339:28   **The ring was like a dentist's instrument**   Earlier, when Dr. Quinn examined Temple, she cried "like a child in a dentist's waiting-room." See entry 283:1//150:7. Popeye's forcing of her mouth links these assaults.°

339:38 **blowing with fireflies** the intermittent glow of the fireflies in the dark.

340:5 **Dont you wish he was the one watching us instead of you?** Temple taunts Popeye with a sexual scenario wherein he is an active performer, but she maintains the triangular nature and the voyeurism of the scene.°

340:10 **I gave you your chance** Temple is repeating Popeye's own words: "I'm giving him his chance" (338:33//231:4). But now she is turning them back on Popeye. She is saying it is Popeye's decision to come to the Grotto; thus, she releases herself of responsibility for what happens.

340:13 **"Shucks," she said, "it didn't leave a mark, even;" drawing the flesh this way and that. "Little runt," she said** Looking in the mirror, Temple unconsciously alludes to the scene of her assault in the bedroom and her rape in the barn among the corn shucks. At this point, Temple is enacting the role of the prostitute, down to the obscene phrase. See entry 340:15//233:8. When she looks in the mirror, that image is what she now sees—a new identity substituted for the old one blotted out during the rape. Given the connection between mouth and vagina in this book, Temple's statement could also mean that her rape has also not left any physical mark on her body.° Popeye is such a "little runt" that he can do no obvious damage to her without the use of some artificial object. Her insult also connects Temple to Little Belle, who has called Horace "Shrimp" (189:19//14:27).

340:15 **She added a phrase, glibly obscene, with a detached parrotlike effect** Temple doesn't fully comprehend the meaning; she is, like a child, parroting the sounds rather than the essence of the words.° This description also casts light on Temple's performance in the courtroom, where she also gives "parrotlike" testimony. The talk is a part of her impersonation of a prostitute, but also suggests that she doesn't fully understand the meaning of her story.°

340:17 **They examined one another's clothes with brief, covert, cold, embracing glances** Even in this alien world Temple sizes up her competition. At the Grotto, she puts herself up against gangsters' molls and professional prostitutes rather than college girls.

340:27 **then her hand flicked toward his armpit** Temple has hidden Popeye's pistol in the room. Now it occurs to her to check his shoulder holster to see if he has another.

340:30 **the rouge spots darkening slowly on her face** Temple's face becomes pale as she realizes Popeye's intentions; the rouge spots appear darker as the blood drains away leaving her pale.

340:32 **"I gave you your chance back there in town," he said. "You took it"** Once again it is *Temple's* chance: that is, she had the choice to make in the first place. Because of her decision to meet Red, his fate has been sealed, and so, according to Popeye, she bears ultimate responsibility for Red's death.

341:13 **the four men** Popeye's men, waiting with him for Red. See entry 380:19//289:21 for parallels to the courtroom scene.

341:31 **her legs felt cold too, like they were not hers. They were sitting at a table** Temple often treats her legs as if they were separate from the rest of her and at fault: "they" get her into trouble. In this passage, the first "they" refers to the legs, the second primarily to Temple and Popeye. See entry 329:7//217:12.

341:40 **He looked like a college boy** This description connects the scene with Temple's earlier behavior at school, where she dates town boys during the week and college boys during the weekend. Here Popeye becomes the town boy and Red the college boy. But now the game is deadly serious.

342:23 **"Give it to me," she whispered** This is a last ditch effort to divert Popeye's attention from Red. Temple means the gun, but she is sexually cajoling him, grinding his shoulder. The pronoun "it" is ambiguous, but given the connection between Popeye's pistol and penis, the provocative request invites a reading in which Temple is asking Popeye to (use the pistol) to arouse her.

342:26 **Suddenly her hand began to steal down his body . . .**

"I forgot," she whispered; "I didn't mean. . . . I didn't . . . ." Temple forgets herself and reaches for Popeye's penis before remembering his impotency: "I didn't mean to touch you there, to remind you of your inadequacy." This movement, however, breaks whatever mood she may have hoped to establish.

342:30 **One of the men at the other table hissed once through his teeth** to alert Popeye that Red is approaching.

342:36 **He was turned a little, facing the two men at the other table** Red is watching Popeye's bodyguards to gauge their reactions to his proximity to their boss.

343:18 **She could hear herself saying I hope it has. I hope it has** Temple hopes to avoid the ugliness of the act. However, as the next lines show, she enjoys the ensuing "bereavement," a self-indulgent display of romantic morbidity.

343:28 **Then she became aware that the orchestra was playing the same tune as when Red was asking her to dance** In her drunkenness, Temple loses track of time. Only a moment has actually passed.

344:8 **The table where the two men had sat was empty** The other two have already gone outside. Caught up entirely in her desire, Temple no longer cares about Popeye's men.

344:13 **She jerked her hand at him; he went out** She signals the waiter and Red comes almost immediately: he has either been sent for or has been watching her, waiting.

344:25 **her mouth gaping in straining protrusion** Temple is apparently preparing to kiss Red, but the overtly grotesque description recalls the image of the "dying fish" gasping out of the water, which also takes us back to the image of "the chemical agony of a world left stark and dying above the tide-edge of the fluid in which it lived and breathed" (332:35//222:14). At this moment, sex and death converge: Temple seems tortured by her passion.

344:27 **It's not my fault. Is it my fault?** that you are likely to get killed if we stay here much longer, but perhaps also that Popeye is not a man and thus can't hold on to her. Temple is responding to Popeye's earlier accusation, "I gave you your chance back there in town . . . . You took it" (340:32// 233:25).

344:33 I told him I was. I said if you bring me here. I gave you your chance I said Temple concocts a version of the things she has supposedly said to Popeye. "I'm leaving you." "If you take me to the Grotto, I'm off with Red." "You've had your chance with me and you've lost it." Clearly some of these statements are implausible.

344:34 And now he's got them there to bump you off Popeye has the four men waiting to kill Red. Temple has picked up underworld slang as part of her new persona.

344:36 Did you know that when you telephoned me? Red wants to know whether Temple was aware of the danger she put him in by setting up this appointment. Obviously Temple was, but didn't care.

344:40 You're a man. You're a man Temple's insistence not only contrasts Red with Popeye, but also harkens back to Ruby's earlier insult that Temple couldn't handle a "real" man. Temple is proving to herself that she can, no matter the cost to others.

345:4 Lifting her bodily he turned so that he faced the door, and slipped his right hand free Red wants to be able to see who comes in; he frees his hand so that he can reach for his gun.

345:7 Dont make me wait. I'm burning up Although Temple is conforming to the "too-hot-to-handle" stereotype, she probably is not suggesting that they have sex in the room. She is, however, begging that they get away from Popeye and *then* have sex. The danger heightens her arousal, but she is also manipulating Red, promising him pleasure in order to get him moving.

345:23 when she found that she was dancing again . . . moving toward the door In her drunkenness, Temple confuses her abduction with the act of dancing. The scene also alludes to her general attitude at college dances, where she passes from one set of arms to another without real recognition of the identities of her partners.

345:40 **"Let it lay," Red said. "I'll pass a million times tonight"** Red is playing craps, a game of dice in which a first throw of seven or eleven wins, but a roll of two, three, or twelve loses the bet. Any other number must be repeated before a seven is thrown. To "pass" is to win a throw. To "crap out" is to lose the bet and the dice. Red is leaving his bet on the table, letting it accumulate with each win. However, both "to pass" and "to crap out" have supplementary meanings of "to die." In *Sanctuary: The Original Text*, Red's awareness of his possible death is underscored: "His face was bold and calm, but there were two white lines at the base of his nostrils and his forehead was damp."°

346:1 **They helped Temple into the car . . . sucked with the profile into darkness by the rush of their passing** The events echo her kidnapping from the Old Frenchman place. In *Requiem for a Nun*, Temple says that Red was "shot from a car while he was slipping up the alley behind the house, to climb up the same drainpipe I could have climbed down at any time and got away, to see me—the one time, the first time, the only time when we thought we had dodged him, fooled him, could be alone together. . . ."° There are other discrepancies between the two books; for example, Temple says that she helped drive Gowan's car when he was too drunk to do it.°

346:6 **The match flipped outward like a dying star in miniature** See Popeye's murder of Tommy: "the sound was no louder than the striking of a match: a short, minor sound shutting down upon the scene, the instant, with a profound finality, completely isolating it" (249:39//102:8).

CHAPTER XXV

347:1 **The tables** the craps tables where Red was playing before his death. Red's funeral is apparently held the day after his murder, Tuesday, June 18.

347:6 **other shapes of ceremonial mortality** displays, probably floral (347:7//242:7), associated with the funeral ceremony.

347:7 **the mass appeared to break in a symbolical wave** of flowers. The flowers are banked to a crest, symbolizing a cascade, like an ocean wave. Faulkner underscores the ostentatiousness of the ceremony.

347:8 **bier** the stand, supported by the trestles, holding the coffin. Faulkner will pun on the word before the scene is out. See entry 350:16//247:6.

347:14 **They moved . . . a little febrile** The waiters recognize the solemnity of the occasion, even take pride in being a part of it. Nevertheless, although the nightclub is decorated and disguised, the raucousness underneath waits to break through.

347:20 **the men in dark suits of decorous restraint, others in the light, bright shades of spring** Some of the mourners attending the funeral dress appropriately; others, perhaps actual customers, unintentionally mock the decorum of the occasion by dressing in party clothes. Faulkner misses few opportunities to portray such desecrations in *Sanctuary*. In one sense, the riotous funeral anticipates the equally-mocking trial yet to come.°

347:24 **matronly figures resembling housewives on a Sunday afternoon excursion** another connection drawn between "proper" and "improper" society. The madams, like Miss Reba, could possibly be mistaken for respectable housewives after church.

347:28 **their white jackets and black shirts resembling photograph negatives** In a negative, dark and light are reversed. Ordinarily, one would expect to see dark jackets and white shirts. Also, a white face would appear dark in a negative. By this reversal or contrast, Faulkner might also be commenting once again on the essential similarities between the two societies depicted in this book, one the dark reversal of the other.

347:32 **bullet-headed** The man has short-cropped hair and his head comes to a point. See description of Uncle Bud at 352:18//250:3 and of the Negro at 367:25//271:8.

347:34 **like a cocoon** The large bouncer threatens to burst through his tight jacket as a moth forces its way through a cocoon.

347:37 **a fat man .... His face gleamed with moisture** Gene's description bears close resemblance to Clarence Snopes, who has clear connections with this realm of society. See entry 307:34//186:15.

348:8 **him** Red.

348:26 **the Blue Danube** Famous waltz by Austrian composer Johann Strauss (1825–1899), who was known as the "King of the Waltz."° The band leader apparently considers the waltz a sophisticated choice for the occasion.

348:27 **dont play no blues** In this broad joke, the proprietor confuses the title of the waltz with the generic concept of "the blues," which is jazzier (although essentially melancholy) in tempo and sound and usually played in quadruple meter (4/4) rather than triple meter (3/4).

348:28 **There's a dead man in that bier** Red is actually *in* the coffin, which is *on* the bier. Faulkner is preparing for the joke to follow. See entry 350:16//247:6.

348:32 **A wop? ... Like hell. Red was an American** A "wop" is a derogatory name for an Italian. The proprietor, recognizing the name as foreign, nevertheless confuses Strauss's nationality.

348:34 **Play I Cant Give You Anything but Love. He always liked that** "I Can't Give You Anything but Love" was written by Jimmy McHugh and was included in the Broadway musical

Blackbirds (1928).° It is interesting that Red, a tough gangster, should like this song, for it is sentimental and sweet, but Faulkner also emphasizes the maudlin in his later description of the three madams. (Recall as well Popeye's devotion to his mother.)

348:38 **Nearer, My God, To Thee** This Protestant hymn, words by Sarah Flower Adams (1805–1848) and music by Lowell Mason (1792–1872), commemorates the martyrdom of the third Christian female saint. Played at Red's wake, it is to remind the guests that they are present at what should be a solemn ritual of death.°

349:13 **Little Rock** Little Rock, Arkansas, 150 miles west of Memphis.

349:21 **In That Haven of Rest** This Anglican Hymn, "The Haven of Rest," was composed by George D. Moore and begins with "My soul in sad exile."°

350:16 **"Beer?" Gene said. "Beer . . . . Is anybody here trying to insult me by———** Gene mistakes "bier" for "beer" and is outraged that a cheap, common drink would be served at Red's funeral.

350:20 **Joe** the proprietor. Faulkner used a character named Joe as a bootlegger in his early sketches "Country Mice" and "Once Aboard the Lugger (I)." Also, in *Mosquitoes*, the gangster Pete (a prototype for Popeye) has an older brother named Joe.

350:33 **mother songs** emotional, sentimental songs which run to bathos. The subject was usually the relationship between a mother and her son: Al Jolson's "Mammy," for example. See 350:34//247:25.

350:34 **Sonny Boy** a mother song, written by B. G. DeSylva, Lew Brown, and Ray Henderson sung by Al Jolson in the film *The Singing Fool* (1928).°

351:12 **He felled the first and whirled and sprang . . . with its face in the center of the wreath** There is a strong element of slapstick, of silent film comic exaggeration, in these antics. Faulkner keeps his readers off balance with the black comedy, preparing for the shock and horror of the tumbling corpse.

351:33 **the snap in the peak** a snap-fastener by which the cloth over the forehead could be fastened to the peak of the cap.°

351:38 **the type rented by the hour by the better class agencies** These cars are rented for the occasion of Red's funeral. However, we do know that Popeye himself owns a touring car (346:3//240:29), so other gangsters might own them as well.

352:1 **taxis, roadsters, sedans** Ferrying the less important members of the procession. A roadster is smaller and less expensive than a touring car, holding two or three people; it has a convertible top (like the touring car). A sedan is closed with two or four doors.

352:10 **each carrying no occupant save the liveried driver** The cars have been rented to carry the ostentatious displays of flowers to the cemetery.

352:16 **a thin woman in sober, severe clothes and gold noseglasses** later identified as Miss Lorraine.

352:17 **a short plump woman in a plumed hat, her face hidden by a handkerchief** later identified as Miss Myrtle.

352:18 **a small bullet-headed boy of five or six** Uncle Bud, as the boy is named, is another pathetic child in *Sanctuary*. He prefigures the character of Otis in *The Reivers*. Both Otis and Bud are from Arkansas, and both are sneaky and underhanded.

352:29 **"Didn't he look sweet?" she wailed. "Didn't he look sweet!"** See Temple's envisioning of her own funeral, with "all the people sitting around the coffin, saying Dont she look sweet. Dont she look sweet" (330:32//219:19).

353:5 **You bite me, you thon bitch** Uncle Bud warns the dog: "Don't you bite me, you son of a bitch."

353:11 **The other woman ... looked like a school-teacher** The cliché of sweet respectability has been complicated by Temple's account of the teacher and her potential for authority and invulnerability. See Temple's fantasy: "I'd talk to him like the teacher does in school, and then . . . I was the teacher" (330:40//219:26).

353:19 **with round cornflower eyes** See Benjy in *The Sound and the Fury*: "his eyes were clear, of the pale sweet blue of cornflowers. . . . "°

353:22 **"We all got to suffer it," Miss Reba said. "Well, may it be a long day."** We all have to die one day, but may it be a long time in coming.

353:28 **I always say it's the greatest pleasure I have to call on Miss Reba** Calling on Miss Reba is the thing in life Miss Myrtle enjoys most, but the "it" could also refer to the good beer Miss Reba serves, which would then change Miss Myrtle's meaning to "What I most enjoy about calling on Miss Reba is the chance to drink her beer."

353:33 **How long's he going to be with you, Miss Myrtle?** The relationship between Miss Myrtle and Uncle Bud is not made clear. There is no reason to assume that he is her uncle, despite the designation (like the use of "Miss," which should denote virginity, or at least singleness, for the three madams); nor is it likely that he is her child. In *The Reivers*, Otis is the nephew of Everbe Corinthia, one of Miss Reba's prostitutes. See entry 325:13//212:2.

353:39 **them two nice young fellows** Virgil and Fonzo.

354:4 **to stop the girls running around the house without no clothes on, and they dont like it** The girls don't like it, but Virgil and Fonzo probably don't like the change either. Miss Reba's concern for the boys' innocence is, of course, comic, but it also reflects on her different attitude towards Temple: she has helped to initiate the girl into the world of "meanness," although, as she later told Horace, "She wasn't born for this kind of life" (331:31//220:28).

354:18 **It must have cost a good piece of jack** jack = money. The slang is especially funny coming from the proper-looking Miss Lorraine.

354:24 **looked at it** at the tankard.

354:27 **Aint you ashamed?** See Popeye to Temple: "Aint you ashamed of yourself?" (274:35//139:1).

355:9 **Miss Myrtle's took again** Miss Myrtle has lost her composure and is weeping, once again. Miss Lorraine says this to Miss Reba, in effect trying to hurry her along with the gin to calm down Miss Myrtle.

355:12 **She groped for a moment, then it touched her hand** The tankard is not where she set it down. Uncle Bud has moved it in order to sneak a drink. Perhaps it touches her hand as he replaces it or as she reaches toward a new position.

355:25 **"It's us girls," Miss Myrtle said. . . . "Expect us not to never look at another man, while they come and go as they please"** Miss Myrtle's comment is on the general fate of women, but also to Temple's specific arrangement with Popeye and Red.

355:32 **a free-hearted spender that never give her a hour's uneasiness or a hard word** Miss Reba will shortly contradict herself (356:33//256:5), but the scene is full of sentimental drunkenness, not logical discourse.

355:39 **He was such a good man** Miss Reba begins to think of Mr. Binford, her late consort.

356:2 **It's when it comes over me like this** When I remember Mr. Binford, I am overcome with grief.

356:4 **He never had no more than Mr Binford had** no more flowers at his funeral.

356:11 **Where you reckon they went, Miss Reba?** The ladies assume that Popeye escaped with Temple after he killed Red.

356:15 **"He goes all the way to Pensacola every summer to see his mother," Miss Myrtle said. "A man that'll do that cant be all bad"** Pensacola is located on the Gulf Coast in extreme west Florida, approximately 350 miles from Memphis. Miss Myrtle is still under the sentimental influences of the mother songs sung at Red's funeral. Still, she has a point. Popeye, in his devotion to his mother, serves as the bankrupt illustration of yet another institution whose appearances have replaced reality—the family and its preservation of values.

356:19 **Me trying to run a respectable house, that's been running a shooting-gallery for twenty years, and him trying to turn it into a peep-show** A shooting-gallery would indicate normal sexual activity wherein men pay to have sex with the women. This slang makes explicit connections between guns and penises. A peep-show, wherein customers pay to watch others have sex (with themselves, other partners of either sex, animals, etc.), is nowhere nearly as respectable on this continuum of perversion. One of the reasons Miss Reba is so angry at Popeye is that he has damaged the reputation of her house.

356:24 **I heard two years ago that he wasn't no good that way** that Popeye was impotent or sexually dysfunctional.

356:26 **I knew it all the time** This would not seem to be true, based on what Miss Reba has earlier said to Temple and Horace. She is saving face as best she can, given the shame Popeye has brought on her house.

356:28 **It's against nature** Miss Reba is being (intentionally or not) ironic: no man would treat a woman well unless he was getting sex from her.

356:33 **The clothes and jewelry that girl bought . . . Having the front of my house watched like it was a. . . . . . .** Recollections of Popeye's stake-out triggers Miss Reba's indignation; ironically, she resents her house being treated like it's a tawdry site for illicit activity. Miss Reba contradicts her earlier romantic description of Popeye and Temple's relationship. She is now retelling the events of Temple's last night, described in Chapter XXIV. Although Popeye manhandles Temple, we never actually see him hit her, so this may be strictly Miss Reba's spicy narrative offering.

357:16 **She laid the other hand to her flat spinster's breast** Faulkner is not saying that Miss Lorraine is a spinster; rather that she has the flat chest associated with the archetypal spinster. Miss Myrtle is once again reminding Miss Reba of the promise of gin under the pretext of concern for Miss Lorraine.

357:24 **First thing I knowed was when Minnie told me there was something funny going on** another contradiction. "I knew it all the time," Miss Reba said earlier (356:26//255:28).

357:3   **Where's my———— beer.**

357:27 **no signs at all the next morning when she cleaned up** no physical evidence that sexual intercourse had taken place in Temple's bed.

357:31 **and she'd get mad and lock the door and wouldn't even let him in** This detail clarifies Temple's degree of control in this relationship. If she can't leave, she at least has the power to lock the door.

357:34 **monkey glands** Dr. Serge Voronoff, Director of Experimental Surgery, Station Physiologique du College de France (Paris), sought to renew sexual prowess by grafting the testicles of monkeys onto human subjects. Dr. Eugen Steinach also performed similar experiments. The topic provided material for jokes during the 1920s.°

358:13 **turn a stud in to your girl** Miss Reba uses the language of husbandry, indicating that Popeye employed Red as stud service for Temple, although not for purposes of impregnation. See 358:25//258:20 and 358:33//258:29 for continuation of the imagery.

358:15 **French joint** a French whorehouse where more unusual sexual practices putatively take place. The question of propriety and appearance continues to be all-important to Miss Reba and her establishment.

358:23 **Every morning for four days that was going on, then they didn't come back** If the week Popeye is absent ends on June 17, the day he takes Temple to the Grotto and kills Red, then the four days would be June 6–9, after Horace's visit on June 3. On the last day, Reba tells Popeye to take Temple and leave. On June 10 Horace calls to check on Temple and Miss Reba offers to "turn them both out on the street and you can have them arrested there." See entry 365:21//286:12.

358:28 **And me trying to get word to him to come and take her out of my house because I didn't want nuttin like that going on in it** one of several instances in which Miss Reba echoes Narcissa in her priorities: "The house where my father and mother and your father and mother, the house where I———I wont have it. I wont have it" (260:32//118:12).

358:35 **Maybe he was cheering for them** as if they were horses running a race.

359:4 **Minnie swung him sharply away from her as he began to vomit** Uncle Bud is sick to his stomach, like Gowan and Horace previously. At the beginning of the next chapter, Horace will be recovering from his own bout of nausea. Noel Polk has argued that the Uncle Bud episode is "a kind of parable of Horace's own childhood [especially in *Sanctuary: The Original Text*], if not actually a dream's distorted representation of it."°

CHAPTER XXVI

360:1 **When the sun rose** Tuesday, June 4. This is the day after Horace visits Miss Reba's brothel and talks to Temple (see Chapter XXIII). See entry 306:5//260:5.

360:5 **feeling quiet and empty for the first time since he had found Popeye watching him across the spring** Horace vomited at the end of Chapter XXIII, and now feels, both physically and emotionally, that he is prepared to settle the various conflicts in his personal and professional lives; with his new resolve, he finally writes Belle asking for the divorce and anticipates winning his court case.

360:7 **four weeks ago** Horace meets Popeye on Tuesday, May 7, at the spring, exactly four weeks earlier.

360:9 **I am too old for this** By "this," Horace means not only the horrors of the trial and Temple's abduction, but also the horrors of his own self-discoveries.

360:10 **so I am sick to death for quiet** anticipates Horace's later realization, "Less oft is peace." See entry 386:38//300:9.

360:19 **I reckon you was settled for the night, maybe?** Snopes slyly suggests that Horace decided to take advantage of Miss Reba's business as long as he was there.

360:33 **The only place he did not investigate . . . Eustace Graham** This is the place Horace should have first looked, another example of his missing the obvious. The District Attorney generally serves the role of prosecutor in state cases. Since Tommy's murder occurred in Yoknapatawpha County, it is Graham's duty to develop the case against Lee Goodwin. Narcissa has waited a week before contacting Eustace, possibly giving Horace time to change his mind. However, the call from Clarence

Snopes and Horace's subsequent trip to Memphis apparently spurs her into final action. See 362:29//264:10.

360:37 **Graham had a club foot** a congenital deformity which sometimes results in the foot looking like a club. Literary sources suggest themselves in this deformity: a boy with a club foot appears in *Madame Bovary*; the crippled king of Thebes in *Oedipus Rex*; and the cloven hoof of the devil, an image Faulkner also used to describe Ab Snopes in "Barn Burning."°

361:24 **It was in the poker game . . . "I pass, Eustace"** The poker game is a simpler version of the sort Faulkner later devised in *Go Down, Moses*. Mr. Harris obviously has a good hand since he is Eustace's "only remaining opponent." When Eustace bets the entire amount of Mr. Harris's earnings, $42, Mr. Harris realizes that Eustace is determined to break him in the game. Still, there is the possibility of a bluff. Eustace has, after all, drawn three cards, indicating that his initial hand was likely not that strong and the odds are against his drawing into a winning hand. But when Mr. Harris learns that Eustace himself dealt the cards, he passes; that is, he forfeits the money he has already bet because he assumes that Eustace has dishonestly given himself the winning hand.

361:39 **he would announce for Congress on his record of convictions** Eustace has a great deal riding on Goodwin's trial, which, at this time, is only for the murder of Tommy. Because Eustace is politically ambitious, he poses a real threat to Senator Clarence Snopes, who has already told Horace, "Between you and me, I'd like to see a good lawyer make a monkey outen that District Attorney. Give a fellow like that a little county office and he gits too big for his pants right away" (308:21// 187:14). With these concerns, Snopes would not be likely to go to Graham with his information on Temple. See entry 363:25// 265:18.

362:4 **a brother-in-arms** a fellow lawyer.

362:6 **even when it does seem. . . . . . .** rather useless to try a man for the killing of a nobody like Tommy. Or perhaps Eustace is also insincerely apologizing for having to best Narcissa's brother in the court of law.

362:10 **Of course, you cant expect——** Horace not to try his best to win the case.
362:12 **Naturally, I——** am confident I will win the case.
362:13 **I suppose you know things about it that he doesn't** Perhaps this is Narcissa's way of telling Eustace that there is more to the case than he is aware of. And Eustace is alert enough to pick up on her hint. See 362:20//264:1.
362:20 **We happen to know that the man is guilty** Eustace is bluffing. Since Goodwin did not kill Tommy, they have no murder weapon, and they do not at this time have Temple to tell her story, all of their evidence is circumstantial. Goodwin's refusal to talk helps but does not prove their case.
362:24 **his business is to——** to win. Since Horace's reputation will be hurt by this foregone loss, Eustace suggests it would be better if he withdrew before the trial started. Horace has plenty of reasons to excuse himself.
362:29 **Three nights ago** It was actually two nights ago, Sunday, June 2. The next day Horace goes to Memphis.
362:38 **clumsy clog-step** A clog-dance is characterized by heavy stamping of feet. Eustace, because of his club foot, undoubtedly wears a special built-up shoe which resembles a clog. His dance step is performed out of joy since Narcissa has given him a much-needed lead in his case.
362:39 **he snapped his hands toward his tie** to hide the excited movement of snapping his fingers. Eustace succeeds by hiding his emotions (as in the poker game), but Narcissa sees right through his pretenses.
363:2 **Court opens the twentieth** In 1929, this would be on a Thursday. Cleanth Brooks argues that the court actually opens on June 10, that the first week and a half are then devoted to impaneling a grand jury, receiving the indictment, impaneling a trial jury, and disposing of all civil cases. The 20th would be the date that Goodwin's actual trial would begin. Brooks also points out that in Lafayette County, court traditionally opened on the second Monday, which, for June 1929, would be the 10th.°
363:4 **I need not assure you that this will be held in strictest**

confidence between us. . . . . . . the fact that Narcissa has brought information to Graham. Like Clarence Snopes with Horace, Eustace creates a sense of conspiracy with Narcissa. But unlike Horace, Narcissa is impervious to such attempts. See 363:16//265:9.

363:8   **That will be the twenty-fourth**   the following Monday. Narcissa is taking the weekend into account.

363:10   **That night she wrote Belle that Horace would be home on the twenty-fourth**   Thus Belle should receive Horace's letter asking for a divorce and Narcissa's letter that Horace is coming home at just about the same time, maybe a day apart.

363:20   **Two days before it opened**   The "it" must be Goodwin's trial itself, since the previous sentence is "He did not see her again before the trial opened." If so, then this event occurs on Tuesday, June 18, one day after Red is murdered.

363:25   **Got hit by a car in Jackson**   On June 4, Snopes tells Horace that he is "Going down to Jackson for a couple of days on a little business" (360:17//261:8). The implication is that he intends to sell Judge Drake information about Temple's whereabouts. Now, two weeks later, Snopes has a black eye, bruised nose, and teeth problems. The roll of bills would suggest that he was successful in his dealings with Judge Drake, as he was with Horace. But the question is, who beats him up? He implies that it happens in Jackson, where the Drakes live, but he also inveighs against the Memphis Jew lawyer. The most likely answer is that Eustace Graham (the one person Snopes would *not* be likely to approach with the information), following up on Narcissa's lead, has contacted his own sources in Memphis. Among these sources is the "jew lawyer," very likely the same lawyer who later shows up at the trial sitting by Graham on the same day Temple appears to testify against Goodwin (375:5//281:26). This is apparently the same Memphis lawyer who visits Popeye in his Alabama jail cell after his arrest (396:25//314:6). This connection would suggest that Eustace learns about Temple through the lawyer. Popeye already knows that Snopes has information on Temple—he catches him looking in the keyhole near the first of the month (323:10//209:8). The Memphis lawyer would want to know *what* Clarence has told both Horace and Judge Drake, how much actual information they have about Temple and Popeye, so that he can complete the frame on Goodwin. The "ten dollars" he gives Clarence, after he has him roughed up, is a double insult.

363:26 **But dont think I never made the bastard pay** Snopes's colloquial double negative can be translated: "Dont for a minute think," he brags, "that the man who hit me with his car got off without making financial restitution." The double negative reinforces the rhetorical understatement of Snopes's brag since, in fact, he was outfinessed.

363:29 **notecase** a billfold.

363:34 **We need laws against them. Drastic laws** Snopes echoes the "There ought to be a law" sentiment pronounced by Popeye, Ruby, and Horace. Given the failure of law throughout the book, and Snopes's own perversion of the legal system, his rant, like Popeye's earlier comment, is ironic.

364:3 **a judge living in the capital of the State of Mississippi and a lawyer that's going to be as big a man as his pa some day, and a judge too** The first reference is to Judge Drake of Jackson. The second is to Horace, whom Snopes constantly addresses as "Judge." Snopes says that Horace will one day, like his deceased father, be a judge and is hoping to flatter with his prediction.

364:13 **"What was you trying to sell to that car when it run over you?" the barber said** The barber jokes that Snopes has confused his two stories, shifting from Jackson to Memphis. Snopes then ends the conversation.

CHAPTER XXVII

365:1 **The trial was set for the twentieth of June** a Thursday. See entry 363:2//264:24. There Eustace says "Court opens"; here, the "trial was set"; and later, "The trial opened" (366:4//296:3).

365:1 **A week after his Memphis visit, Horace telephoned Miss Reba** Horace made the visit to Miss Reba's on June 3. This call is probably made on June 10, at which time Temple still remains at the house.

365:8 **"It'll be only a bailiff," Horace said. "Someone to hand a paper into her own hand"** The bailiff is a court official who has the power to serve warrants and summons. Horace would send the bailiff to call Temple to court as his witness in the trial. The summons would have to be handed directly to Temple. When Temple does appear in court, however, it is not as Horace's witness, and she seems to have been brought to the trial by extra-legal means.

365:12 **full-blowed cop** "Full-blown" means fully developed, displaying all the significant characteristics. Here it means a policeman dressed in his uniform. Such a sight, Miss Reba suggests, could frighten away her customers.

365:21 **jay cops** "Jay" means hick or rustic; thus, an official from Yoknapatawpha County, who might not know how to behave, who might not appreciate the understanding Miss Reba has with the local authorities.

365:21 **You telephone me and I'll turn them both out on the street and you can have them arrested there** "Them" refers to Temple and Popeye. By now Miss Reba knows the reason Popeye keeps Temple in the house and why Popeye brought

Red to the room, a situation of which she disapproves. See entry 358.23. She is more than willing to get them out of her establishment, even to the point of setting up an arrest, since she doesn't like business troubles or "unnatural" brothel practices.

365:24 **On the night of the nineteenth** a Wednesday. This is two days after Popeye kills Red, one day after Red's funeral, one day after Clarence Snopes appears beaten up in Jefferson, and one day before the beginning of Lee Goodwin's trial. One might question Horace's judgment in waiting so near to the beginning of the trial to check on his witness. If these calculations are correct, he has let nine days pass since last calling Miss Reba. Perhaps he is fearful of tipping his hand, and Miss Reba has told him to keep his distance, but he is aware that Clarence Snopes is not to be trusted and should be alert for that reason alone.

365:25 **He had some trouble in getting in touch with her** Miss Reba clearly no longer wants to talk to Horace. She has now gotten rid of Temple and Popeye (they apparently leave on the 17th, after Red's murder) and does not want to be further involved in what has become, especially with Red's death, a very ugly and potentially dangerous situation.

365:26 **"They're gone," she said. "Both of them. Dont you read no papers?"** Miss Reba does not specifically say that Temple has left with Popeye but implies that Horace would have known as much if he had kept up with the events in Memphis, Popeye's murder of Red in particular. But Horace need not have connected Red's murder to Popeye (or Temple). He visits Temple on the 3rd, Popeye brings Red for the first time on the 6th, Horace calls on the 10th but there is no evidence that Miss Reba tells him anything, although Minnie apparently told Miss Reba what was going on and Miss Reba put a stop to it by confronting Popeye on the 9th. See entry 358:23//258:19. There is no evidence that Popeye is even suspected in Red's murder, but Miss Reba might be suggesting that names were cited in the paper.

365:32 I may need her Horace still plans to use Temple only as a last resort to save Goodwin. Ostensibly, he does not want to expose her unnecessarily to public shame. Since the charge is still murder, if Temple comes in, then the whole question of rape possibly enters into it and thus complicates Horace's case. So Horace, in fact, plays it smart, just as he is apparently keeping his own earlier involvement with Lee and Ruby quiet. We don't actually know whether or in what detail Temple described the rape to Horace. He seems as shocked and horrified by the corncob as the other courtroom observers. In *Sanctuary: The Original Text*, when Horace hears Temple has left he thinks, "'Thank God. . . . Better that he should hang [. . .] than to expose . . . . than to expose . . . . I cannot even face the picture,' he told himself."°

365:34 He heard the receiver thud onto the table . . . the wire clicked in his ear Miss Reba fumbles the receiver in an attempt to hang up. Horace can hear her call for Minnie before she, or Minnie, replaces the receiver and disconnects the line. Since Horace does not also hang up, the long distance operator comes onto the line (Horace is calling from Jefferson to Memphis).

366:2 detached Delsarteish voice Francois Delsarte (1811–1871), the inventor of a program of elocution exercises. The long distance operator is speaking in an artificial, affected manner, as evidenced by Faulkner's representation of her words. See 366:3//269:2.

366:3 Pine Bluff dizzent. . . . Enkyew! Pine Bluff, Arkansas, is the next big city to Memphis and thus on the long distance relay. "Pine Bluff doesn't answer. . . . Thank you."

366:4 On the table lay the sparse objects . . . a stoneware jug containing corn whiskey Eustace is offering evidence related to Tommy's murder and Lee's moonshining, not sufficient in Horace's mind to require Temple to testify. He still feels the burden of proof is on the prosecution and the evidence displayed remains circumstantial.

366:9 the child lying on her lap a possible play for sympathy on Horace's part, emphasizing the mother and child. However, the defense attorney will use the common law marriage against Goodwin in cross examination.

366:10 **She repeated the story as she had told it to him on the day after the child was ill** It isn't clear whether Ruby actually testifies in court about Temple at the Old Frenchman place. If she were to repeat the story exactly as she told Horace, the girl's role must be included, although she need not be identified (Ruby does know who Temple is; see entry 215:22//54:12). Moreover, since Ruby was not at the house when the murder took place, what exact defense can she give for Goodwin? She cannot swear that he didn't do it, but she *can* testify that she saw Popeye and the girl leave together, that she and Goodwin did call the police, that Popeye is a known gangster, that Goodwin had no motive to kill Tommy, and that Popeye possibly did.

366:14 **She sat erect in the chair ... the purple ornament on her shoulder** Compare to description of Temple when she testifies. See entry 376:21//284:12. Ruby is clothed to look poor but honest, respectable. Temple will appear in Beale Street finery, but both women wear a similar "purple ornament."

366:31 **I waive, your Honor** Graham does not contest Horace's objection to the question. His goal is to thwart Ruby's credibility, and his question fuels the prejudices of the jury and turns the presence of the child against Ruby. Horace's vigorous objection, however, shows that at this point in the trial, at least, he is still attempting to be an effective defense lawyer.

366:33 **Goodwin said bitterly: "Well, you've said you would kill me someday, but I didn't think you meant it"** Goodwin directs this to Ruby. Goodwin believes that if Ruby has implicated Popeye as the murderer, she has made it inevitable that Popeye will kill him in revenge.

367:5 **Dont you see how that explodes their case?** It is unclear how Ruby's testimony could have had this effect. She can say that she saw Popeye leaving, but how can she know that this is before or after Tommy's murder? Popeye has already told her that he was leaving on Sunday (185:20//9:25), has already established his alibi. Unless she mentions the girl, her story would seem to carry relatively little weight. Horace's confidence may serve to bolster her, but is unwarranted.

367:6 **The best they can hope for now is a hung jury** A mistrial would be declared if the jury cannot agree unanimously either to acquit or convict. The prosecution could then decide whether or not to retry. Horace seems so certain of victory at this point that he considers the hung jury to be the prosecutor's best hope

367:11 **Tonight?** Ruby seems surprised by the timing, though she is planning to pay Horace with sex. Horace, however, has not yet made that connection and, as he explains, is concerned with preparing her for a possible cross examination. Ruby must wonder whether Horace isn't rushing things a bit, but actually, if Horace *were* expecting sex, it would make sense to do it before Lee was released from prison. Horace has predicted that "he'll walk out of that jail tomorrow a free man." See entry 370:22//275:14.

367:31 **Where the good folks live** The mad woman speaks like a Shakespearean fool in this scene. Given *Sanctuary*'s examination of moral bankruptcy, this assertion is appropriate. Goodwin is innocent of this crime, and the jailer and his wife are among the few Jeffersonians to show Ruby any kindness.

367:31 **When you get a husband, keep him in jail where he cant bother you** One wonders how Horace reacts to this statement and its applicability to his own life. See Horace's last scene in the book (Chap. XXX), in which he, at Belle's orders, locks himself in the house with her, shuts the door to future escape. It further suggests that once the husband is locked up, the wife can do as she pleases.

367:33 **a small flask** The old lady sells magic potions and spells (317:2//200:2).

368:2 **Why not get into the corner, and we'll put the mattress over you** Horace sarcastically suggests that Goodwin should hide in the corner covered by the mattress to avoid being shot by Popeye. Horace doesn't feel that Popeye is a real threat.

368:5   **You promised I wouldn't hang, didn't you?**   Goodwin thinks that Popeye will shoot him before the courts can hang him.

368:10   **I know that he and I are fools, but I expected better of you**   Horace is making a gender joke here, indicating that males are basically simple but that Ruby, as a woman, should have more intrinsic wisdom. For another example of Horace's stereotyping of women, see entry 370:17//275:9.

368:22   **I reckon I better stay**   Ruby must think that the main reason Horace wants her to leave is so that he might have sex for his payment. Her going to the jail and wanting to stay there is a sign of her primary loyalty to Lee.

368:31   **his brown wrists folded into the faded sleeves of his shirt**   He has his arms crossed (369:27//274:6).

368:35   **They'd know you never had the guts to kill anybody**   Horace is trying to shame Lee out of his supposed paranoia. As Ruby told Temple, Goodwin has already killed another soldier over a native woman, although Horace probably does not know it. (Neither do we know whether Eustace Graham has this information and is prepared to use it.)

368:38   **We could sleep here, if there wasn't so much noise going on**   Horace's constant talking rather than jail noise, probably. Goodwin is nothing if not sardonic.

369:10   **the bottle was gone**   Ruby is warming it beneath her legs (369:30//274:9).

369:33   **Shall we lay him down?**   him = Goodwin, who has gone to sleep sitting up in the chair.

369:38   **the imaginary scene**   the cross examination likely to occur the next day.

369:39   **If he should ask you anything you cant answer in the exact words you've learned tonight, just say nothing for a moment**   Horace is drilling Ruby in her answers, a common legal tactic, one that is probably being used on Temple as well. See entry 377:34//286:2. He is saying that if Ruby becomes confused, she should wait for Horace to intervene, deflect the question in some way.

370:17   **O tempora! O mores! O hell!**   Horace quotes the Roman orator Cicero—"O, what times! O, what standards!" from *In Catilinam*), adding his own conclusion. He is expressing his utter exasperation with Ruby and, by the extension he then makes, with all women—"stupid mammals"—who expect the worst from men.

370:19 **that any man, every man———— doesn't have sex in mind for everything he does.**

370:22 **It wouldn't have done you any good if you hadn't waited** Ruby is not "stupid" enough to pay Horace for his services until that service has been performed.

371:9 **When they knew he was guilty** Goodwin was clearly guilty of murdering the soldier (219:3//59:4). He is innocent of murdering Tommy.

372:2 **And this is the sort of animal I wasted a year over. I guess that was why I didn't** Ruby chooses not to "let go, go on with him [the pawing soldier], get drunk and never sober up again." The pronoun "this" refers to the drunken soldier, who reminds her of Goodwin in the worst way. To go with the soldier would be no better than to stay with Lee.

372:6 **trying to make me** trying to talk her into having sex with them.

372:10 **Childs'** Childs' was a chain of restaurants. F. Scott Fitzgerald mentions Childs' in his short story "May Day."°

372:11 **We didn't know that a lawyer couldn't do anything for a federal prisoner** By "federal prisoner," Ruby means a prisoner under military justice. In court martial proceedings the defendant would normally be represented by a military lawyer, not a civilian one.

372:20 **I was at the ship to meet him** in New York. Ruby has traveled across the continent, from San Francisco to New York, to be with Goodwin.

372:22 **for killing that soldier three years ago** Lee comes back after the Armistice in 1918. Therefore, he must have killed the other soldier in 1915.

372:22 **Then I got a lawyer to get a Congressman to get him out** The suggestion is that the lawyer bribes or unduly influences the Congressman, thus revealing the spread of corruption up the ladder of authority.

373:8 **"You've certainly done enough not to miss it," Horace said. "I suppose you'll believe us, after this."** "It" must refer to "nightmare" or to the fate Goodwin has projected for himself. Horace means that Goodwin has devoted himself to nightmare scenarios long enough and has gone out of his way to condemn himself in the trial, both by refusing to testify and (although Horace still discounts the possibility) by making himself available to Popeye. Horace hopes that, after the trial is over and Goodwin is set free, he will then see that his fears are unfounded. By saying "us," however, Horace is assuming Ruby's agreement, although it seems likely that Ruby has accepted Lee's fate.

373:12 **do you think for one minute that man is going to let me walk out of that door and up the street and into that courthouse, after yesterday?** Now that Ruby has, apparently, revealed Popeye's presence at Goodwin's place, Lee assumes that Popeye expects Lee to give more evidence about Popeye in order to save himself.

373:14 **What sort of men have you lived with all your life? In a nursery? I wouldn't do that, myself** Goodwin's question echoes Horace's earlier question to Ruby: "What kind of men have you known?" (371:6//276:8). He turns the question right back on Horace. But the question also recalls Ruby's challenge to Temple at the Old Frenchman place: "Man? You've never seen a real man. You dont know what it is to be wanted by a real man" (219:21//59:22). Like Temple, Horace has been "playing at it." As Goodwin's "nursery" comment suggests, Horace is just as innocent and perhaps even infantile as Temple herself. As Goodwin suggests, a "real" man would certainly kill another to protect himself, and Popeye is, in this sense at least, a "real" man.

373:17 **If he does, he has sprung his own trap** If Popeye does kill Goodwin, then he will surely hang for the murder. See entry 398:4//316:8.

373:20 **the next time you want to play dice with a man's neck** The image of "playing at it" continues here. Goodwin finally confronts Horace with his inadequacy, declaring that Horace is simply too naive to be gambling with ruthless professionals for Lee's life. See Red's final moments at the crap table, entry 345:40//240:26.

373:29 **Just tell that goddamned deputy not to walk too close to me** because he might be hit accidentally by a bullet aimed at Goodwin.

373:37 **jim-jams** nervous agitation; the "willies."

374:1 **They walked on in the fresh sunlight . . . long since fallen** Once again, nature is deceptive, lulling Horace into a false belief in goodness, rightness. The scene is similar to the Sunday morning at the Old Frenchman place. With the coming of daylight, people should be safe; but in both cases, this proof of security is proven false.

374:6 **I've been paid** by the greater awareness of life, perhaps of himself, that he has gathered through this experience. Horace thinks that he is about to prove himself a man, a successful lawyer who sees to it that justice is done. His first 43 years have been "an apprenticeship," but now he feels ready to take on a grown man's job.

374:8 **Forty-three years. Half again as long as you have lived** Thus Horace surmises that Ruby is in her early thirties. She would have been in her teens when she met Goodwin.

374:11 **And you know that he———that———** "He" is ambiguous. Ruby may be asking whether Horace really knows that Goodwin will be found innocent and released. Or "he" may refer to Popeye, in which case Ruby is asking whether Horace knows for a fact that Popeye will not be coming to Jefferson to kill Lee, that she has done the correct thing in testifying as she has.

374:12 **We dreamed that away, too. God is foolish at times, but at least He's a gentleman** Horace assures Ruby that a guilty verdict is as unlikely as Lee's fears that Popeye will kill him. That is, foolish, inexplicable things happen in life, but goodness finally wins out.

374:14 **"I always thought of Him as a man," the woman said** For Ruby men have always been cruel, demanding, unfair. She expects no more from God.

374:23 **bald heads . . . a sunbonnet or a flowered hat** Faulkner makes a distinction between the countrymen with shaggy or recently-cut hair (which reveals their red necks) and the slick, oiled hair of the townsmen, who wear shirts with collars. Although women are present, the audience is largely male.

374:31 **that unmistakable odor of courtrooms** The courtroom, like the brothel, has its own particular smell.

374:33 **and withal a certain clumsy stability in lieu of anything better** The whole book is an outcry against the complete failure of the legal system, yet Horace, at this point, still believes that justice works in its own graceless fashion.

375:3 **The Bench was empty** The judge has not yet entered the courtroom. But the scene also symbolizes the lack of justice in the events to come.

375:5 **a man picking his teeth** Faulkner repeats this description just below. The man, a "Jew lawyer from Memphis" (375:12//282:3), is both indifferent and predatory. He seems indifferent because he knows the verdict is a foregone conclusion; he picks his teeth because he is bored and because he has already, in effect, consumed Goodwin in this trial. See entry 375:12//282:3.

375:8 **a tan palm beach suit** a very fashionable outfit worn in warm weather. The suit, along with the "smart leather briefcase" and the "straw hat with a red-and-tan band," suggests the lawyer's sophistication and urbane style.

375:12 **A Jew lawyer from Memphis** Horace's identification recalls Clarence Snopes's tirade against "jew lawyers": "And the lowest kind of jew lawyer is a Memphis jew lawyer." See entry 363:25//265:18. Later, when Popeye is awaiting execution, he is visited by a "Memphis lawyer" (396:25//314:6). Though no direct evidence suggests that these three are the same man, Faulkner creates that possibility. The "Memphis lawyer" who visits Popeye is clearly someone he knows, someone who works for him. It would make sense for Popeye's lawyer to attend

Goodwin's trial, especially if Ruby has now implicated Popeye in the crime. So the lawyer in each case is very likely the same man. When Horace identifies him as a "Jew lawyer from Memphis," he does not necessarily mean it in the derogatory sense that Snopes did. Horace simply realizes that the legal top guns have been called out.°

Also, the presence of the lawyer proves both Goodwin and Horace wrong. Goodwin expected Popeye himself to come to town to prevent Goodwin from testifying by murdering him. Horace felt there was no danger of anyone showing up at the trial. Perhaps after Red's murder, Popeye left—with or without Temple. He apparently has been keeping up with the trial (perhaps through Eustace Graham), and when Ruby testifies about his presence at the Old Frenchman place, he sends Temple in as his defense. It seems clear from later events that Temple's name has not been brought up in the trial. Now Eustace Graham uses Temple not only to place the blame for Tommy's murder on Goodwin, but also to assure his conviction by adding the charge of rape. The Memphis lawyer apparently has accompanied Temple to Jefferson: together they act as Popeye's agents. The implication is that if Ruby had followed Goodwin's plan and not mentioned Popeye, then Popeye would not have needed to send Temple into court. In effect, Ruby, under Horace's influence, has assured her husband's conviction.

375:15 **She will have on a black hat** to indicate solemnity, mourning, someone's conception of virginity violated.

375:19 **the bailiff** courtroom official deputized and charged with overseeing court processes.

375:27 **"Is this your witness, Mr Benbow?"** . . . **"I do, your Honor."** Horace has apparently listed Temple as a witness for the defense. Now he realizes that Temple's testimony will be used against his client. Nevertheless, now that she has shown up in court, he has to examine her in an effort to mitigate the damage her testimony is sure to bring about.

CHAPTER XXVIII

376:3 **corn-cob** Although Faulkner noted the presence of corn-cobs in the crib (see 249:11//101:9, for example), the reader here learns for the first time, along with Horace and the spectators, exactly how Temple was raped. Her earlier rebuke to Popeye—"You couldn't fool me but once, could you?" (339:12//231:25)—now makes sense.°

376:4 **dark brownish paint** the stain of Temple's blood.

376:4 **The reason this was not offered sooner . . . from the record** Note that Eustace now refers to Ruby as Lee's "wife," when he earlier made the point that she was his mistress, or at least common-law partner. Possibly her testimony is now seen as so damaging that Eustace wants to strengthen it by making her a more credible witness, by underlining her closeness to Goodwin: we know that Ruby has identified Popeye, given Lee's reaction (366:33//270:6), and she must have also mentioned the girl. Still, she would not have known that Popeye had raped Temple with a corncob, or, for that matter, that Temple had been raped at all. She would have known, based on Lee's account, that Popeye had killed Tommy and, based on her own witnessing, that Popeye had taken Temple with him when he left. Eustace is saying also that apparently the law officials had discovered the blood-stained corncob earlier, when, one assumes, they first investigated the crime, but that they had no way of knowing its significance until Ruby, the day before, placed the girl at the site of the crime. If this were true, Eustace would in the intervening time have had to find Temple, had her examined by a gynecologist, had the corncob tested by the chemist, and all the rest, a very unlikely scenario. It thus seems clear that Eustace has known about Temple and the rape, strongly suggesting collusion with Popeye's lawyer, who is present in the courtroom.

376:11 **this is no longer a matter for the hangman, but for a bonfire of gasoline——** an incredibly prejudicial statement, obvious pandering to the jury on Eustace's part. In other words, the crime is so horrendous that simple, legal hanging is insufficient; the defendant deserves to be burned alive. Eustace is encouraging the townspeople to take the law into their own hands, as they indeed will.

376:15 **Strike out the phrase beginning 'who says that', mister clerk** The judge, however, leaves in Graham's paean to womanhood, a sentiment guaranteed to influence the jury's final decision. The "mister clerk" would be the Clerk of Courts, who maintains court records. But the judge here seems to be calling on the court stenographer, who records the admissible testimony, rather than the clerk of courts. Eustace knows the effect the words will have on the jury, despite the judge's order to disregard.

376:20 **her hair escaped in tight red curls like clots of resin** Probably resin from a pine tree, which dries into reddish solids—hence the comparison to Temple's "tight red curls." "Clots" also evoke the image of dried blood. See entry 273:4// 136:4.

376:21 **The hat bore a rhinestone ornament . . . a shoulder knot of purple.** Temple is not conventionally dressed or made up for this courtroom appearance. She is, apparently, dressed in the clothes Popeye bought for her. The platinum purse, the hat with the rhinestone ornament, the black silk dress all come from the Memphis underground. In addition, the "shoulder knot of purple" links her visually with Ruby Lamar, who also wears "the purple ornament on her shoulder" (366:16// 269:14); more indirectly, even the platinum bag "laying" in her lap recalls the inert child in Ruby's lap. See entry 376:24// 284:15.

376:24 **Her hands lay motionless . . . on their sides as though**

empty Temple is twice before described in a similar manner. While she is alone in the bedroom of the Old Frenchman place, she sits with "her legs tucked under her, erect, her hands lying in her lap, her hat tilted on the back of her head" (226:14// 69:6). Later, after she watches Popeye kill Tommy, she "sat there, her legs straight before her, her hands limp and palm-up on her lap" (250:1//102:10). The imagery suggests that Temple is as much a victim in the courtroom as she was in each of the two previous episodes. The palms-up attitude indicates passivity. She certainly seems more the marionette than the avenger. (Temple has on several occasions been depicted as a puppet controlled by others—when Popeye grabs her by the neck, for example.) Her normally kinetic legs are now almost lifeless. She is arranged, like a corpse. As André Bleikasten has noted, Temple is "itemized and displayed in a random arrangement of inert fetish objects—a *nature morte*, a still life ritually offered to the gaping crowd in the courtroom, its deadness matched by their white cadaverous faces."° See entry 376:27// 284:18.

376:27 **Above the ranked intent faces white and pallid** the faces of the crowd at the trial. Because of segregation, the spectators in the main courtroom would have been white, but these faces are also "pallid" because of the emotion and tension of the testimony about to be given. The comparison to the "floating bellies of dead fish" also reveals Faulkner's (or maybe Temple's) contempt for them.

376:30 **her gaze fixed on something at the back of the room** Temple seems "detached." Some critics believe she expects Popeye to enter; or perhaps his men are there to keep her in line through their sheer presence. Jay Watson has argued that this is part of the prosecution strategy and that Temple is part of a carefully orchestrated forensics.° However, she is more likely in a state of mild shock, fearful, as the "cringing" description suggests. See entry 380:2//289:3.

376:30 **Her face was quite pale . . . from purple paper and pasted there** Compare to earlier description at Miss Reba's, when Temple first reveals herself to Horace: "Her head was tousled, her face puffed, two spots of rouge on her cheekbones and her mouth painted into a savage cupid's bow" (326:36). Temple is dressed and made up like the caricature of the whore, a doll-faced slut. She has become less life-like, more mechanical and artificial, through her stay with Popeye. When Temple is first described, Faulkner notes her "bold painted mouth" (198:22//29:13), but now the mouth is also "symbolical and cryptic" as if her lips are sealed but still tell a story, serving as a sign for the world she is representing. The question is why Eustace allows Temple to go on the stand looking like this. If Eustace has had access to Temple long enough to coach her in her answers, he certainly could have dressed her differently if he had so chosen. For instance, if he wanted to argue that her rape was an atrocious desecration of womanhood, wouldn't he want to show her as the fragile, ruined innocent? More likely, his intention is to shock the jury at Temple's expense, to show them her complete and total degradation. Clearly there is no attempt to conceal her identity as Horace had offered: she is "Temple Drake."

377:2 **moving also, into the line of her vision again** The reader is shut out of Temple's inner life here. Her face is a mask, her mouth is sealed, her actions are controlled. Graham is obviously trying to keep her attention focused on him and not on whom or whatever she is looking for or at in the back of the courtroom. In one sense, Temple is like Goodwin here: both seem to be expecting someone to show up. Goodwin expects Popeye, and it is possible that Temple does also, although it is extremely unlikely that Popeye would appear in the Jefferson courtroom. Nevertheless, Popeye has proved to be a ubiquitous figure in Temple's recent life, appearing out of nowhere in the bedroom at the Old Frenchman place, in the barn crib, at Miss Reba's brothel, in the street in front of the house: she has not been able to escape him in the past, and, like Goodwin, she might very well be looking for his almost supernatural presence here as well. Popeye casts a long and inclusive shadow in the novel. Though it is possible that Temple is watching for her father, Judge Drake, who will, in fact, soon enter the room, she continues to search the back of the room after her father enters. See entry 379:31//288:22. All the other major players in her immediate experience, with the exceptions of Gowan and Miss Reba, are either present already or dead.

377:4 **Let these good men, these fathers and husbands, hear what you have to say and right your wrong for you** Eustace plays to the proprietariness of the all-male jury. By extension, he intends to include the men of the town, whose honor he has already challenged in his earlier remark. Ruby's account of her own father, who also sought to "right her wrong" by killing her lover, has foreshadowed Eustace's tactic.

377:7 **The Court glanced at Horace, his eyebrows raised** The Judge realizes that Eustace's statement is prejudicial and looks questioningly at Horace, fully expecting him to object.

377:8 **He sat with his head bent a little, his hands clutched in his lap** Horace's posture parallels Temple's: both assume the position of helplessness. Horace's posture certainly shows that he has lost control of the situation, that he is awaiting the inevitable blow, as of the knife blade or guillotine mentioned earlier.

377:12 **Eighteen** Temple was earlier described as being seventeen. She has apparently had her birthday during her abduction and come of age.

377:14 **Memphis** Temple would be expected to answer Jackson, where her family lives.

377:22 **My father** Temple is responding to the earlier question "Have you relations there?" (377:19//285:17).

377:27 **You are your father's only daughter?** This point has already been stressed. Eustace is underscoring the outrage to womanhood and appealing to the paternalistic and fraternalistic prejudices of the court and the audience: virgin daughters are priceless in this society, and this one has been ruined. The judge will again look to Horace anticipating an objection.

377:34 **giving her parrotlike answers** Faulkner does not tell us

Temple's specific answer to this question. It is possible that she gives Miss Reba's house, although there appears to be no shock in the courtroom at her reply.° Perhaps she gives a fictitious address, even through Graham's strategy would make this unnecessary. Her answer is "parrotlike" because she has, as previously suggested, been coached in her answers, or, perhaps, because she does not totally comprehend the significance of her words. Earlier, for example, when Temple cursed, trying out her role as whore, she "added a phrase, glibly obscene, with a detached parrotlike effect" (340:15//238:19). Later, when she throws herself at Red in the Grotto, she "began to grind against him, dragging at his head, murmuring to him in parrotlike underworld epithet" (344:40//239:16). In both cases, she seems to be making prepared noises rather than responding authentically.

377:38 **He thought I was in school** This is not true. In fact, Horace could point to the newspaper notice that Clarence Snopes mentions to Horace, the one that says Temple has left school (301:18//176:13). He could also refer to the detective who was searching for her shortly after her disappearance.

377:40 **you dared not———** face your father because of the shame, or show your face in proper society. See her actions in Dumfries (276:3//140:19).

378:1 **"I object!" Horace said. "The question is lead———"** Horace finally objects that Eustace is leading the witness. But, as the judge notes, Graham has done this at least twice before.

378:8 **I was in the crib** The multiple meanings of the word all come into play in Temple's simple statement. The crib conjures up the baby's crib (signifying Temple's loss of childhood innocence), the crib in the barn (where the assault takes place, a locale associated with animals), and the crib of Miss Reba's house of prostitution (where illicit sex occurs). Dressed now as a prostitute, Temple starkly illustrates how fragile respectability is, how easily the innocent child of any of the men in the courtroom could likewise be snatched away, abused, and forever ruined.

378:10 **Some newcomers entered** probably Judge Drake and Temple's brothers.

378:15 **From a short distance her eyes, the two spots of rouge and her mouth, were like five meaningless objects in a small heart-shaped dish** Though Temple's face is "heart-shaped," she is almost completely objectified at this point. Her face is a container, its features "meaningless" because she seems without thought or volition.

378:21 **In the crib** It is possible that Temple did see Goodwin in the crib if he came in to see what had happened to Tommy. However, it is much more likely that Lee waited until Popeye and Temple left before he went to check. Temple's perjury has been variously ascribed to confusion, lying, and revenge on the patriarchy.°

378:25 **From him** In one sense, as discussed earlier, Temple was indeed hiding from Goodwin, as she was from all the men at the Old Frenchman place. In the description to follow, Temple recounts the facts but replaces Popeye with Goodwin. Since she never actually accuses Goodwin by name—it is always "he"—she may feel that she is telling the truth. We don't know that she looks at Goodwin when Eustace points in his direction.

379:4 **"Yes. He said he———" "Wait. What did he do to Tommy?"** This is the third time Eustace prevents Temple from finishing her statement. See 378:31//287:10 and 378:33//287:12. The question is why. She apparently intends to say that Tommy had promised to protect her. Eustace may want to give the impression that Temple had no one to turn to.

379:8 **At once the girl's gaze went to the back of the room and became fixed there** Up until this point Temple has been searching the room, looking for someone. Now, following the mention of the entrance of the newcomers, her gaze becomes "fixed."

379:19 **I shall no longer subject this ruined defenseless child to the agony of———** Eustace's ploy is to get Temple off the stand before Horace can challenge her story. If he did, however, he would immediately be seen as attacking the victim. Judge Drake's entrance will effectively preempt any possible chance Horace might have had to cross-examine.

379:24 **He had neat white hair . . . a slender black stick in the other** Judge Drake is nearly a caricature of the Southern plantation owner, dressed in white (one assumes) linen, and is thus a contrast to Popeye (her other Daddy) and his black suits. On the other hand, Judge Drake is also described as having "dark skin," his suit is "snugly' fit," and he carries "a slender black stick" (recalling Temple's vision of Popeye's "little black thing like a nigger boy, kind of" [331:1//219:27]). The image also links Judge Drake to Pap and his walking stick.

379:30 **He passed the witness stand without a glance at the witness** Temple, that is. If Judge Drake has not yet met with his daughter, then his action reveals the coldness of his attitude towards her. He does not attempt to comfort her or to support her.

379:31 **who still gazed at something in the back of the room** The "something" is unclear. It can't be her father, since she won't even turn her head to keep him in sight. See entry 379:32//288:23. It could be her brothers, who are still standing in the back; but it is as if she were still waiting for someone to show up.

379:32 **walking right through her line of vision like a runner crossing a tape** Her "line of vision" is so intense that her father must, in a sense, break through it. Compare to her watching Popeye cross through the crib to kill Tommy and to her seeing Ruby beside the road as Popeye drives her away. In these moments, Temple is unnaturally still.

379:35 **the old man** Throughout this description Judge Drake is called "the old man," perhaps to underscore his connection with Pap.

379:37 **do you waive——— the right to cross-examine.**

379:40 **the six people at the counsel table** The six are identified at 380:34//290:6.

380:2 **gazing like a drugged person** Faulkner's simile is provocative, especially given Temple's behavior. Some critics have entertained the idea that she is actually drugged. It would make her more easily controlled, would help explain her blank eyes, her general sluggishness, her "immobility," her unusual concentration on the back of the room.

380:8 **She put her hand in his and rose ... moved down the aisle** The platinum bag links Temple to her life at Miss Reba's. In keeping with her general lassitude, she makes no move to catch it as it falls from her lap, and her father spurns it with a kick which places it next to the spittoon, illustrating his disgust. As others have noted, the entire scene is a parody or rather an inversion of the wedding ceremony: the father walks down the aisle alone, reclaims his daughter, and then takes (or forces) her back into the family. See entries 380:19//289:21; 380:30//289:28.

380:19 **She began to cringe back ... in that shrinking and rapt abasement** Temple's actions are similar to those she sometimes exhibits with Popeye; she is controlled by her father much as Popeye controlled her, minus only the hand to the neck. See also her reaction to Red at the Grotto (344:19//238:23). But this reaction is a "cringing" away from rather than toward. She seems to be fearful of her four brothers waiting at the end of the aisle. In her state, it is possible that she doesn't even recognize them. She might very well be thinking of Popeye's four henchmen at the Grotto. The word "abasement" is worth noting: Temple is without will, without self-respect or sense of purpose.°

380:30 **in a close body the group passed through the door and disappeared** Temple is absorbed by the male bodies almost as if she were ingested. She is forcibly reconstituted as a part of the family.

CHAPTER XXIX

381:1 **The jury was out eight minutes** The author never actually gives the court's verdict, but the very brevity of its deliberations leaves no doubt of its conclusion. See 395:7//312:7 for comparison to Popeye's trial. The date is Friday, June 21.

381:9 **I mean, to the house, or out home?** Narcissa asks whether Horace wants to go to the Benbow house in town or to the Sartoris estate in the country. She also suggests that Horace return to his former home in Kinston. Horace's reply—"Home .... I dont care. Just home" (381:15//292:5) indicates his woeful indifference; earlier he was careful to make a distinction between the two places.

381:11 **She was driving the car** Horace cannot drive. Narcissa is even in this way in control.

381:12 **in a new dark dress with a severe white collar, a dark hat** Narcissa's wardrobe deviates from her signature whites. She seems here the soul of sobriety, almost a puritan matron.

381:17 **the blackguard boys and youths** "Blackguard" = villainous, unprincipled, or foul-mouthed. These young men have apparently cursed, heckled, and threatened Goodwin as he was escorted back to his cell.

381:19 **Beside the gate the woman stood ... sitting in the car beside his sister** Horace's post-trial "scenario" for Goodwin—the pathetic wife and child, the humble fare—is almost mawkish and certainly at chilling odds with the reality facing Goodwin. When paralleling his own fate with Goodwin's, he seems more self-pitying than warranted, given his role in his client's doom.

381:25 **in parallel and diminishing retrograde** The cotton fields/plants on either side of the road seem drawn away, both spatially and temporally, like passing through a tunnel.

381:28 **You'd almost think there was some purpose to it** Horace's final sardonic statement on nature and its revelation of order and rightness. At the beginning of the book, he sees Spring as the "female season" and postulates his theory of its conspiratorial sexual essence. Although he feared it, Horace at least acknowledged some design to it. Now, having failed and been failed by the system of justice and moral order, Horace, a betrayed idealist, denies any overriding purpose to the universe.

381:30 **quite gently** Now that Narcissa has won, she can afford to be nice to her brother. She treats him like an invalid. And he reacts in kind.

382:1 **I intended to stop here** that is, to stop on the porch. He did not leave the house with the intention of walking back to town. Horace, dazed, abdicates all responsibility for his actions. See next entry.

382:1 **He watched himself cross the porch** Horace is behaving much as did Temple, observing his movements, his body, as if he were separate from them. In one sense he is in a state of shock, as was Temple. On the other hand, by simply walking away from the house he does what Temple did not do at both the old Frenchman place and Miss Reba's. However, by leaving his sister's house at this time, Horace puts himself in the middle of crisis.

382:15 **He was a fat man** Although unnamed, the sheriff bears resemblance to Wat Kennedy, the sheriff in *Light in August*: "a fat, comfortable man with a hard, canny head and a benevolent aspect."° Like Sheriff Kennedy, the sheriff in *Sanctuary* attempts to conceal his own thoughts. Though he is worried about the crowd, he banks on his understanding of mob psychology.

382:32 **The drummers sat ... the south-bound train ran at one oclock** The salesmen are waiting to take the night train. By working during the day and then taking the train overnight, they save the cost of a hotel room for the evening.

382:34 **They're going to let him get away with it, are they?** Although Faulkner has not actually told us what the verdict is, there is no doubt that Goodwin has been found guilty of the crime of murder. Since he was not actually charged with Temple's rape, her testimony concerning her assault should not have been considered in determining Goodwin's guilt in the murder of Tommy, although it obviously was. To the drummer, the town's failure to act on its own, to avenge itself on Goodwin, is a disgrace. We might remember, however, that Temple is not actually a citizen of Jefferson (neither is the drummer): her home is in Jackson and she has been living in Oxford. Jefferson adopts her as a symbol of what could happen to their own women.

382:35 **What kind of folks have you got here? . . . Who was she?** All three of the drummers who speak here are from out of town. They know next to nothing about the people involved in the trial. Their protest is of a general nature, more morbid curiosity than moral outrage. See entry 383:2//294:14.

383:2 **She was some baby. Jeez. I wouldn't have used no cob** The slang "baby" takes us back to the crib in which the rape occurred. The drummer's comment betrays the sanctimony of moral outrage. He is not offended by the idea of the rape itself; but since Temple is attractive to him, he brags he wouldn't have employed a cob for sex with her. Horace never identifies himself, nor does he challenge these drummers' statements that foment the lynching. See entry 385:27//298:17.

383:5 **turned the chairs back into the wall** The porter places them against and facing the wall for the night so he can sweep, a sign that the porch is closed for the evening.

383:8 **Yes. Have you got a report on it yet?** Though Horace has no clothes with him and seems not to have any plan in mind, he appears serious about wanting to catch the train since he asks if it's running on time and apparently agrees to be awakened before it arrives. A train heading southwest would get him to Kinston, but it is unclear if he has decided at this time to return.

383:24 **It was not a sound Horace heard now; it was something in the air which the sound of the running feet died into** This "something in the air" is probably fire. It would not be a "sound" to Horace since he is not completely aware of hearing it. It seems to be more of a physical sensation than an aural one.

383:29 **Then he had passed it** The "it" is the voice Horace hears. Since he never actually sees the speaker, the voice functions like the invisible bird in the opening scene.

383:29 **"I scared him," Horace said. "He's just from St. Louis, maybe, and he's not used to this"** Horace's running down the hall towards the stairs alarms a man in one of the hotel rooms. That man apparently assumes the hotel is on fire, but Horace simply wants to know what is going on outside in the square.

383:35 **three other men passed the hotel running** These dressed men might be the drummers, who have not gone to bed or who are expecting an early train. Another possibility is that these men are dressed (as opposed to the hotel proprietor who is still in his nightshirt) because they have been forewarned or alerted to the planned lynching and are running to witness or take part in it.

383:39 **"It is a fire," Horace said** The stress would likely be on the word "is": Horace did not really expect a fire to be the focus of this pandemonium. He may, in fact, be relieved that it is nothing more. But he does not, at this time, fully apprehend the cause of the fire which will occur to him in several successive shocks. See entry 384:5//295:28.

384:5 **then he heard the sound, of the fire; the furious sound of gasoline** Faulkner employs unusual punctuation: the comma after "sound" forces us to pause, just as Horace does as he attempts to identify the source. He has expected the sound of burning, but because of the gasoline the fire is roaring much louder than normal.

384:8 **Against the flames black figures showed, antic** The crowd is portrayed as frightfully clownish, even ludicrous. There is an air of perverse celebration in the actions, the sense of a pagan ritual. The date, June 22, is the summer solstice, which was celebrated with Midsummer fires.° Faulkner here underscores the irony of these "Christian" people performing such a barbaric act. In *Light in August,* Faulkner describes the crowd watching the burning of Joanna Burden's house as participating in "an emotional barbecue, a Roman holiday almost."°

384:10 **he saw a man turn and run, a mass of flames** One of the lynchers is also, apparently, killed in the riot. He has been dousing the flames with more coal oil and the container explodes. The continual emphasis on chaotic "running" which appears throughout this section echoes Temple's furious and purposeless movement at the Old Frenchman place.

384:16 **but from the central mass of fire there came no sound at all** This is, of course, Lee Goodwin. Goodwin is likely dead by this time, given the atrocities he is subject to. However, he has also been presented as a stoic character, and the contrast between his suffering silence and the other man's pitiful screams are significant. He is something like Joe Christmas, who is shot and castrated by Percy Grimm in *Light in August*: "He just lay there, with his eyes open and empty of everything save consciousness, and with something, a shadow, about his mouth. For a long moment he looked up at them with peaceful and unfathomable and unbearable eyes."° Both Goodwin and Christmas establish the still point at the center of the storm.

384:17 **It was now indistinguishable** Goodwin's body is a part of the flames. The fire is burning so hotly that Goodwin himself cannot be seen.

384:19 **the ends of a few posts and planks** Goodwin, in other words, has been burned at the stake, at a wooden pyre.

384:27 **Do to the lawyer what we did to him. What he did to her. Only we never used a cob. We made him wish we had used a cob** The crowd of men has apparently impaled Goodwin with a stake before burning him alive. Castration is also likely since he is being punished for a sex crime more than for the murder of Tommy. The men in the crowd have thus raped Goodwin, sodomized him, proving themselves as capable of the unspeakable as Popeye. The statement "Only we never used a cob" echoes the drummer's earlier aside, "Jeez. I wouldn't have used no cob" (383:2//294:14). The crowd is also, as their comments show, willing to do the same thing to Horace.

384:30 **Horace couldn't hear them** See Temple in the barn: "it was as though sound and silence had become inverted. She could hear silence in a thick rustling as he moved toward her through it, thrusting it aside . . ." (250:11//102:19).

384:31 **though it still swirled upward unabated, as though it were living upon itself** as though the fire would continue to burn forever, feeding itself with its own matter, undiminishing.

384:34 **roaring silently out of a peaceful void** Horace has been searching for peace throughout the whole book. "Lest oft is peace," he will shortly say (386:39//300:10). Here he simply withdraws from the world, disengages himself from the events surrounding him—again, much as did Temple. The imagery here invokes that used at the end of Chapter XXIII, in which Horace identifies with Temple at the moment of rape: "she watched something black and furious go roaring out of her pale body" (333:27//223:17).

CHAPTER XXX

385:3 **waxed ends** Similar to hair pomade, moustache wax was used to shape and groom large moustaches.

385:7 **hack** Although a hack could refer to a carriage, here it means a car, hired transportation such as that Horace takes to and from the station in Jefferson. "After the horse era passed, he bought a car, still meeting the trains" (385:11//298:1).

385:8 **Prince Albert coat** a long, double-breasted frock coat named after Prince Albert Edward (1841–1910), later Edward VII.

385:12 **the top hat was replaced by a cap . . . New York tenement district** The tenement district would be the lower east side of Manhattan. The aristocratic dress of Southern gentry is displaced by immigrant clothing indicating a significant loss of status.

385:15 **Here you are** The driver has been expecting Horace, as is made clear by his following statement: "You are one train late"; the statement confirms Narcissa's control. The date is probably Monday, June 24th. See entry 385:20//298:10.

385:20 **She got in this morning. I took her home. Your wife** Belle, after Horace's desertion, had "gone back home to Kentucky" (253:22//107:12). Narcissa has already written Belle to tell her Horace would "be home on the twenty-fourth" (363:10//265:3).

385:23 **When did you expect her? . . . .** The old man is fishing for information. He pretends that he believes Horace and Belle had planned their arrivals. The extended ellipses suggest that the old man is waiting for Horace to fill in the blanks.

385:24 **"I see where they burned that fellow over at Jefferson. I guess you saw it".... "I heard about it"** The driver has read about the lynching in the papers. When he asks, "I guess you saw it," he could mean "I guess you read it in the papers also" or "since you were in Jefferson, I guess you witnessed it firsthand," more likely the second than the first. However, the driver's statement gives no indication that he is aware of Horace's participation in the trial. Horace is evasive; in fact, he lies about his involvement and attempts to deflect further discussion of the matter.

385:27 **We got to protect our girls. Might need them ourselves** Again, the chivalric jest of the good male citizen is marked by crude sexual irony. The driver displays not moral disapproval but patriarchal possessiveness.

386:1 **which he had brought into town with him on the morning when she had asked him the name of the District Attorney** When Horace moved into the Benbow house on May 10, he had no suitcase. Narcissa asks Horace about Eustace Graham on Monday, May 27.

386:4 **a fairish piece of lawn** a fairly large yard.

386:6 **the rose colored shade at his wife's windows** The rose color captures both a sickly romanticism and a disturbing sexuality. Horace is about to be engulfed once again by Belle's suffocating femininity. It also connects the house, and Belle's room, with Miss Reba's house in the Memphis red-light district and Temple's room in it, which was distinguished by a lamp shade and the covering of a slop jar, both made of "fluted rose-colored paper" (286:37//155:16).

386:7 **He entered the house from the back** a sign of defeat, of creeping back home. He doesn't want to be seen, which is also probably the reason he asked the driver to let him out at the corner rather than deliver him to the front door.

386:8 **She was reading in bed ... an open box of chocolates** Faulkner paints a very broad, stereotypical picture of Belle as the lazy and spoiled wife.

386:14 **Did you lock the back door?** Belle completely ignores

Horace's announcement cum apology. The effect is to suggest that she has not missed Horace and that he actually doesn't count except for routine chores. See entry 387:28//301:10.

386:15   **Yes, I knew she would be**   out for the entire evening. This "she" refers to Little Belle, as becomes clearer below.

386:15   **Have you tonight.......**   As the next lines make clear, Horace is asking whether Belle has spoken to Little Belle tonight, to check on her safety.

386:19   **house party**   a social affair at which people would spend the night, although some form of chaperone would be assumed.

386:24   **I talked to her night before last. Go lock the back door**   Belle is much less concerned about her daughter than is Horace. She also either has not listened to Horace, who has already said he has locked the door, or knows him too well to believe it. She treats him like a child or a servant. Locking the door will, supposedly, keep danger and threat out. Since it will also keep Horace in, in effect she has told Horace to close his own cell.

386:25   **I'll just.......**   check on her. Just to be sure.

386:27   **The number was on a rural line; it took some time**   probably a party line, shared by more than one household. Horace must wait until the line is free before he can place his call.

386:30   **"Night is hard on old people," he said quietly, holding the receiver. "Summer nights are hard on them"**   Horace, in surrender and self-pity, is apparently speaking of himself, although he is only 43. This observation is similar to his earlier comment on Spring: "You'd almost think there was some purpose to it" (381:27//292:18).

386:32   **Something should be done about it. A law**   Presumably Horace is now being ironic: he is also surely aware how ineffectual all laws have been in his recent past. Note that this lament echoes Popeye's earlier statements.

386:38   **He began to say something out of a book he had read: "Less oft is peace. Less oft is peace," he said**   The quotation comes from Percy Shelley's poem "To Jane: The Recollection" (1822):

> Though thou art ever fair and kind,
> The forests ever green,
> Less oft is peace in Shelley's mind,
> Than calm in waters, seen.°

Horace obviously knows that his attempt to escape from this kind of domestic entrapment has failed, even as he looks at the open door. He also knows that he is doomed to unhappiness because of his failure of courage. In the absence of moral courage, it is not surprising Horace reverts to a bookish, romantic idea as a kind of mantra.

387:11 **Hello, Horace; I want you to meet a———** It is unclear what Little Belle's male friend is about to say, but, based on earlier portraits of college-age students in the book, it is no doubt crude and suggestive. Little Belle is surrounded by party hubbub, and her companion is apparently drunk.

387:14 **It's Horace! I live with him!** Little Belle still doesn't identify Horace as her step-father, another variation on the "It's just Horace" attitude displayed in the grape arbor.

387:23 **I dont know. I just———** got home myself.

387:28 **"Lock the back door," she said** This is the last we see of Horace, as he is ordered to confine himself in the Kinston house with Belle, who is likely to be obeyed. See entry 398:4//316:8.

CHAPTER XXXI

Faulkner breaks the narrative strategy he has used throughout the rest of the novel by changing the narrative voice in this chapter. The account becomes more authoritatively detached, creating the effect of high naturalism. Heretofore, the characters—Horace, Temple, Ruby, for example—have told their own stories. Since Popeye would never do this, the author, using an almost casebook technique, does it for him. Faulkner added the account of Popeye's childhood when he revised the galleys in November and early December of 1930; it was the most extended addition he made to the book. Faulkner would use this narrative technique in the much longer flashback explaining Joe Christmas in his next novel, *Light in August.*

388:1 **Pensacola** Pensacola is a seaport in the Florida panhandle, about 350 miles from Memphis. Highway 78 would take Popeye straight from Memphis through Holly Springs and New Albany, Mississippi, to Birmingham on the way to Pensacola, about 200 miles beyond.

388:4 **He was arrested in August** approximately two months after the trial and mob execution of Lee Goodwin. No clues as to what prompts Popeye's arrest are given. Perhaps simply being from out-of-state is enough.

388:6 **on the night when Red had been killed** Faulkner still does not tell the reader that Popeye actually killed Red. It is an interesting omission, rather like Joe Christmas's murder of Joanna Burden: we never see Joe do it but assume that he did. Popeye is nevertheless unable to give a truthful alibi, since to do so would implicate him in Red's death, as explained above (388:4//302:4). He could, of course, simply lie and have others back him up, as his lawyer will later suggest.

388:7 **Each summer Popeye went to see his mother** The narrator confirms what Miss Myrtle has already said (356:15//25:17). The episode is further evidence of the parallel Faulkner draws between underworld and proper society: Popeye the thug dutifully visits his mother with a pleasing fiction about his life.

388:10 **His father had been a professional strike breaker hired by the street railway company to break a strike in 1900** The decades of the late 19th and early 20th centuries were periods of intense labor disputes. Strike breakers were often hired by management to foment trouble for the strikers and to protect the scabs, newly hired workers who would keep the lines operating during the strike. A strike breaker would, of course, be considered a traitorous and despicable person, especially a professional one who traveled around taking advantage of the difficulties of others.

388:18 **By who?** Popeye's father is bragging that he is too valuable a tool for management to fire. He can break the rules with the knowledge that either side would happily hire his strong-arm services. He has no loyalty to either management or labor.

388:34 **I dont dare to tell them** her parents. She has a mother and a step-father, the "second husband of her mother" (389:19//304:17).

188:39 **just as lief** just as inclined; as soon this or that.

389:2 **foot-bell** the trolley bell operated by a foot peddle.

389:7 **She had a Christmas card from him; a picture, with a bell and an embossed wreath in gilt** a Christmas bell, obviously, but its appeal is sentimentally connected with the trolley bell with which he would signal to her during their courtship and marriage.

389:14 **She did not go to a doctor, because an old negro woman told her what was wrong** This could mean that Popeye's mother goes to a midwife or perhaps a conjure woman for medical advice, a not unusual practice among the poor who could not afford the luxury of a traditional doctor unless it was absolutely necessary; but since her mother runs a boarding house, it is not likely that simple lack of money prevents her from seeking professional medical treatment. It may be that the woman tells Popeye's mother that she is suffering from a venereal disease, which seems likely from later details, and that Popeye's mother refuses to go the doctor out of shame or fear.

389:15 **Popeye was born on the Christmas day on which the card was received** This statement does not necessarily mean that Popeye is born on Christmas Day itself in 1900 but rather any day within the Christmas season; if in fact he is a Christmas Day baby, the irony of Popeye's life increases: the obverse to the Christ child. It is, in fact, unlikely that mail would be delivered on Christmas Day. This chronology establishes Popeye as only 28 years old when he is executed.

389:16 **At first they thought he was blind . . . he did not learn to walk and talk until he was about four years old** Symptoms associated with syphilis. (The adult Popeye is also impotent, another effect of the disease.) An obvious comparison can be made between baby Popeye and the Goodwin baby, which is also clearly very ill.

389:19 **the second husband of her mother, an undersized, snuffy man** Popeye's mother's stepfather; married to her mother, the owner of the boarding house. "Snuffy" may mean a man who takes snuff but most likely means temperamental, quick to anger.

389:23 **with a check signed in blank to pay a twelve dollar butcher's bill** The recipient and the amount of payment have not been filled in, although the check itself has been signed. Thus, the stepfather simply fills in the amount and makes himself the payee. Like Popeye's father, he disappears.

389:30 **he found a smudge in his waste-basket** where a fire had been started but had not successfully caught flame.

389:33 **the firemen found the grandmother in the attic . . . the child asleep in a discarded mattress nearby** Excelsior is wood shavings used for packing. Deserted by her second husband, the grandmother has begun to lose her mind and has been setting the fires, perhaps putting them out as well, as in the wastebasket mentioned earlier. Or it could be that when she heard the firemen coming she tried to put it out to deflect suspicion.

389:37 **"Them bastards are trying to get him," the old woman said. "They set the house on fire"** The "bastards" are some unnamed enemy; the "him" would refer to baby Popeye. There is no evidence that the grandmother is herself trying to kill the baby, at least not consciously, since she will later make sure Popeye is safe when she does finally burn down the house with herself in it.

390:7 **She would watch all the fires; she would not allow a match in the house** "she" = the daughter. She suspects her mother of setting the fires and stays in the house to monitor her. This background intensifies Popeye's subsequent connection with matches.

390:11 **eggs cooked in olive oil** Olive oil would be more easily digested by the baby than would butter or lard. But this is also probably a reference to E. C. Segar's comic strip *Thimble Theatre*, in which both Popeye the Sailor and Olive Oyl were characters, which had been running over ten years when Faulkner added this history of his Popeye's life. Olive Oyl was an established figure in the strip; Popeye the Sailor had first appeared on January 17, 1929 and had already become Olive's suitor by November, 1930, when Faulkner was revising the galleys.°

390:27 **A woman got out and entered a store, leaving a negro driver behind the wheel** Although the Negro works for the woman, he would not ordinarily be allowed to enter the store, which caters to whites, to do the shopping. He does, however, expect to be called in to pay the bill and carry the groceries. See 390:33//306:11.

390:36 **I want a half a dollar. He busted the bottle** he = the grocer's boy. The grandmother is sufficiently deranged that she addresses the driver as if he were able to settle the store's debt to her.

390:37 **Seem like to me you folks would see that folks got what they buy, folks that been trading here long as we is** The Negro assumes that the old woman works in the store and is requiring money for a broken item. But his understanding seems to be that the grocer's boy broke the bottle after his mistress had purchased it, and the store is forcing her to buy another one for an extra fifty cents. He correctly thinks this is unfair to the customer. The "we" reflects the driver's sense of belonging to (working for) a wealthy white mistress, and his indignation is directed at the store's "hired help."

391:7 **"That'll be a dollar and a quarter," she said. The negro gave her the money. She took it and passed them and crossed the room** The grandmother, still pretending to be an employee, takes the money from the Negro for the items handed him by his employer. The Negro assumes that he is paying per item as each is chosen, rather than paying for them all at once. The grandmother now has $1.75 from the Negro.

391:9 **There was a bottle of imported Italian olive oil, with a price tag. "I got twenty-eight cents more," she said** The imported olive oil is more expensive than the regular fifty cent brand they normally buy. It apparently costs $1.47, which leaves the grandmother with twenty-eight cents, which she then uses to buy seven bars of soap at four cents each.

391:26 **"You ought to be in vaudeville," the policeman said** The policeman gives her a pat response to what he thinks is a corny joke when, in effect, she is telling the truth.

391:27 **You'd bring down the house** If she were in vaudeville, she would threaten the theatre with collapse because of the thunderous laughter and applause.

391:28 **"I am," the woman said. "I bring down the house"** I am in vaudeville: a comedian. I do bring down the house, with fire.

391:29 **The poor house?** an institution, usually government-supported, for the destitute. The policeman comments on her shabby appearance.

391:32 **Calvin Coolidge** President of the United States from 1923–29. This scene, however, takes place around 1903 or 1904 since Popeye is described as three years old. Coolidge would not have been well-known enough at this time to warrant the kind of joke the policeman will tell. This oversight suggests the haste with which Faulkner revised the novel.

391:34 **Oh. That's why you had so much trouble shopping** The policeman implies that Coolidge would not be worth much in a trade. In 1929, the present time of *Sanctuary* and the first year of the Depression, that would likely be true.

392:2   **"Them bastards," she said. "They thought they would get him. But I told them I would show them. I told them so."**   It is unclear whether the grandmother wants people to think that the baby has perished in the fire. Perhaps the grandmother now believes that the baby was in the house.

392:13   **the disease**   syphilis.

392:25   **But he will never be any older than he is now**   Popeye's genitals will remain stunted; at this time he also appears to be retarded.

393:15   **He told her that his business was being night clerk in hotels; that, following his profession, he would move from town to town, as a doctor or a lawyer might**   Popeye cares what his mother thinks. Since he does want her to be proud of him, he lies to her, speaks of himself as a professional who travels on the job, much as his father did.

393:19   **that summer**   The narrative returns to the present time of the novel, 1929.

393:36   **What do I want with a lawyer? I never was in—— What's the name of this dump?**   Popeye's initial response is the same as Lee Goodwin's. Since he is innocent, let them prove he did it.

394:4   **somewhere down the corridor a negro was singing**   See the Negro prisoner in the Jefferson jail.°

394:5   **Popeye lay on the cot, his feet crossed in small, gleaming black shoes. "For Christ's sake," he said**   Like both Temple and Lee, Popeye finds himself locked in a room/jail cell, forced to contemplate his fate. His oath—more irritated than worried—indicates his exasperation at this turn of events.

394:12   **a stranger**   the lawyer.

394:16   **Any of you ginneys want a one-day job?**   "Ginney" means gin-drinkers, drunks: see "all ginned up on free whiskey" (348:23//244:21). Popeye displays his contempt by sarcastically offering them the job of defending him for one day. At this point he seems to assume that he will be found innocent without any trouble.

394:20 **a young man just out of law school** one as inexperienced as Horace as a trial lawyer.

394:21 **"And I wont bother about being sprung," Popeye said. "Get it over with all at once."** He doesn't want to be let out on bail to await a later trial.

395:1 **Get out and walk it off** Popeye intimates that his attorney needs to "sober up" since he strikes Popeye as too earnest/intoxicated with the process.

395:1 **Popeye lounged in his chair, looking out the window above the jury's heads** Compare to the lawyer at Goodwin's trial who "gazed lazily out a window above the ranked heads, picking his teeth" (375:10//282:1). Popeye is as confident of the jury's verdict as the lawyer was.

395:7 **The jury was out eight minutes** the same length of time it took the Jefferson jury to find Lee Goodwin guilty (381:1//291:1).

395:9 **he looked back at them in a slow silence for several moments. "Well, for Christ's sake," he said** the third time Popeye has used this oath. He seems genuinely surprised by the verdict. He apparently truly expected to be found innocent since he *was* innocent. Like Lee, but even more like Horace, Popeye at heart expects the law to do the right thing.

395:16 **Go take a pill** calm down. Take a tranquilizer.

395:21 **Probably got a Memphis lawyer already there outside the supreme court door now, waiting for a wire** the state supreme court. The District Attorney rightly suspects that Popeye has political influence in the state. He assumes the lawyer is waiting on a telegram to appeal Popeye's conviction.

395:23 **It's them thugs like that that have made justice a laughingstock, until even when we get a conviction, everybody knows it wont hold** The irony is that all elements of society in the book have conspired to make a laughing-stock of justice: that Popeye should be set free for this particular crime makes his execution yet another miscarriage of justice.

395:32 **Ed Pinaud** a commercial line of toiletries sold at the time of the novel.

395:34 **It had been a gray summer, a little cool** The line anticipates the beginning of Temple's section of the chapter (398:6//316:10).

396:7 **The turnkey said: "They might not a sent your telegram. You want me to send another one for you?"** The turnkey assumes that Popeye has tried to send for a good lawyer to defend him. He can't understand Popeye's lack of concern. Popeye's overtipping may have enlisted the jailer on Popeye's side, but his suspicion that the system may have betrayed the prisoner is worth noting.

396:16 **When he had six days left** before his scheduled execution.

396:19 **his eyes round and soft as those prehensile tips on a child's toy arrows** like rubber suction cups on toy arrows. This detail harkens back to the original description of Popeye's eyes ("two knobs of soft black rubber" [181:32//4:24]) and underscores Popeye's ability to hold one with his gaze.

396:25 **a Memphis lawyer** Faulkner does not specify which Memphis lawyer, but the specificity of the referee makes it likely the same one that attended Goodwin's trial. See entry 375:12//282:3.

396:34 **Are you so tired of dragging down jack that. . . .** tired of making money. Popeye does seem to be tired of everything: he makes money and now has nothing of value to spend it on except his old mother. Not only does he refuse to defend himself, he orders the lawyer not to interfere with the execution; see entry 396:36//314:17.

396:35 **You, the smartest—— bootlegger, gangster, in Memphis.**

396:36 **I told you once. I've got enough on you** See Miss Reba's threat to Dr. Quinn. Popeye knows enough about the lawyer's shady and illegal dealings to cause him trouble if the lawyer attempts to appeal Popeye's verdict. He is determined to die; see entry 396:40//314:22.

396:40   **"Them durn hicks," Popeye said. "Jesus Christ.......
Beat it, now," he said. "I told you. I'm all right"**   Clearly Popeye is exasperated and perhaps baffled by the preposterous turn of events. He still can't quite believe that these "hicks" have found him guilty. Perhaps Popeye recognizes that there is a poetic justice to his conviction and faces his death with existential acceptance. Or, lacking love, passion, and meaning in his life, perhaps Popeye simply accepts death as inevitable and sees no need to postpone it. The world is as "goofy" as he found the Old Frenchman place to be.°

397:10   **twelve marks at spaced intervals . . . beside the others**   This is the night before Popeye's execution, which is scheduled for six in the morning (397:32//315:25). Each of these marks represents one hour; each cigarette stub represents a passage of fifteen minutes ("All the spaces were filled save the twelfth one. It was three quarters complete" [397:17//315:9]). Popeye counts down his remaining time with cigarettes, one of his few pleasures. But the detail also reminds us of Horace and the stinking drops of shrimp residue which mark his own life's passage, and the Negro prisoner's song.

397:28   **I dont know exactly, but I can give you a list————them tickets. . . . . . .**   The turnkey offers to show Popeye the receipts for the purchases he has made with the hundred dollars. It makes no sense to return the unspent money to the doomed Popeye, but the offer does show the turnkey's sense of pity and, perhaps, justice. He doesn't know how else to express his regret at Popeye's fate. Popeye does invite some slight sympathy, at least from the jailer, here at the end.

397:30   **Buy yourself a hoop**   a wooden or metal hoop, a child's toy which the child would roll using a stick. In other words, Popeye tells the turnkey in a joking contemptuous manner to keep the change.

398:3   **Fix my hair, Jack**   Popeye's vanity reasserts itself. He is concerned that he look good when he dies. Compare to Joe Christmas, who goes to a barber shop shortly before his capture for Joanna Burden's murder in *Light in August*, and Eula

Snopes, who goes to the beauty parlor before committing suicide in *The Town*.

398:4 **"sure," the sheriff said. "I'll fix it for you;" springing the trap** the trap door on the scaffold. The scene replays Popeye's earlier entrance into Temple's crib through the trap door of the barn loft. This abrupt closure also juxtaposes with the end of Horace's story in the novel. Horace is left preparing to lock the back door, thus imprisoning himself in the house with Belle. Popeye is also jailed but is freed through execution by the opening of a door.° The idea of the "trap" takes us back to Horace's initial comments about female nature and its "green-snared promise of unease." Both Horace and Popeye have been caught in versions of this trap.

398:6 **It had been a gray day, a gray summer, a gray year** In the Fall of 1925, Faulkner lived for several months in Paris. On 6 September 1925 he wrote his mother, "I have just written such a beautiful thing that I am about to bust—2000 words about the Luxembourg gardens and death. It has a thin thread of plot, about a young woman, and it is poetry though written in prose form. I have worked on it for two whole days and every word is perfect. I haven't slept hardly for two nights, thinking about it, comparing words, accepting and rejecting them, then changing again. But now it is perfect—a jewel. I am going to put it away for a week, then show it to someone for an opinion. So tomorrow I will wake up feeling rotten, I expect. Reaction. But its worth it, to have done a thing like this."° The ending of *Sanctuary* likely derives from this earlier experiment.

398:7 **Luxembourg Gardens** Located on the Left Bank of the Seine in Paris. Faulkner roomed "just around the corner from the Luxembourg gardens, where I can sit and write and watch the children."° The Gardens are often mentioned in Faulkner's letters home during this time.

398:13 **spurious Greek balustrade** The Luxembourg Palace, designed by Salomon deBrosse, is in an imitative Greek architectural style.

398:16 **passed the pool where the children and an old man in a**

shabby brown overcoat sailed toy boats On Sunday, August 16, 1925 Faulkner wrote his mother: "I came back toward home, stopping at the Luxembourg Gardens to watch the children sailing boats on the pool. There is a man rents boats—toy ones—and even grown people sail them, while their friends look on. . . . And there was an old old man, bent and rheumatic, sailing a boat too. He hobbled along around the pool, but he couldnt keep up with his boat, so other people would very kindly stop it and send it back across to him."°

398:20 **collected four sous** a fee for public seating.

398:22 **Massenet and Scriabin, and Berlioz like a thin coating of tortured Tschaikovsky on a slice of stale bread** Massenet, Jules Emile Frederic (1842–1912), French composer; Scriabin, Alexander (1872–1915), Russian composer; Berlioz, Louis Hector (1803–1869), French composer; Tschaikovsky, Peter Ilich (1840–90), Russian composer. See Faulkner's letter to his mother on September 22, 1925: "The Belgian Military Orchestra (all Continental bands are military and covered with epaulets and medals—for silence, probably—and swords) is in Paris and there is to be a musical combat between them and the French trombone battlers this afternoon. So I am staying over today to hear it. The bandstand is outdoors, in a grove of chestnut trees in the Luxembourg Gardens. It's lovely, the way the music sounds. And these people really love good music. The bands play Massenet and Chopin and Berlioz and Wagner, and the kids are quiet, listening, and taxi-drivers stop their cars to hear it, and even day laborers are there rubbing elbows with members of the Senate and tourists and beggars and murderers and descendants of the house of Orleans."° The strained simile of "a thin coating of tortured Tschaikovsky on a slice of stale bread" is a reminder of Faulkner's apprentice writings, when he sometimes attempted such self-consciously artistic conceits. In *Mosquitoes* (1927), he placed some of them in the mouths of his dilettantish characters who spoke of Chopin as "snow rotting under a dead moon" (185) and Berlioz as "Swedenborg on a French holiday" (186).

398:27 **Temple yawned behind her hand ... sullen and discontented and sad** Unlike Faulkner, who found great pleasure in the Luxembourg Gardens, Temple appears bored by the music and the charming surroundings. For the last time in the novel she checks herself in a mirror which apparently reduces the size of its image since her entire face appears "in miniature." Note that her face is not blank or unfeeling but "sullen and discontented and sad." This focus constitutes the third ending in this chapter. Horace gives up, Popeye takes death, Temple resigns herself to living. Although some critics have seen Temple as narcissistic and vain in this scene, she has, in fact, changed radically from the first of the book.° Then she was full of speed and vitality; now she is shrunken and unhappy, a puppet or pet under her father's control.° Also, compare her yawn to Popeye's yawning at his trial (395:2//312:2). See 398:29//317:17.

398:29 **Beside her father sat** Cf. the image Temple forms of Pap during Popeye's assault (250:14//102:22). Temple appears to be imprisoned rather than protected by her father with his stick and the "rigid bar" of his moustache. In that sense, her fate is similar to that of Horace.

398:33 **she seemed to follow with her eyes ... the season of rain and death** Her eyes move around the park, from the band to the statues and on to the sky itself which, in images out of Eliot, confirms her sense of loss and futility. Like Popeye, Temple is surely aware of her doom, as the repetition of "dying ... dead ... death" in the sentence insists. *Sanctuary* ends, in Michel Gresset's term, on a "dying fall," a terribly sad and pessimistic note, and is perhaps the most forlorn of all of Faulkner's conclusions.°

APPENDIX

A Chronology for *Sanctuary*

Cleanth Brooks's "Chronology of Events in *Sanctuary*" (*The Yoknapatawpha Country*, 387–89) serves as our basic guide to the sometimes ambiguous sequencing of events in the novel. As Brooks points out, the year is clearly 1929, and there are several specific dates given in the text. Temple is raped on Sunday, May 12, Red is killed on Monday, June 17, Horace calls Miss Reba's on Wednesday, June 19, Goodwin's trial starts on Thursday, June 20, Horace apparently returns home on Monday, June 24. Other dates are derived from other clues or explanations in the text, although some of these are clearer and more reliable than others. For example, Horace arrives at the Old Frenchman place on the Tuesday before the Sunday Temple is raped; therefore, he would have been there on May 7. He leaves Kinston on the previous Friday, May 3, arrives at his sister's on Wednesday, May 8, moves into the Benbow home in Jefferson on Friday, May 10, and so on. Brooks points out that the day after Horace interviews Temple at Miss Reba's is, in Horace's reckoning, "four weeks" after encountering Popeye at the spring. If we take the phrase literally, that would make the interview date Monday, June 3, a date which, in terms of the Horace-Temple story, seems consistent with other events. However, before taking Horace to see Temple, Miss Reba tells him about Clarence Snopes's visits to her house and his encounter with Popeye. She says Snopes "turned up here about two weeks ago.... Come in looking for two boys and sat around the dining-room blowing his head off and feeling the girls' behinds..." (323). If we accept June 3 as the interview date and take Miss Reba literally, then Snopes would have first come to Memphis around Monday, May 20 (she does say "about" two weeks), before Virgil and Fonzo even arrive in Memphis, not knowing where they will stay, and before Clarence has any reason to be looking for Temple. Obviously a choice has to be made here, and not all of the events can be thoroughly explained (Brooks omits Clarence's early visits and much of Virgil and Fonzo's adventures from his Chronology). In other words, the Chronology which follows makes certain assumptions

APPENDIX

which seem best supported by our reading of the story. For the most part this chronology coincides with Prof. Brooks's, although for some approximate dates we have suggested different possibilities and have tried to add to the events Brooks has provided.

What this chronology reveals is the fascinating overlap and counterpoint of events in *Sanctuary*. The reader comes to realize, for example, that Temple is kept at Miss Reba's brothel for over five weeks; that Fonzo and Virgil are also there during much of that time, their experiences providing a comic variation on Temple's nightmare; that Horace and Narcissa both write Belle on the same day, Horace asking for a divorce and Narcissa announcing Horace's return; that Horace leaves Temple with Popeye for over two weeks even after knowing what Popeye did to her; that it is *after* Horace's visit that Popeye begins bringing Red to Temple's bed; and that Judge Drake, her father, apparently also knows of her whereabouts for over two weeks before the trial and does nothing about it. As we have noted, Temple has every right to feel abandoned and angry.

For all of the rethinking and rewriting and restructuring Faulkner did on this novel, and despite the haste in which he apparently did it, *Sanctuary* is a carefully arranged and plotted work. While not all the questions are answered in the Chronology, it does underscore the complexity of the narrative and the thoughtful intention with which it was finally arranged.

Thursday, May 2: Horace Benbow admonishes his step-daughter Little Belle for her dating practices, sees her doubled reflection in the mirror as she pretends remorse [188//13].

Friday, May 3: Horace leaves home and begins to hitchhike to Jefferson [188//13, 191//17].

Saturday, May 4: Horace's wife Belle wires his sister Narcissa Sartoris that Horace has left and announces her own intentions to return to her family in Kentucky [253//107].

Tuesday, May 7: Horace encounters Popeye at the spring, is taken to the Old Frenchman place where he gets drunk [188–92//13–19].

Wednesday, May 8: After midnight, Horace is given a ride to Jefferson on Popeye's truck carrying bootleg whiskey [192–94//19–21]; arrives at his sister's home four miles from Jefferson, stays two days [195//23, 253//107].

Thursday, May 9: Horace tells Narcissa and Miss Jenny why he left Belle and describes his night at the Old Frenchman place [253–55//107–109].

APPENDIX

Friday, May 10: Horace moves into the Benbow family home in Jefferson [255]; Gowan Stevens takes Temple Drake to the university dance, makes plans to meet her in Taylor and take her to the college baseball game in Starkville the next day [197//26]; Gowan gets drunk in the company of three town boys [202//34].

Saturday, May 11: Temple leaves the train in Taylor and finds Gowan drunk; Gowan takes her to the Old Frenchman place against her will and wrecks the car [203-05//35-37]; after several frightening experiences, Temple spends the night in the barn [235-36//81-82]. Horace strolls around downtown Jefferson at noon [256-57//112-13].

Sunday, May 12 [date given: 377//285]: Gowan abandons Temple after hiring car to pick her up [238//85]; Temple thinks she has survived the worst but is then frightened by Lee Goodwin and returns to the barn where she asks Tommy to protect her; Popeye sneaks into the barn, kills Tommy, rapes Temple, and takes her to Reba Rivers's brothel in Memphis [239-52//87-105, 273-83//137-50]; Ruby Lamar calls the sheriff from Tull's house and Goodwin is arrested [251-52//105-06].

Monday, May 13: Tommy's body is put on display in Jefferson [257//113]; Horace first takes Ruby and the baby to the Benbow home, but, after talking to his sister and Miss Jenny, moves them into a local hotel [259-65//116-125]; Temple is retroactively withdrawn from school around this date (on May 25, the postal clerk tells Horace, "She quit school about two weeks ago" [297//171]).

Tuesday, May 14: Around this date the Jackson newspaper announces that Temple Drake has gone to Michigan to stay with aunt [301//176]. ("It was in the papers couple days later," according to Clarence Snopes [301//176]).

Sunday, May 19: Horace goes to visit sister; Miss Jenny shows him Gowan's letter to Narcissa [266//126, 269//131].

Monday, May 20: Clarence Snopes shows up at Miss Reba's "looking for two boys" [323//209]. ("He turned up here about two weeks ago," according to Miss Reba on June 3; see entry 323.10//209.8 for further discussion.)

Wednesday, May 22: Snopes returns to Miss Reba's "couple of nights later [323//209].

Thursday, May 23: Horace tries to convince Goodwin to reveal Popeye's presence at Old Frenchman place [271//133]. ("He's only got two days more," Horace says of the Negro murderer, who is executed on Saturday, May 25; see entry 258.1//114.1.)

Friday, May 24: Goodwin baby is sick and Horace is summoned to the hotel; Ruby tells Horace about Temple [272//135, 290-93//161-65]; Horace

APPENDIX

goes to Sartoris and tells Miss Jenny about Gowan's role, returns to town and looks at Little Belle's picture [293–94//165–166].

Saturday, May 25: The Negro wife-murderer is hanged [269//131, 271//134]; Horace takes the early morning train to Oxford, learns Temple has quit school and that a detective has been asking about her, sees Temple's name in bathroom stall [295–98//167–170]; on return trip meets Clarence Snopes and incites his interest in Temple [299–301//171–173]; sees Clarence talk to Virgil Winbush and Fonzo Snopes in Holly Springs [302//178]; reaches Jefferson at 8:20 and learns that Ruby and the child have been forced from the hotel and are staying at the jail [303–04//179–80]; Virgil and Fonzo wind up at Miss Reba's [309–312//188–91].

Sunday, May 26: Horace goes again to Sartoris, learns that Narcissa is behind Ruby's removal from the hotel, and spends the night to avoid having to face Ruby; Narcissa encourages him to drop the case, but he refuses [305–07//182–84].

Monday, May 27: Narcissa asks identity of District Attorney [307//184]; Horace meets Clarence Snopes on his way to Memphis [307–08//184–85].

Tuesday, May 28 (or Wednesday, May 29): "On the third day" Miss Reba asks Virgil and Fonzo if she can use their room during the day [313//194].

Wednesday, May 29: "On the third day of his search" Horace finds place for Ruby and the baby [317//201]; Virgil and Fonzo find undergarment in their room [314//198].

Thursday, May 30: Horace has telephone installed [317//201, 318//202].

Friday, May 31 or Saturday, June 1: Popeye finds Clarence peering through keyhole to Temple's room at Miss Reba's, burns him with match [323–24//209–10]; see entry 323.10//209.8 for further discussion.

Sunday, June 2: Clarence Snopes calls Narcissa looking for Horace [362//264]; Clarence calls Horace and comes to his house with news of Temple [318–21//202–206]; see entries 318.5//202.3, 363.2//264.24.

Monday, June 3: Horace goes to Memphis and interviews Temple at Miss Reba's; a nervous Clarence Snopes meets him outside the door [322//206].

Tuesday, June 4 ["four weeks" since Horace encountered Popeye at the spring]: Horace returns to Jefferson in early morning, becomes sick [332–33//222–24], writes Belle asking for divorce [360//260]; Narcissa takes information to Eustace Graham, writes Belle telling her Horace will return on the 24th [360–63//260–63]; Horace meets Clarence Snopes on his way to Jackson [360//260].

APPENDIX

Wednesday, June 5: Virgil and Fonzo are taken to a brothel by another barber student ("On the twelfth day") [314//198].
Thursday, June 6: Popeye brings Red to Temple for four days [357–58// 257–58]; see entry 358.23//258.19 for further discussion.
Friday, June 7: Virgil and Fonzo return to brothel, find Clarence Snopes at Miss Reba's on their return [315–16//198–99].
Sunday, June 9: Miss Reba confronts Popeye over the arrangement with Red; Popeye doesn't return for a week [357–58//257–58].
Monday, June 10: Horace calls Reba to check on Temple; Miss Reba offers to "turn them both out on the street and you can have them arrested there" [365//268].
Monday, June 17 [date given 388//303]: Temple calls Red and arranges to meet him at the Grotto; Popeye appears and gives her the choice to meet Red or not, then takes her to Grotto; Red is killed; Popeye and Temple leave Miss Reba's [334–46//225–241].
Tuesday, June 18: Red's funeral is held at the Grotto; Miss Reba entertains Misses Myrtle and Lorraine and Uncle Bud [347–59//242–59]; "Two days before court" a beaten and bruised Clarence Snopes shows up in Jefferson complaining about a "Memphis jew lawyer" [363–64//265–66].
Wednesday, June 19 [date given, 365//268]: Horace calls Reba again, learns that Temple has fled.
Thursday, June 20 [date given, 363//265, 365//267]: Goodwin's trial opens; Ruby testifies, against Goodwin's wishes, that Popeye was at the Old Frenchman place; Horace rehearses Ruby all night for next day's testimony [365–74//267–281].
Friday, June 21: Temple appears and names Goodwin as the murderer; Eustace Graham reveals the details of Temple's rape [374–80//280–84]; Goodwin is convicted of Tommy's murder [381]; Narcissa takes Horace to Sartoris [381//290]; that night Horace walks back into town [382// 291].
Saturday, June 22: In the early morning hours Goodwin is lynched by mob; Horace barely escapes his own lynching [383–84//292–93].
Monday, June 24: Horace returns to Belle in Kinston [363//264, 385–87// 293–95].
August: Popeye is arrested and falsely convicted for murder of Alabama policeman, is hanged [388–98//303–316].
Autumn: Temple in Paris.

NOTES

Title

Meriwether and Millgate, eds. *Lion in the Garden*, 169; *The Town*, 27.

Chapter I

181:2   Blotner, *Faulkner: A Biography, One Volume Edition* 176; Inge 169; "The Big Shot," *Uncollected Stories* 504.
181:2   *Sanctuary: The Original Text* 21.
181:12   See McHaney, "Frazier's Slain Kings" 223–45, for further discussion of this opening scene.
181:14   Polk, "Afterword" 303–04.
181:22   Brown 187; "Barn Burning," *Collected Stories* 8.
181:25   Stevens 76; *The Sound and the Fury* 136.
182:26   Blotner records an instance where, when asked which character Faulkner would play in the film version of *Sanctuary*, he replied, "the cob." See Blotner, *Faulkner: A Biography* 292.
182:29   *Sanctuary: The Original Text* 50.
182:30   See Polk, "The Space Between *Sanctuary*" 16–35, for further discussion of the two versions of *Sanctuary*.
182:32   Cherrington 3, 2.
183:22   See McHaney, "Literary Modernism" 160–67, for a discussion of Faulkner's style in the context of modernism.
184:1   *Sanctuary: The Original Text* 47.
184:4   Flaubert 342. See also Bleikasten, "'Cet affreux goût d'encre': Emma Bovary's Ghost in *Sanctuary*" 36–56; Guerard 63–80; and Yonce 439–42.
184:12   *The Hamlet* 731.
184:22   Brown 72.
185:20   Blotner 99–101.
185:25   *Requiem for a Nun* 616.

185:26 As Michael Millgate and others have noted, Faulkner uses these honored names ironically by giving them to these characters (113–23).
185:33 *Sanctuary: The Original Text* 52–53.

Chapter II

187:18 *Sanctuary: The Original Text* 54.
188:24 Eliot 51; Guerard 63–80.
189:15 *Sanctuary: The Original Text* 15.
190:11 *Sanctuary: The Original Text* 18.
191:12 *Flags in the Dust* 402–04; Eliot 3.
193:13 Matthews 246–65.

Chapter III

195:1 *Sanctuary: The Original Text* 63; *Flags in the Dust* 418–19, 426; *Sanctuary: The Original Text* 59, 426; *Collected Stories* 740.
195:5 *Collected Stories* 727–44; *Sanctuary: The Original Text* 59.
195:8 Brooks 389.
195:16 Brooks 449; *Sanctuary: The Original Text* 44.
196:10 *Flags in the Dust* 57, 31.
196:22 *Flags in the Dust* 191.
196:32 *Sanctuary: The Original Text* 37–38.
197:4 *Sanctuary: The Original Text* 38.
197:29 Blotner, *Faulkner: A Biography*, 2 v. 608.

Chapter IV

198:6 Diaz-Diocaretz 235–69.
198:7 Carvel Collins included these sketches in *William Faulkner: Early Prose and Poetry*.
198:35 *The International Cyclopedia of Music and Musicians* 764.
200:27 Blotner, *Faulkner: A Biography* 608–609.
200:30 Brown 32.
202:14 Bleikasten, "Terror and Nausea: Bodies in *Sanctuary*" 17–29; also see Gresset, *Fascination* 157–182, and Polk, "The Space Between *Sanctuary*."
202:39 Reed 11–26.
204:40 Wentworth and Flexner 13, 254.

Chapter V

206:11 *The Marionettes* 2; *Mosquitoes* 235; *The Sound and the Fury* 88–89.
207:4 *Mosquitoes* 144, 25.

Chapter VI

209:24 *Sanctuary: The Original Text* 49.
212:4 For further discussion of the gothic elements in the novel, see M. Kerr, "*Sanctuary*: The Persecuted Maiden" 81–101. See also Frazier 114–24; Heller, "Mirrored Worlds" 247–59.

Chapter VII

216:15 For Noel Polk's discussion on *Sanctuary* nightmares see "The Space Between Sanctuary" 16–35.
219:8 Traditionally presidents and governors pardon. But congressional constitutional power extends to military law and is not subject to review by federal courts. Military cases are reviewed at least once by a Detention Review Board or by the Judge Advocate General, a review notorious for its liberality and highly subject to political pressure. See Mayers 386, and Schiller 250.

Chapter VIII

226:16 For further discussion of Temple's youth as a motivating factor in her actions, see Muhlenfeld 43–55.
226:25 Ross 45–51.
226:8 Brown 145.
227:5 Olga W. Vickery argues, "In Ruby's spare room, her fear almost forgotten in her excitement and anticipation, Temple goes through a self-conscious ritual of preparing for her victimization and self-sacrifice" (108).
227:26 Brown 177.

Chapter IX

236:5 Eliot, "The Waste Land" 51.

Chapter X

238:30   *Sanctuary: The Original Text* 141.

Chapter XI

239:30   Moore 121–33.
240:32   Brown 81.
241:2   *Requiem for a Nun* 576.
243:39   Guerard 109–35.

Chapter XIII

249:38   Silencers were patented in 1897 and were adapted from Hiram Percy Maxim's automobile muffler. They were outlawed in 1937. The Maxim family, including Sir Hiram Stevens Maxim and his brother Hudson Maxim, can be credited for the first fully automatic gun, a steam-propelled flying machine, gun cartridges, and torpedo propellants.
250:18   Matthews; see also Parker 59–86.

Chapter XIV

251:31   *Sanctuary: The Original Text* 141.

Chapter XV

253:33   *Sanctuary: The Original Text* 44.

Chapter XVI

258:16   Brown 101.
263:38   Polk, "The Space Between *Sanctuary*."

Chapter XVII

266:6   For an interesting account of prison life in the 1930s, see Taylor 94–95.

   The black murderer, who is scheduled to be executed, is perhaps allowed to use that room in the days leading up to his execution for "conjugal visits" that were granted by the prison system as a racist accommodation of the promiscuity believed to be "natural" among Negroes. Viewed as a penal managerial tool of the 20s and 30s, these "conjugal visits" were extended to black prisoners, regardless of marital status, in the Mississippi Penitentiary to "keep them in line." At Parchman, the central administration building housed black prostitutes during the day, who then trafficked with the black prisoners in the field camps at night.

One prisoner, referring to the practice of housing prostitutes at the penitentiary specifically so that the black prisoners could have sex, records: "Hell, nobody knows when it started. It just started. You gotta understand, mister, that back in them days niggers were pretty simple creatures. Give a nigger some pork, some greens, some cornbread and some poontang ever now and then and he would work for you. And workin' was what it was all about back then. I never saw it, but I heard tell of truckloads of whores bein' brought up from Cleveland at dusk. The cons who had a good day got to get 'em some right there between the rows. In my day we got civilized—put 'em in little houses and told everybody that them whores was wives. That kept the Baptists off our backs."

White prisoners were excluded from these privileges based on their assumed "moral superiority."

266:21   Brooks 387.

Chapter XVIII

277:4   Miller 31.
277:39   Blotner, *Faulkner: A Biography* 330.
278:1   Miller 45. A revolt triggered by his refusal to enforce prohibition laws forced Crump to resign as mayor in 1916. His political machine facilitated Memphis vice and as a supplier of money, votes, and patronage, he expanded his base during segregation by allowing blacks to vote.

According to the *Encyclopedia of Southern Culture* Crump, campaigning on a promise to clean up Beale Street, hired W. C. Handy's band in 1909 to lure black votes. The result, "The Memphis Blues," ironically mocks Crump's campaign strategy: "Mister Crump won't 'low no easy riders here/ Mister Crump won't 'low no easy riders here/ I don't care what Mister Crump don't 'low/ I'm gwine bar'l-house anyhow—/ Mister Crump can go an' catch hisself some air!"

279:3   Elizabeth Kerr notes that Miss Reba's brothel "is a place of entrapment or imprisonment, prominent among the scenes of enclosure in *Sanctuary*"; she further compares the house to the Old Frenchman place and to the Sartoris estate ("The Persecuted Maiden" 85). See also 503–15.

282:37 Masons, a fraternal order ostensibly dedicated to a moral life and good citizenship, used tools as its symbol and "the building of King Solomon's Temple as a vehicle for the lessons" (*Encyclopedia of Southern Culture* 491). The organization attracted prominent citizens who officially opposed saloons which corrupted the poor (Dumenil 87, 77–78).

283:5 See Guerard 109–35.
284:10 *Mosquitoes* 321.
284:32 *As I Lay Dying* 52.
285:6 Guerard 109–35.
285:40 Blotner 269.
286:40 Rossky 503–15.

Chapter XIX

293:26 *Sanctuary: The Original Text* 36.
295:32 Adams and Coleman 177.
297:26 Brown 233.
299:22 *Flags in the Dust* 256; *Selected Letters* 423.
300:25 *The Mansion* 64–65.
301:19 Lindsey and Evans xiiii, xxv, 147.

Chapter XX

307:15 *Flags in the Dust* 136.

Chapter XXI

309:35 Brown, *Glossary* 90.
312:39 Blotner 189–90, also see picture of Estelle Franklin in Shanghai 41.
316:31 *The Reivers* 91.

Chapter XXII

318:5 Brooks 391.

Chapter XXIII

323:10 *The Mansion* 75.
326:17 *Sanctuary: The Original Text* 255.
329:7 See Tanner 233–367.
330:25 Bleikasten, "'Cet affreux goût d'encre'" 36.
333:28 There have been numerous Freudian interpretations of *Sanctuary*, starting with Kubie 218, 272. For other examples see Adamowski 36–51; Polk, "The Spaces Between *Sanctuary*"; and Wilson 441–60.

Chapter XXIV

335:6 Brown 221.
339:28 Bleikasten, "Terror and Nausea" 23–26.
340:5 Gresset 157–82.
340:13 Bleikasten 23–26.
340:15 See Kirchdorfer 51–53; for an interesting argument about calculation in legal tactics in *Sanctuary*; see Watson 47–66.
345:40 *Sanctuary: The Original Text* 235.
346:1 *Requiem for a Nun* 132; 118.

Chapter XXV

347:20 For further discussion, see Calvin S. Brown, "*Sanctuary*: From Confrontation to Peaceful Void" 27–52; Frazier, and Heller.
348:26 Thompson and Harris 1809–10.
348:34 Ewen 268.
348:38 Bailey 462.
349:21 Diehl 999; Rousselle surmised that Faulkner invented the hymn (62).
350:34 Ewen 283–84. Written in an hour, "Sonny Boy" was produced for Al Jolson by the three songwriters who were striving for maximum maudliness (Goldman 167).
351:33 Brown, *Glossary* 181.
353:19 *The Sound and the Fury* 342.
357:34 See Haire. Also of note is "Monkey Man Blues." Published in Chicago in 1935, it includes the lyrics "I been doing the same thing baby: ever since nineteen and twelve/ . . . . /Because when I try to love you right baby: seems like my loving won't do" (*Blues Lyric Poetry* 173).
359:4 Polk, "The Space Between Sanctuary" 26.

Chapter XXVI

360:37 See Dawn Trouard, "Not Listening to the Best of All Possible Talk: Generation X Goes to the Luxembourg Gardens," *Faulkner in Cultural Context* (forthcoming), Ed. Donald Kartiganer and Ann J. Abadie (Jackson: UP of Mississippi).
363:2 Brooks 391.

Chapter XXVII

365:32 *Sanctuary: The Original Text* 260.
372:10 Fitzgerald 83–126.
375:12 For further discussion of the lawyer, see Chappell 331–38.

Chapter XXVIII

376:3 See Parker 59–86, for further discussion of the withheld information.
376:24 Bleikasten, "Terror and Nausea" 44.
376:30 Watson 47–66.
377:34 Brooks 123–24.
378:21 See Brooks 123–24; Urgo 435–44; Muhlenfeld 43–55.
380:19 For sympathetic attempts to explain Temple's testimony at the trial, see Urgo 435–44; Cox 301–24; Muhlenfeld 43–55.

Chapter XXIX

382:15 *Light in August* 611.
384:8 McHaney, "Frazier's Slain Kings" 223–45; *Light in August* 612.
384:16 *Light in August* 742.

Chapter XXX

386:8 Grossman 436–38. The phrase is also quoted by Gavin Stevens in *Knight's Gambit* (1949).

Chapter XXXI

390:11 Inge 169.
394:4 Chappell 331–38.

396:40 Wilson 451.
398:4   See Ellstrom 63–73.
398:6   *Selected Letters of William Faulkner* 17.
398:7   *Selected Letters* 13.
398:16 *Selected Letters* 12.
398:22 *Selected Letters* 23.
398:27 Muhlenfeld 43–55; Trouard.
398:33 Gresset, "Of Sailboats and Kites" 57–72; Trouard offers a more sanguine rendering of this scene.

BIBLIOGRAPHY

Adamowski, T. H. "Faulkner's Popeye: The 'Other' as Self." Canfield 32–48.
Adams, James Truslow, and R.V. Coleman, eds. *Dictionary of American History*. New York: Scribner's, 1940.
Bailey, Edward Albert. *The Gospel in Hymns: Backgrounds and Interpretations*. New York: Overlook, 1989.
Bassett, John E. "*Sanctuary:* Personal Fantasies and Social Fictions." *South Carolina Review* 13 (1981): 73–82.
Black, Henry Campbell. *Black's Law Dictionary*. Rev. ed. St Paul: West, 1968.
Bleikasten, André. "'Cet affreux gout d'encre': Emma Bovary's Ghost in *Sanctuary*." Gresset and Polk 36–56.
———. "Terror and Nausea: Bodies in *Sanctuary*." *The Faulkner Journal* 1 (1985): 17–29.
Bloom, Harold, ed. *William Faulkner's* Sanctuary: *Modern Critical Interpretations*. New York: Chelsea, 1988.
Blotner, Joseph. *Faulkner: A Biography*. 2 vols. New York: Random House, 1974.
———. *Faulkner: A Biography, One Volume Edition*. New York: Random House, 1984.
Boon, Kevin A. "Temple Defiled: The Brainwashing of Temple Drake in Faulkner's *Sanctuary*." *The Faulkner Journal* 6.2 (1991): 33–50.
Borgström, Greta I. "The Roaring Twenties and William Faulkner's *Sanctuary*." *Moderna Språk* 62.3 (1968): 237–48.
Bradley, Ian, ed. *The Book of Hymns*. Woodstock: Overlook, 1989.
Bravo, Maria Elena. "Los parientes faulknerianos de Pasual Duarte." *Nueva Estafeta* 50 (1983): 39–49.
Brooks, Cleanth. *William Faulkner: The Yoknapatawpha Country*. New Haven: Yale UP, 1963.
Brown, Calvin S. *A Glossary of Faulkner's South*. New Haven: Yale UP, 1976.
———. "*Sanctuary:* From Confrontation to Peaceful Void." Bloom 27–52.
Brown, James. "Shaping the World of *Sanctuary*." *University of Kansas City Review* 25 (1985): 137–42.

Brown, Theron, and Hezekiah Butterworth. *Hymns of Christian Devotion*. New York: American Tract Society, 1906.

Buchanan, Ron. "'I want you to be human': The Potential Sexuality of Narcissa Benbow." *Mississippi Quarterly* 41.3 (1988): 447–58.

Campbell, Harry Modean. "Faulkner's *Sanctuary*." *Explicator* 4.8 (1946): Q61.

Canfield, John Douglas, ed. *Twentieth Century Interpretations of Sanctuary: A Collection of Critical Essays*. Englewood Cliffs: Prentice, 1982.

Carothers, James B. "'The Dead Tranquil Queens': Sculptors and Sculpture in Faulkner's Fiction." *The Artist and His Masks*. Ed. Agostino Lombardo. Rome: Bulzoni Editore, 1991. 65–79.

Chapdelaine, Annick. "Le problem de la traduction du comique: Étude du cas de *Sanctuaire* de William Faulkner." *Bulletin de l'ACLA* 12 (1990): 51–66.

Chappel, Charles. "The Memphis Lawyer and His Spine: Another Piece in the *Sanctuary* Puzzle." *Essays in Literature* 13 (1986): 331–38.

Cherrington, Ernest Hurst, ed. *The Anti-Saloon Year Book 1929: An Encyclopedia of Facts and Figures Dealing with the Liquor Traffic and the Temperance Reform*. N.p., n.p., 1929.

Cohen, Phillip. "'A Cheap Idea . . . Deliberately Conceived to Make Money': The Biographical Context of William Faulkner's Introduction to *Sanctuary*." *The Faulkner Journal* 3.2 (1988): 54–66.

Cox, Diane Luce. "A Measure of Innocence: *Sanctuary*'s Temple Drake." *Mississippi Quarterly* 39.3 (1986): 301–24.

Creighton, Joanne V. "Self-Destructive Evil in *Sanctuary*." *Twentieth Century Literature* 18 (1972): 259–70.

Cypher, James R. "The Tangled Sexuality of Temple Drake." *American Imago* 19.3 (1962): 243–52.

Diaz-Diocartez, Myriam. "Faulkner's Hen-House: Woman as Bounded Text." Fowler and Abadie, *Faulkner and Women* 235–69.

———. "'Look What He Has Already Done to Me': Modality and Temple Drake." *Faulkner's Discourse: An International Symposium*. Ed. Lothar Hönnighausen. Tubingen: Niemayer, 1989. 214–22.

Diehl, Katharine Smith. *Hymns and Tunes: An Index*. New York: Scarecrow, 1966.

Dorland's Illustrated Medical Dictionary. 27th ed. Philadelphia: Saunders, 1988.

Duffield, Samuel Willoughby. *English Hymns: Their Authors and History*. 10th ed. New York: Funk, 1886.

Dumenil, Lynn. *Freemasonry and American Culture: 1880–1930*. Princeton: Princeton UP, 1984.

Eliot, T. S. "The Waste Land." 1922. *Collected Poems: 1909–1962.* New York: Harcourt, 1963. 51.
———. "The Love Song of J. Alfred Prufrock." 1917. *Collected Poems: 1909–1962.* 3.
Ellstrom, Karen Aubrey. "Faulkner's Closing of the Doors in *Sanctuary.*" *Notes on Mississippi Writers* 20.2 (1988): 63–73.
Emery, Michael James. "U.S. Horror: Gothicism in the Work of William Faulkner, Thomas Pynchon, and Stanley Kubrick." *DAI* 50 (1990): 3227A.
Encyclopedia of Southern Culture. Ed. Charles Reagan Wilson and William Ferris. Chapel Hill: U of North Carolina P, 1989.
Encyclopedia of Southern History. Ed. David C. Roller and Robert W. Twyman. Baton Rouge: Louisiana State UP, 1979.
Ewen, David. *Panorama of American Popular Music.* Englewood Cliffs: Prentice, 1957.
Eschliman, Herbert R. "A Deconstruction of Faulkner's *Sanctuary.*" *Publications of the Missouri Philological Association* 8 (1983): 1–5.
———. "Faulkner's *Sanctuary*" *Explicator* 4 (Nov. 1945): Q8.
Faulkner, William. *Absalom! Absalom!* 1936. *Faulkner: Novels 1936–1940.* New York: Library of America, 1990.
———. *Collected Stories of William Faulkner.* New York: Random House, 1950.
———. *Flags in the Dust.* Ed. Douglas Day. New York: Random House, 1973.
———. *Go Down, Moses.* 1942. *Faulkner: Novels 1942–1954.* New York: Library of America, 1994.
———. *The Hamlet.* 1940. *Faulkner: Novels 1936–1940.* New York: Library of America, 1990.
———. *If I Forget Thee, Jerusalem.* 1939. Originally published under title *The Wild Palms. Faulkner: Novels 1936–1940.* New York: Library of America, 1985.
———. *Light in August.* 1932. *Faulkner: Novels 1930–1935.* New York: Library of America, 1985.
———. *The Mansion.* New York: Random House, 1959.
———. *The Marionettes.* 1920. Ed. Noel Polk. Charlottesville: U of Virginia P, 1979.
———. *Mosquitoes.* New York: Boni, 1927.
———. *Pylon.* 1935. *Faulkner: Novels 1930–35.* New York: Library of America, 1985.
———. *The Reivers.* New York: Random House, 1962.
———. *Requiem for a Nun.* 1951. *Faulkner: Novels 1942–1954.* New York: Library of America, 1985.

BIBLIOGRAPHY

―――. *Sanctuary.* 1931. *Faulkner: Novels 1930–1935.* New York: Library of America, 1985.

―――. *Sanctuary: The Original Text.* Ed. Noel Polk. New York: Random House, 1981.

―――. *Selected Letters of William Faulkner.* Ed. Joseph Blotner. New York: Random House, 1978.

―――. *The Sound and the Fury.* 1929. New York: Vintage International, 1987.

―――. *Uncollected Stories of William Faulkner.* Ed. Joseph Blotner. New York: Random House, 1979.

―――. *The Unvanquished.* 1938. *Faulkner: Novels 1936–1940.* New York: Library of America, 1990.

Fiedler, Leslie. "Pop Goes the Faulkner: In Quest of *Sanctuary.*" Fowler and Abadie, *Faulkner and Popular Culture* 75–92.

Fitzgerald, F. Scott. "May Day." *The Stories of F. Scott Fitzgerald.* New York: Scribner's, 1951. 83–126.

Flaubert, Gustave. *Madame Bovary.* 1857. Trans. Eleanor May Aveling. 1886. London: Dent, 1928.

Fletcher, John. "Faulkner, Gulliver, and the Problem of Evil." *Orion Blinded: Essays on Claude Simon.* Ed. Randi Birn and Karen Gould. Lewisburg: London: Bucknell UP; Associated UP, 1981: 239–47.

Flynn, Robert. "The Dialectic of *Sanctuary.*" *Modern Fiction Studies* 2 (1956): 109–13.

Folks, Jeffrey. "Women at the 'Crossing of the Ways': Faulkner's Portrayal of Temple Drake." *Heir and Prototype: Original and Derived Characterizations in Faulkner.* Ed. Dan Ford. Conway: U of Central Arkansas P, 1987. 59–69.

Fowler, Doreen. "Time and Punishment in Faulkner's *Requiem for a Nun.*" *Renascence* 38 (1986): 245–55.

Fowler, Doreen and Ann J. Abadie, eds. *Faulkner and Humor: Faulkner and Yoknapatawpha, 1984.* Jackson: UP of Mississippi, 1986.

―――. *Faulkner and Popular Culture: Faulkner and Yoknapatawpha, 1989.* Jackson: UP of Mississippi, 1990.

―――. *Faulkner and Women: Faulkner and Yoknapatawpha, 1985.* Jackson: UP of Mississippi, 1986.

Frazier, David. "Gothicism in *Sanctuary*: The Black Pall and the Crap Table." Canfield 49–58.

Gold, Analee. *Ninety Years of Fashion.* New York: Fairchild, 1991.

Goldman, Herbert G. *Jolson: The Legend Comes to Life.* New York: Oxford UP, 1988.

Gresset, Michel. "Of Sailboats and Kites: The 'Dying Fall' in Faulkner's *Sanctuary* and Beckett's *Murphy*." Gresset and Polk 57–72.

Gresset, Michel, and Noel Polk eds. *Intertextuality in Faulkner*. Jackson: UP of Mississippi, 1985.

Grossman, Joel M. "The Source of Faulkner's 'Lest Oft is Peace.'" *American Literature* 47 (1975): 436–38.

Guerard, Albert J. "Sanctuary and Faulkner's Misogyny." Bloom 63–80. Rpt. of "Forbidden Games: Faulkner—Sanctuary." *The Triumph of the Novel: Dickens, Dostoevsky, Faulkner*. New York: Oxford UP, 1979.

Haire, Norman. *Rejuvenation: The Work of Steinach, Voronoff, and Others*. New York: Macmillan, 1925.

Hashiguchi, Yasuo. "Popeye Extenuated." *Kiyusha American Literature* 5 (1962): 1–9.

Heller, Terry. "Notes on Technique in Black Humor." *Black Humor: Critical Essays*. Ed. Alan R. Pratt. New York: Garland, 1993. 197–214.

———. "Mirrored Worlds and the Gothic in Faulkner's *Sanctuary*." *Mississippi Quarterly* 42.3 (1989): 247–59.

———. "Terror and Empathy in Faulkner's *Sanctuary*." *Arizona Quarterly* 40 (1984): 344–84.

Hönnighausen, Lothar, and André Bleikasten. "*Madame Bovary* et le martin-pecheur de Caroline: Regionalisme et modernisme dans *Sanctuaire*." *Europe: Revue Litteraire Mensuelle* 70 (1992): 45–56.

Hurd, Myles. "Faulkner's Horace Benbow: The Burden of Characterization and the Confusion of Meaning in *Sanctuary*." *CLA Journal* 23.4 (1980): 416–30.

Hymns for the Celebration of Life. Boston: Beacon, 1964.

Inge, M. Thomas. "Faulkner Reads the Funny Papers." Fowler and Abadie, *Faulkner and Humor* 153–90.

Ikedo, Shiro. "Some Contrasts in *Sanctuary*." *Kyushu American Literature* 27 (1986): 29–37.

Kerr, Elizabeth M. "The Creative Evolution of *Sanctuary*." *Faulkner Studies* 7.1 (1980): 14–28.

———. "*Sanctuary*: The Persecuted Maiden, or, Vice Triumphant." Bloom 81–101.

Kingman, Daniel. *American Music: A Panorama*. New York: Shirmir, 1979.

Kinney, Arthur F. "Faulkner's Narrative Poetics and *Collected Stories*." *Faulkner Studies* 7.1 (1980): 58–79.

———. "*Sanctuary*: Style as Vision." Canfield 109–19.

Kirchdorfer, Ulf. "Temple as a Parrot." *The Faulkner Journal* 6.2 (1991): 51-53.
Knights, Pamela E. "The Cost of Singlemindedness: Consciousness in *Sanctuary*." *The Faulkner Journal* 5.1 (1989): 3-10.
Kubie, Lawrence. "William Faulkner's *Sanctuary*: An Analysis." Canfield 25-31.
Lindsey, Ben B. and Wainright Evans. *The Companionate Marriage*. Garden City: Garden City, 1929.
Lippman, Carlee. "William Faulkner and Patrick Susskind: Speaking the Unspeakable." *Literary Half Yearly* 32 (1991): 73-85.
Lyday, Lance. "Faulkner's Miss Reba and Shakespeare's Drunken Porter." *Lamar Journal of the Humanities* 16 (1990): 69-80.
———. "*Sanctuary*: Faulkner's *Inferno*." *Mississippi Quarterly* 35.3 (1982): 243-53.
Machinek, Anna. "William Faulkner and the Gothic Tradition." *Kwatalnik Neofilogiczny* 36.2 (1989): 105-14.
Madden, David. "Photographs in the 1929 Version of *Sanctuary*. " Fowler and Abadie, *Faulkner and Popular Culture* 93-109.
Malraux, André. "Préface a *Sanctuaire* de William Faulkner." *La Nouvelle Revue Française* 41 (1933): 744-47.
Mason, Robert L. "A Defense of Faulkner's *Sanctuary*." *Georgia Review* 21.4 (1967): 430-37.
Matthews, John T. "The Elliptical Nature of *Sanctuary*." *Novel: A Forum on Fiction* 17.3 (1984): 246-65.
Mayers, Lewis. *The American Legal System*. Rev. ed. New York: Harper, 1964.
McHaney, Thomas L. "*Sanctuary* and Frazier's Slain Kings." *Mississippi Quarterly* 24.3 (1971): 223-45.
———. "Literary Modernism: The South Goes Modern and Keeps on Going." *Critical Essays on American Modernism*. Ed. Michael J. Hoffman and Patrick D. Murphy. NY: G. K. Hall, 1992. 160-67.
Meriwether, James B. "The Manuscript of Faulkner's Introduction to *Sanctuary*." *Mississippi Quarterly* 36.3 (1984): 475-81.
Meriwether, James B. and Michael Millgate, eds. *Lion in the Garden: Interviews with William Faulkner, 1926-1962*. New York: Random, 1968.
Miller, William D. *Mr. Crump of Memphis*. Baton Rouge: Louisiana State UP, 1964.
Millgate, Michael. *The Achievement of William Faulkner*. New York: Random House, 1965.

———. "Undue Process: William Faulkner's *Sanctuary*." *Rough Justice: Essays on Crime in Literature.* Ed. L. M. Friedland. Toronto: U of Toronto P, 1991. 157–69.
Moore, Robert R. "Desire and Despair: Temple Drake's Self-Victimization." Fowler and Abadie, *Faulkner and Women* 112–27.
Moulinoux, Nicole. "Absalom: Variantes gothiques." *Du fantastique en littérature: Figures et figurations: Elements pour une poetique du fantastique sur quelques exemples anglo-saxons.* Ed. Max Duperray. Aix-en-Provence: U de Provence P, 1990. 141–52.
Muhlenfeld, Elisabeth. "Bewildered Witness: Temple Drake in *Sanctuary*." *The Faulkner Journal* 1 (1986): 43–55.
Nishiyami, Tamotsu. "Temple Drake's Perjury in *Sanctuary*." *Kyushu American Literature* 28 (1987): 76–79.
Norton, Mary Beth, et al. *A People and a Nation: A History of the United States.* 2nd. ed. 2 vols. Boston: Houghton, 1986.
Parker, Robert Dale. "Watching Something Happening Told: *Sanctuary*." *Faulkner and the Novelistic Imagination.* Urbana: U of Illinois P, 1985.
Perry, Marvin, et al. *Western Civilization: Ideas, Politics, and Society.* 3rd. ed. Boston: Houghton, 1986.
Pettey, Homer B. "Reading and Raping in *Sanctuary*." *The Faulkner Journal* 3.1 (1987): 71–84.
Pilkington, James Penn. "Faulkner's *Sanctuary*." *Explicator* 4.8 (1946): Q61.
———. "Spring's Futility: *Sanctuary*." *The Heart of Yoknapatawpha.* Jackson: UP of Mississippi, 1981. 111–34.
Polk, Noel. "Children of the Dark House." *Children of the Dark House.* Jackson: UP of Mississippi, 1996.
———. "The Space Between *Sanctuary*." *Intertextuality in Faulkner.* Gresset and Polk 16–35.
Polk, Noel and John D. Hart, eds. *Sanctuary: Corrected First Edition Text, Library of America, 1985: A Concordance to the Novel.* Ann Arbor: Faulkner Concordance Advisory Board and U Microfilms International: Research P, 1990.
———. *Sanctuary: The Original Text, 1981: A Concordance to the Novel* (Ann Arbor: Faulkner Concordance Advisory Board and U Microfilms International: Research P, 1990).
Ono, Kiyoyuki. "Sanctuary of the Heart: An Interpretation of *Sanctuary*." *William Faulkner: Materials, Studies, and Criticism* 4 (1982): 63–78.
———. "Kokoro to Yu Seiiki." *Ogoshi Kazugo: Ryokyo Taikan Kinen Ronbunshu.* Ed. Yasuo Suga. Kyoto: Apollonsha, 1980. 915–28.

Reed, Joseph W. *Faulkner's Narrative*. New Haven: Yale, 1973.
Roberts, Diane. "Ravished Belles: Stories of Rape and Resistance in *Flags in the Dust* and *Sanctuary*." *The Faulkner Journal* 4.1-2 (1989): 21-35.
Ross, Stephen M. *Fiction's Inexhaustible Voice*. Athens: U of Georgia P, 1989.
Rossky, William. "The Pattern of Nightmare in *Sanctuary*; or, Miss Reba's Dogs." *Modern Fiction Studies* 15 (Winter 1969): 503-15.
Rousselle, Melinda McLeod. *Annotations to William Faulkner's Sanctuary*. New York: Garland, 1989.
Santraud, Jeanne Marie. "La femme écarlate." *L'Arc*. Le Revest: Saint Martin, France, 1983. 59-71.
Schafer, William J. "Faulkner's *Sanctuary*: The Blackness of Fairytale." *Durham University Journal* 52 (1991): 217-22.
Schiller, Arthur A. *Military Law and Defense Legislation*. St. Paul: West, 1941.
Seed, David. "The Evidence of Things Seen and Unseen: William Faulkner's *Sanctuary*." *American Horror Fiction: From Brockden Brown to Stephen King*. Ed. Brian Docherty. New York: St. Martin's, 1990. 73-91.
Seidel, Kathryn Lee. "From Journalist to Masochist: A New Look at Temple Drake." *Journal of Evolutionary Psychology* 5 (1985): 27-35.
Sherrill, John B. "*Sanctuary* as Tragedy." *Arizona Quarterly* 43 (1987): 119-32.
Slabey, Robert M. "Faulkner's *Sanctuary*." *Explicator* 21, Item 45.
Stevens, Wallace. "Anecdote of the Jar." *Collected Poems*. New York: Knopf, 1954. 76.
Strong, Amy Lovell. "Machines and Machinations: Controlling Desires in Faulkner's *Sanctuary*." *The Faulkner Journal* 9.1-2 (1993/1994): 69-82.
Taft, Michael, ed. *Blues Lyric Poetry: An Anthology*. New York: Garland, 1983.
Tanaka, Hisao. "*Sanctuary*: A World of Ordered Chaos." *Hiroshima Studies in English Language and Literature* 29 (1984): 34-46.
Tanner, Laura E. *Intimate Violence: Reading Rape and Torture in Twentieth-Century Fiction*. Bloomington: Indiana UP, 1994.
———. "Reading Rape: *Sanctuary* and the Women of Brewster Place." *American Literature* 62 (1990): 559-82.
Tanner, Tony. "Flaubert's Madame Bovary." *Adultery in the Novel*. Baltimore: Johns Hopkins UP, 1979.
Taylor, William Banks. *Brokered Justice: Race, Politics, and Mississippi Prisons, 1798-1992*. Columbus: Ohio State UP, 1993.
Tebbetts, Terrell L. "Faulkner's Two Dantes: To the Inferno and Back." *Publications of the Mississippi Philological Association* (1988): 155-61.
Terraine, John. *To Win a War: 1918 The Year of Victory*. London: Sedgwick, 1978.

Thompson, Oscar, and G. W. Harris, eds. *The International Cyclopedia of Music and Musicians.* New York: Dodd, 1943.

Toles, George. "The Space Between: A Study of Faulkner's *Sanctuary.*" Canfield. 120–28.

Trouard, Dawn. "Not Listening to the Best of All Possible Talk: Generation X Goes to the Luxembourg Gardens." *Faulkner in Cultural Context: Faulkner and Yoknapatawpha, 1995.* Ed. Donald Kartiganer and Ann J. Abadie. Jackson: UP of Mississippi. Forthcoming.

Urgo, Joseph R. *Novel Frames: Literature as Guide to Race, Sex, and History in American Culture.* Jackson: UP of Mississippi, 1991.

Vanderwerken, David L. "Lost in the Whorehouse: The Comic Chapters of *Sanctuary.*" *Conference of College Teachers of English Studies.* Sept. 1989. Denton, TX, 34–38.

Vickery, Olga W. *The Novels of William Faulkner.* Baton Rouge: Louisiana State UP, 1959.

Watson, Jay. "The Failure of Forensic Storytelling in *Sanctuary.*" *The Faulkner Journal* 6.1 (1990): 47–66.

Wentworth, Harold and Stuart Berg Flexner, eds. *Dictionary of American Slang.* New York: Crowell, 1975.

Weinstein, Philip M. "Precarious Sanctuaries: Protection and Exposure in Faulkner's Fiction." Canfield 129–33.

Williams, Aubrey. "William Faulkner's 'Temple' of Innocence." Canfield 59–69.

Williams, David. "The Profaned Temple." Canfield 93–107

Wilson, Andrew J. "The Corruption in Looking: William Faulkner's *Sanctuary* as a Detective Novel." *Mississippi Quarterly* 47.3 (1995): 441–60.

Yin, Hum Sue and Larry Young. "Alcohol, Faulkner, and *Sanctuary.*" *Publications of the Arkansas Philological Association* 19 (1993): 37–51.

Yonce, Margaret. "'His True Penelope Was Flaubert': *Madame Bovary* and *Sanctuary.*" *Mississippi Quarterly.* 29.3 (1976): 439–42.

Young, Daniel T. "Narcissa Benbow's Strange Love/s: William Faulkner." *American Declarations of Love.* Ed. Ann Massa. New York: St. Martin's, 1990. 88–103.

Zeng, Dawei. "Woolf's *To the Lighthouse* and Faulkner's *Sanctuary*: An Analysis of Stylistic Features." *Waiguoyo* 39 (1985): 37–44.

INDEX

Absalom, Absalom!, 184:12, 299:14
"An Empress Passed," 195:1 (second entry)
As I Lay Dying, 237:19, 250:18, 284:32
Automatic pistol, 192:37 (second entry), 249:38, 250:7, 254:40, 334:34, 340:27, 342:23
Automobile, 199:9, 205:1, 221:9, 222:7, 275:4, 351:38, 352:1, 381:11, 385:7

Banknotes, 335:6
Baptists, 267:15, 321:22, 321:24
"Barn Burning," 360:37
Battle of Vicksburg, the, 184:19, 264:1
Berlioz, Louis Hector, 398:22
"Big Shot, The," 181:2 (first entry)
Binford, Lloyd T., 285:40
Birmingham, Alabama, 388:1
Blackjacks, 200:30
Blackstone, Sir William, 261:11
"Blue Danube," 348:26
Blues, the, 348:27
Bodily functions, 202:23, 214:6, 239:22, 241:20, 242:5, 242:23
Bonsack, James, 182:24
Bundren, Darl, 284:32

Burden, Joanna, 384:8, 388:6, 398:3
Byron, George Gordon, Lord, 309:1 (second entry)

Chastity belt, 329:19, 329:27
Children (child-like qualities), 188:17, 189:26, 195:16, 212:3, 213:12, 218:40, 219:17, 226:16, 250:1, 253:18, 255:4, 276:40, 282:8, 282:21, 290:27, 293:26 (second entry), 325:13, 332:11, 340:15
Childs' (restaurant), 372:10
Chopin, Frederic Francois, 398:22
Christmas, Joe, 204:22 (second entry), 384:16, 388:6
Cicero, 370:17
Cigarettes (smoking), 181:17, 182:24, 207:38, 208:19, 208:21, 267:33, 334:13, 397:10
Civil War, 184:16
Clari, The Maid of Milan, 198:25
Commentaries on the Law of England, 261:11
Coolidge, Calvin, 391:32
Corn-cob, 376:3, 376:4
"Country Mice," 350:20
Craps, 345:40

INDEX

Crump, Edward Hull, 278:1
Cubism, 181:12, 183:22

de Spain, Manfred, 300:25
Delsarte, Francois, 366:2
Delta, Mississippi, the, 189:40, 190:1
Dog-trot cabin, 184:22
Dollar Watch, 183:12
Drummers, 265:1, 382:32, 382:34, 382:35, 382:36
Dueling, 197:4
Dumfries, Mississippi, 275:14

Eighteenth Amendment, 182:32 (second entry)
Elgar, Sir Edward, 269:29
Eliot, T. S., 188:24, 191:12, 208:17, 236:5 (first entry), 398:33
Erskine, Albert, 299:22
Eyes (vision, blindness), 183:5, 199:4, 202:32, 208:10, 223:2, 238:27, 248:37, 250:18, 284:19, 297:24, 308:30, 376:30 (first entry), 377:2, 378:15, 379:8, 379:31, 379:32, 384:16, 396:19, 398:33

Fairchild, Dawson, 284:10
Fairy tale, 206:11, 214:19, 240:33, 242:25
Fastidiousness, 182:11, 187:36, 190:11, 196:3, 209:5, 238:16, 241:36, 251:20, 272:9, 307:38, 398:3, 398:27
Fate, 181:2, 197:29, 204:32, 209:37, 211:2, 250:14 (first entry), 268:6, 338:36, 340:32, 396:40

Faulkner, Estelle Oldham, 190:20, 312:29
Flags in the Dust, 182:30 (first entry), 188:28, 191:12, 191:18, 195:1 (second entry), 195:4, 195:7, 196:10, 196:22, 253:6 (first entry), 253:33, 263:32, 299:22, 307:15, 309:1 (second entry)
Flaubert, Gustave, 184:4
Ford, Henry, 205:1
Fort Leavenworth, Kansas, 219:5
Freemasons, Order of, 282:37
Frenchman's Bend, 184:12, 184:15
Freud, Sigmund, 333:28

Garbo, Greta, 336:5
Gayoso Hotel, 309:35
Genesis, 284:12
Gilbert, John, 336:5
Go Down, Moses, 361:24
God, 214:11, 374:12, 374:14
Grant, Ulysses S., 184:19
Grape Arbor, 188:20 (first entry), 189:30
Grenier, Louis, 184:12
Grimm, Percy, 384:16
Grotto (nightclub), 338:36, 339:5, 377:34, 380:19

Hamlet, The, 184:12, 184:16, 237:19, 299:14, 299:22
Hanging (Popeye's), 397:10, 398:3, 398:4
"Haven of Rest, The," 349:21
Heaven-Tree, 258:16
Holly Springs, Mississippi, 300:23, 388:1
Hunkering, 182:11

• 276 •

INDEX

"I Can't Give You Anything But Love," 348:34
If I Forget Thee, Jerusalem (*The Wild Palms*), 190:1
Impotency, 298:21, 339:12, 342:26, 356:24, 389:16, 392:25
Incest, 188:33, 195:7, 293:33, 293:39, 338:39
Infants, infant imagery, 215:9, 216:32, 217:6, 219:17, 219:24, 221:31, 272:25, 285:34, 290:7, 373:14

Jackson, Mississippi, 215:22
Jefferson, Mississippi, 181:2 (second entry), 182:31, 184:12, 185:12, 253:6 (second entry)
Jezebel, 218:32
Jim Crow laws, 295:32
Jolson, Al, 350:33, 350:34

Kennedy, Wat, 382:15
Kidnapping, 204:14, 275:14, 275:23
Kinston, Mississippi, 182:30 (second entry), 253:6 (second entry), 253:37, 381:9

Lamar, Lucius Quintus Cincinnatus, 185:25
Lee, Robert E., 185:26
Light in August, 204:22 (second entry), 382:15, 384:8, 384:16, [first note, Chapter XXXI], 398:3
Lindsey, Judge Benjamin, 301:19
"Lizards in Jamshyd's Courtyard," 184:16

"Love Song of J. Alfred Prufrock, The," 191:12
Luxembourg Gardens, 398:6, 398:7, 398:13, 398:16, 398:22, 398:27
Lynching (Goodwin's), 384:8, 384:16, 384:27, 385:24, 385:27

Madame Bovary, 184:4, 202:14, 333:26, 360:37
Mannigoe, Nancy, 195:19
Mansion, The, 237:19, 277:39, 299:22, 300:25, 309:1 (second entry), 309:9, 323:10
Marionettes, The, 206:11
Marriage, 190:20, 196:32, 196:38, 207:7, 212:15, 252:2, 267:6, 292:2, 293:26 (first entry), 301:19, 322:22, 367:31, 376:4, 380:8, 386:38, 387:28
Massenet, Jules Emile Frederic, 398:22
McHugh, Jimmy, 348:34
Memphis lawyer, 363:25, 375:5, 375:12, 395:21, 396:25
Memphis, Tennessee, 181:2 (first entry), 185:12, 185:20 (first entry), 185:22, 277:4, 277:16, 278:1, 310:27, 388:1
Milton, John, 284:12
Mississippi A & M, 197:29
Mitchell, Harry, 188:28, 253:6 (first entry)
Modernism, 183:22
Monkey glands, 357:34
Monte Carlo, Monaco, 322:31
Moonshining, 182:32 (second entry), 187:10, 193:39 (both entries), 194:31, 209:24 (second

INDEX

entry), 210:38, 290:27, 290:34, 294:6, 317:3, 366:4
Mosquitoes, 206:11, 207:4, 284:10, 350:20, 398:22
Mother songs, 350:33

Narcissus myth, 181:12
Nature, 188:21 (second entry), 188:23, 188:24, 188:28, 189:30, 202:39, 239:30, 253:28, 274:3, 274:8, 374:1, 381:28
"Nearer, My God, To Thee," 348:38
New Albany, Mississippi, 388:1
New Orleans, Louisiana, 189:1

Oedipus Rex, 350:37
Old Frenchman place, 181:2 (second entry), 183:15 (first entry), 184:12, 187:10, 188:7, 206:29, 317:3, 374:1
"Old Man," 190:1
"Once Aboard the Lugger (I)," 350:20
Orange stick, 192:14, 254:30
Oxford, England, 196:22
Oxford, Mississippi, 182:31, 184:19, 188:36, 196:22
Oyl, Olive, 390:11

Paradise Lost, 284:12
Paris, France, 398:6
Payne, John Howard, 198:25
Pemberton, John C., 184:19
Pensacola, Florida, 356:15, 388:1
Pershing, Gen. John Joseph, 255:5 (second entry)
Philippines, 219:4, 255:5 (first entry)

Pine Bluff, Arkansas, 366:3
"Pomp and Circumstance," 269:29
Popeye the sailor, 181:2 (first entry), 182:9, 390:11
Priest, Lucius, 277:39, 279:3
Prostitution, 184:39, 185:20 (second entry), 185:22, 198:6, 199:35, 212:36, 219:9, 219:17, 219:26, 230:27, 237:14, 254:30, 279:3, 279:21, 279:23, 312:31, 313:39, 315:12, 315:19, 316:20, 325:13, 326:36, 331:25, 356:19, 358:15, 376:21, 376:30 (second entry), 378:8, 380:8, 386:6
Pumphrey, Neal Karens, 181:2 (first entry)

Ratliff, V. K., 299:22
Reflections (mirrors, water), 181:12, 181:14 (second entry), 189:26, 274:26, 281:34, 285:1, 294:29, 337:22, 340:13, 398:27
Reivers, The, 277:39, 278:11, 279:3, 316:31, 352:18, 353:33
Requiem for a Nun, 181:2 (first entry), 184:12, 185:25, 195:19, 241:2, 346:1
Ripley, Mississippi, 182:31

Sanctuary (concept of), 3
Sanctuary: The Original Text, 181:2 (second entry), 182:29, 184:1, 184:21, 185:33, 187:18, 188:35, 189:15, 190:11, 195:1 (second entry), 195:7, 195:16, 196:32, 197:4, 209:24 (first entry), 238:30, 251:31, 253:33, 283:5,

INDEX

288:22, 293:26 (second entry), 326:17, 345:40, 365:32
Sartoris, Bayard II, 195:4
Sartoris, Bayard III, 195:1 (second entry), 195:16, 307:15
Sartoris, Col. John, 195:4
Saturday Evening Post, The, 184:16
Scriabin, Alexander, 398:22
Segar, E. C., 181:2 (first entry), 390:11
Shack, the, 201:23
Shelley, Percy, 386:38
Shrimp, 189:18, 191:12, 191:18, 191:19, 340:13
Silencing (of Temple Drake), 213:17, 274:26, 327:20, 376:30 (second entry), 377:34, 379:4, 379:19
Snopes, Ab, 360:37
"Sonny Boy," 350:34
Sorghum, 187:36
Sound and the Fury, The, 206:11, 263:38, 281:23, 353:19
Starkville, Mississippi, 197:29, 200:27
Steinach, Dr. Eugen, 357:34
Stevens, Gavin [title note], 195:19
Stevens, Wallace, 181:25
Strauss, Johann, 348:26
Strike breakers, 388:10
Sugar daddy, 338:39
Sutpen, Thomas, 184:12
Swedenborg, Emanuel, 398:22
Syphilis, 389:16, 392:13

Taft, William Howard, 255:5 (first entry)
Taylor, Mississippi, 200:24, 203:30

"There Was a Queen," 195:1 (second entry), 195:4, 195:5
Thimble Theatre, 181:2 (first entry), 390:11
"Through the Window," 195:1 (second entry)
Time (concept of), 258:18, 281:27, 283:10, 283:31, 284:32, 288:22, 332:32, 397:10
"To Jane: The Recollection," 386:38
Town, The [title note], 195:19, 237:19, 299:22, 309:1 (second entry), 398:3
Trial (Goodwin's), 318:5, 326:17, 331:25, 362:20, 363:2, 365:1, 365:32, 366:10, 367:5, 367:6, 375:12, 376:4, 376:24, 376:30 (first and second entries), 377:4, 379:4, 379:19, 381:1, 382:34
Trial (Popeye's), 394:16, 395:1, 395:7, 395:9, 396:40
Tschaikovsky, Peter Ilich, 398:22
Tulane University, 189:1
Tull, Vernon, 238:30, 251:32

University of Mississippi, 188:36, 196:22, 197:29, 198:6, 198:17 (both entries), 297:26
University of Virginia, 195:34, 196:18
Unvanquished, The, 195:4, 264:1, 299:14

Varner, Eula, 398:3
Varner, Will, 184:12, 300:25
Vomiting, 202:14, 202:23, 284:25, 333:20, 333:31, 359:4, 360:5

INDEX

Voronoff, Dr. Serge, 357:34
Voyeurism, 181:1, 187:36, 188:21
  (second entry), 188:23, 188:24,
  189:26, 195:7, 198:25, 204:9,
  227:5, 242:15, 242:39, 253:12,
  340:5

Wagner, Richard, 398:22
Waste Land, The, 188:24, 236:5
World War I, 219:6, 255:6

Yoknapatawpha County, Mississippi,
  182:31, 184:12, 184:19

www.ingramcontent.com/pod-product-compliance
Lightning Source LLC
Chambersburg PA
CBHW030336240426

43661CB00052B/1651